THE ENTREPRENEUR'S PLAYBOOK

FEATURING INDUSTRY SECRETS FROM
70 SUCCESSFUL ONLINE MARKETERS

PROMINENCE PUBLISHING

Published by Prominence Publishing, www.prominencepublishing.com

Edited by Barb Kelly, www.subject-matters.ca.

ISBN: 978-1-988925-77-6

Operation Underground Railroad:

The publisher and authors of this book are proud to donate 100% of the Amazon royalties to Operation Underground Railroad. They are the world's experts on rescuing women and children from slavery. More information can be found here: https://ourrescue.org.

Contents

Foreword By Greg Reid 1

Preface By Kevin Steven Quinn 3

Introduction By Randy Stratford 5

Chapter 1

The Value Ladder Explained By Alan Dean 8

Chapter 2

Selling Your Digital Services By Megan Flanagan 12

Chapter 3

Media Secrets By Lori McNeil 16

Chapter 4

The Essentials of Starting a Business By Matt Rodak 20

Chapter 5

Cold Email Marketing/Big Data By Robert Raff 24

Chapter 6

The Three Principles Of E-Commerce Success By Earnest Epps 29

Chapter 7

Emotional Intelligence In Digital Marketing By Page Nielson 33

Chapter 8

Promotion Through Signature Stories By Pierre-Francois Rio 37

Chapter 9

Five Shifts To Successful Selling By Allie Bjerk 41

Chapter 10

How to Write a Client-Attracting Book to Use as a Marketing Tool

By Suzanne Doyle-Ingram 45

Chapter 11

Relationship Building In The Digital Age By Andrew Izumi 50

Chapter 12

Why Do Most Businesses Fail and Only A Few Succeed?

By Mike Lasswell 53

Chapter 13

Masterful Messaging By Christa Nichols 58

Chapter 14

How To Spark Life Into A New Or Dying Business By Anton Gray 62

Chapter 15

Strategic Consultancy: The Creation Of Blue Oceans By Trevor Wood 66

Chapter 16

Parentpreneur By Lisa Kuntze 70

Chapter 17

The Power of Outsourcing By Travis Linares 74

Chapter 18

Beat Burnout By Kelly Shockley 78

Chapter 19

Become A Successful Health And Wellness Entrepreneur

By Brittani Feinberg 83

Chapter 20

The Unfair Advantage of Butterfly Marketing By Mike Filsaime 88

Chapter 21

Getting Business Credit Funding By Joe Lawrence 92

Chapter 22

Tax Hacks By Carlotta Thompson 97

Chapter 23

Patenting Your Ideas Without an Attorney By Laurel Bloomfield 101

Chapter 24

Understanding Google's Marketing Platform By Petra Manos 105

Chapter 25

SEO: Search Engine Optimization By Lisa Gaal 110

Chapter 26

Planning Your Strategic Marketing Schedule By Laurie Shields 114

Chapter 27

Masterminding By Jenny Hansen Lane 118

Chapter 28

What Preschoolers Can Teach Us About Marketing By Lynley Hipps 122

Chapter 29

Lead Generation By Robert Segelquist 127

Chapter 30

Email Secrets By Clint Whitney 131

Chapter 31

Escape Your 9-5 With One Simple Sales Funnel By Blake Nubar 136

Chapter 32

Challenge Funnels By Austin Ford 140

Chapter 33

Content Marketing – "Content is Not King" By Becky Koyle 146

Chapter 34

How To Acquire High-Ticket Clients By Bryan Fuentes 150

Chapter 35

Influencer Marketing By Latasha Mitchell 155

Chapter 36

Business Growth and Marketing By Tammy Donnell 159

Chapter 37

Messenger Bots By Larissa Banting 165

Chapter 38

How To Build A Passive Income Using Automation And Systems

By Spencer Meecham 169

Chapter 39

Drop-Shipping on Amazon and eBay By Waseem Rahman 174

Chapter 40

How To Use Instagram For Business By Kelly Sturtevant 179

Chapter 41

Pinterest By Tereza Toledo 184

Chapter 42

Solo Ads By Wayne Crowe 188

Chapter 43

Podcasting: Scale Your Influence and Create Authority

By Ruth O'Neill 192

Chapter 44

Monetizing Your Podcast: Create Predictable Profits On Autopilot

By Evans Putman 196

Chapter 45

YouTube: A Recipe For Success By Lyndon Scott 200

Chapter 46

Subscription Boxes By Jessica Principe 205

Chapter 47

A Six-Step Framework For Creating Live Events By Justin Stephens 209

Chapter 48

Ad Scaling Secrets By Dan Ryder 212

Chapter 49

Modern Multi-Level Marketing Tactics By Coulton Woods 218

Chapter 50

Facebook Engagement By Kevin Steven Quinn 222

Chapter 51

Facebook Ads By Jessica Walman 226

Chapter 52

Facebook Group Profits By Chantelle Page Turner 231

Chapter 53

The VIP Visibility Formula: Show Up, Be Seen, and Get Paid

By Yael Bendahan 235

Chapter 54

Publishing: Get Your Audience to Love You and Buy By Kris Russo 240

Chapter 55

The Future of TV is Connected By Angie Norris 245

Chapter 56

The Art Of The Interview By Shannon Houchin 248

Chapter 57

Nine-To-Five Freedom: The Switch From Employee To Entrepreneur

By Bryan Rhodes 253

Chapter 58

Reinventing Virtual Summits By Mark Stern 257

Chapter 59

Drop-Shipping and Retail Arbitrage By Tommy Wang 262

Chapter 60

Arbitrage And Amazon By Nate McCallister 267

Chapter 61

Fulfillment By Amazon (FBA) By Siru Pihlajavesi 272

Chapter 62

Shopify By Kim Calera 276

Chapter 63

Etsy By Kathy Walls 280

Chapter 64

Blogging By Ilir Salihi 283

Chapter 65

Starting A Digital Agency By Serena Schwartz 288

Chapter 66

Print On Demand By Cody Neer 293

Chapter 67

Affiliate Marketing By Paul Mottley 297

Chapter 68

How To Create A Successful Online Course By Melissa Duran 301

Chapter 69

LinkedIn By Lindsay Mustain 305

Chapter 70

Door-To-Door Sales Funnels By Jackson Rucker 309

Foreword

By Greg Reid

"There is a difference in being interested and being committed."

When I wrote *Three Feet from Gold,* I knew I had to share the years of knowledge, purpose, and passion I had learned from great thought leaders, with others.

Entrepreneurs know all too well what it's like to be committed. Or should. Even as kids, we had dreams. As adults, it's about taking action on those dreams. Unless you write them down, they're only dreams. Once written, they become goals. You can take action on goals. And that's where the magic happens.

All those lessons learned that came to us as failures prepared us for greatness. But that success comes to those who never quit. How many times have you stepped back from a situation and realized your path needed to change? In that change, however, is where you were able to find a different solution.

Did you know that 20% of small businesses fail in the first year? And that 50% of them fail by year five? Successful entrepreneurs collaborate. Collaboration can play an integral role in not only launching a dream but finding a miracle.

The average CEO reads sixty books a year. That's five books a month. Knowledge is key to an entrepreneur's success. When you become successful, you will find others whom you can mentor. Share with them the lessons you have learned.

The Entrepreneur's Playbook is one of those books that is going to move you. So much so, you're going to want to share this with someone you know who is launching their own business online.

Never quit. You might only be three feet from gold.

Here's to your success.

Greg Reid

www.gregreid.com

PREFACE

By Kevin Steven Quinn

Last year, I started filming Facebook Live videos from my kitchen every week. Each Friday, while I cooked a meal in my air fryer, I discussed digital marketing ideas. This led me to have a following around these Facebook Lives.

Facebook friends kept asking, "Are you going Live with your air fryer today?" They loved my Facebook Lives. So, sure enough, I kept it up; every Friday I'd go live while cooking with my air fryer. Air Fryer Fridays were born. The audience that consisted of *my* friends started to build an new audience of *their* friends. A ripple effect took over as friends of friends were tuning in. Engagement was happening!

The Facebook Algorithm loved it. So much so, that hundreds of people were either tuning in live or watching a replay of the video. A monster was created: A madman with an air fryer.

Months later, a joke about this became a book idea, we joked about calling it *Air Fryer Secrets*. A book on digital marketing and digital products. This book is the A to Z, and all points in between, "how to" for building an online digital marketing business. Whether you have an idea or have no idea at all, experts cover their niche in each chapter to help you out.

So many people wanted to write a chapter in the book, we had to start turning some away. 70 authors are in this book. Of course, a book filled with marketers meant we had some wicked smart people who thought, *Air Fryer Secrets* sounded more like a cookbook than a marketing book and didn't have the right ring we needed. So, *The Entrepreneurs' Playbook* was born.

Want to know how to run Facebook Ads? We have a chapter for you. Don't know what a sales funnel is? There's a chapter. How to build an audience with a YouTube channel? Again, that's covered. 70 authors and 70 different niches, all to help you develop your online business.

◊

When I first started digital marketing in June 2018, I had absolutely no clue what I was doing. I was a software developer for a company and an agency introduced me to a sales funnel.

"Hey Kevin, you should be using Click Funnels to build a lead-generation page for your company."

It sounded like Greek to me.

The agency had some amazing ideas and planned to help the business build our following. When the time came to sign the contract, the agency was already too busy to take us on as a client. So, I decided to figure out how to use sales funnels on my own.

I joined Facebook groups, watched a lot of YouTube videos, and purchased digital courses about sales funnels and marketing. I asked a lot of questions. I tested. Launched. Failed. Repeated the process until I found success. I built Facebook engagement on my personal page. I created a couple of Facebook groups. I launched one sales funnel. And another. And another. I've launched close to 100 sales funnels in a year-and-a-half. I'm self-taught, with no agency help. And, man, would I have loved to have a book like this to help me out on my journey. It would have shortened the learning curve and taken me where I needed to go that much faster.

This book will help you in so many ways. From mindset development to creating a finished product and monetize it: a course, an offer, a book and more. This book is for anyone, no matter where you're at on your entrepreneurial journey. You'll find value learning from people who have made millions in different ways. Let those experts shorten the learning curve for you.

You have to know where you are, where you're headed and what you need to do to ensure that you're successful on your entrepreneurial journey. Thank you for purchasing this book. You're going to love it.

Kevin Steven Quinn

INTRODUCTION

By Randy Stratford

The fact that you have not only picked up, but actually cracked the cover and started reading this book says something about you.

I'm guessing you're the adventurous type. You're willing to take a risk and take a shot at new things. And, for the right opportunity, you're probably even willing to go all in.

There's something about the adventurous soul. An unsettled something inside that not only wants more but hungers for more. The rush to be involved in digital commerce may be the closest thing in the 21st Century to the gold rushes of the 19th Century. There's definitely a rush going on and it has been for some time. The question is, do you want in on the adventure?

Are You A '49er?

If you were alive at the time of the famous California Gold Rush (1848-1855), would you have essentially dropped everything and headed west to an unknown land for the opportunity of a lifetime?

Remember, you couldn't hop on a plane and land in San Francisco within days or hours of your decision. And, if you didn't like what you saw after arriving you couldn't just hop on the next flight back to where you came from and pick up where you left off. No, these were decisions that changed the course of one's life forever.

What life would you be leaving? Where, exactly, would you go? Where would you live? What would you do when you got there? Would you even know how to mine for gold? When you finally did arrive after weeks or months of traversing the wild frontier, San Francisco would be a foreign place.

In 1846, San Francisco's population was only 200; that's probably less than the number of students at the elementary school you attended. Within six years, over 300,000 of the famed '49ers poured in daily by land and sea, creating a veritable deluge of immigrants. Most were Americans, but tens of thousands poured in from Europe, China, Australia, and Latin America.

The ripple effects are nothing short of staggering. One random discovery of a few flakes of gold at Sutter's Mill triggered a movement that would forever change the history of California, the nation -- even the world.

Digital Is The New Rush

This book is not about the Gold Rush of 1849. It's about a new kind of rush, happening right now, in our time, right before our eyes. This rush is digital commerce.

Now, typically a rush involves some type of scarcity. People rush in to snatch a commodity or product up as quickly as they can before it all disappears. But, unlike gold or land, digital resources are the opposite of scarce. Digital seems to be everywhere. Every advancement in technology seems to unlock more of it. What's currently underway is bigger, better, and will change the world more than all gold rushes before it, combined.

You already know digital/online technology has changed the world and will continue evolving for at least the rest of your life. This is the place to be. You just need to stake your claim. You've got the desire and the drive. You just need your shot. You want the shot, but you don't want to blow it when you take it.

You've probably heard the quote by hockey star Wayne Gretzky, *"You miss 100% of the shots you don't take."* It's one of those simple truisms. You won't succeed unless you try. But how does that other saying go? "If at first you don't succeed..." Yep. "Try, try again." It's all about trying; sometimes, over and over again.

The Journey Begins With One Step

This is your shot. The time is now. Starting a business of your own has never been easier. You can have your location for $12 per year (it's called a website). Who would have thought that, in less than one generation, a guy could start a website to sell books, called Amazon, and end up becoming the richest man in the world (all without opening a single store)?

This book is written by a group of entrepreneurs who, not too long ago, were just like you. They felt the yearn to stake their claim. And, they acted. And, having tried many things and failed at many, but succeeded in some, they are here to tell their stories and share their secrets.

At first, reading this book may seem like drinking from a firehose – overwhelming. It's not designed to be read from cover to cover, like a novel. It's more like a reference book. Not all of the chapters or strategies will align with you and your business. Start with what you want, then try some of the other stuff later. There's a lot of actionable information here. The key is starting. Take that first step into the unknown, not sure of where you're going, then take another step. The path will appear as you move forward.

A Gift For You

I'm writing a book, *Digital Is The New Gold*, that delves deeper into the digital commerce rush. As a bonus for reading The Entrepreneur's Playbook, you qualify for an **Insiders' Discount** (so it's practically free)! Just fill out the form at www.digitalgoldbook.com.

About Randy Stratford

Randy Stratford is an entrepreneur to the core. He has a passion for startups and is most fulfilled by helping businesses, partners, and investors find breakthrough success.

Mr. Stratford's formal education is primarily financial. He earned a bachelor's and a master's degree in Accounting and became a CPA with a global Big 4 firm. He is currently a Certified Financial Planner (CFP®) and is licensed in real estate (Broker), securities, and insurance.

Mr. Stratford's work experience ranges from pre-teen paper routes to Fortune 500 companies and he has held positions from entry-level to President/CEO. He has been a founder or co-founder of multiple companies, and has built and led companies from startup concept to eight-figures in annual revenue with over 150 employees.

He is a dedicated family man. For leisure, he enjoys playing golf, snowboarding, photography, watching sports, and diving into new business ideas and opportunities.

CHAPTER ONE

The Value Ladder Explained

By Alan Dean

Baby, guess what?"

"What, dear?" I responded to my wife, knowing she was about to drop some sort of bomb on me.

"We got a new cat!" She said excitedly.

"What do you mean we got a new cat?"

"Well, you see, I was shopping at the grocery store and when I came out, I heard this soft little *meow* coming from under my car. To my surprise, I found a baby kitten there. It was all alone with nowhere to go and I felt bad, so I brought it home!"

"That's great, dear," I said sarcastically.

Not only is my wife an animal lover, but she also adores cats. This kitten wasn't more than a few weeks old. If left alone, I am sure the chance of it surviving was slim. So, home with my wife came the cat. My wife and children promptly sat around that first night debating on a name for the cat. They ultimately decided on the name Chance, as they felt like he had been given a second chance at life.

The next day, my wife decided to take Chance to the vet to get him checked out. I guess it was perfect timing or fate, I don't know, but she had recently received a coupon in the mail from a veterinarian offering a $100 check-up for only $60. So, off to the vet went Chance.

Upon arrival, they were greeted by the helpful and caring staff and taken back to an exam room. That's when it all started.

"Mrs. Dean, would you like us to trim his nails for you? We can do that while he is here for $5."

"Yes, please. Thanks for offering."

"Mrs. Dean, since we don't know where this kitten came from and he has no chip or ID tag, we have no idea if he has ever been treated before. We would like to do a simple test to see if he has any ringworm, if that's ok. The test is only $18."

"Sure, that would be fine. Go ahead."

Next came a test for heartworms. Then shots. And so on, until the bill went from a special discounted rate of $60 to over $300. And that didn't include any future shots, office visits, having him neutered, micro-chipped, or any flea/heartworm prevention.

That's when they brought out the big guns. They told my wife that all of the necessary shots, vaccinations, neutering and everything else necessary to ensure this sweet little bundle of grocery store joy would grow strong and healthy would cost around $800. However, they have this convenient little payment plan of $79/month for ten months that takes care of everything our Chance would need for the year and even included unlimited office visits. Rather than pay $300+ for her initial visit, my wife walked out paying $79. She had just signed up to spend $800 but she left happier than a camel on hump day

In this chapter, we are going to talk about a very simple, yet very powerful concept that Chance's vet understood very well and with which you may or may not be familiar: the Value Ladder (VL).

What is a Value Ladder?

In its simplest form, a VL is a roadmap of the products and/or services that you offer customers in ascending order of value and price.

Before you even think about building your sales ads or sales funnels, you must take the time to map and create your VL. It will help bring structure and clarity to your offers and help you determine the best way to promote them. By carefully constructing VLs, I have personally been able to sell millions of dollars' worth of products and services in my professional career.

If you took your car in for a $60 oil change and ended up being slapped with an $800 repair bill, you would probably be extremely upset and leave the mechanic shop angry, possibly even refusing to return. So, why did my wife leave the veterinarian's office happy after going from a $60 bill to an $800 bill?

The answer is simple. The veterinarian provided *value*. Not only did they provide value; they also provided value at carefully calculated intervals throughout the visit. There are two things to remember concerning a VL:

1. When value is presented correctly, price becomes irrelevant to the customer.
2. The second yes is always easier than the first yes.

Here is what a typical VL looks like:

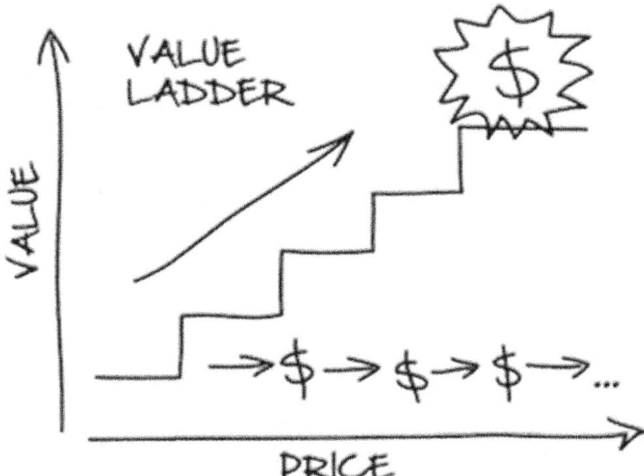

The left vertical axis represents value; the bottom, horizontal axis represents price. In an ideal scenario, as the value goes up, the price goes up in a correlated fashion. Eventually, you will hit the top step of your VL (shown with the big $ sign). This is your highest-priced offering and is your top sale. It is the one thing you hope every customer will purchase.

Now if this was Burger King™ and we could all have it our way, we would just sell everyone our highest-priced item every time. But the cold, hard truth is we just can't do that.

To make top sales, you have to establish a relationship with your customers. You have to build trust. You have to provide value. If the veterinarian had gone straight to the $800 offer as soon as my wife walked in the door, she would have left as quickly as she came in. However, the staff loved her kitten. They established a relationship. They started with a small ticket item ($5 nail clipping) and slowly and methodically worked their way up to the $800 offer.

This brings me to the most important part of any VL: **The lifeblood of any company is a continuity program.** Continuity exists when you charge a customer on a daily, weekly, monthly, or yearly basis until the customer decides to cancel. That is Monthly Recurring Revenue (MRR), and it provides a constant stream of income for your business, day in and day out.

The vet is collecting $79/month from my wife now because their carefully constructed VL ended with a continuity offer. When her ten months are up, I am sure they will get her right back on board with their next continuity program. And you know what? I bet she will sign up for it faster than a politician's promise on election day because they've provided her with good value and service for ten months. They have cared for her baby and, as I mentioned before, every subsequent *yes* is an easier sell.

Moving Forward

No matter what your VL contains, your priority should involve being more creative and adding more value to your offer than your competitors. While crafting your VL, remember these three simple things:

Faster is Always Better

Add additional value to your offer by increasing the speed at which you deliver your product(s) or service(s). These days, everyone is impatient; they make impulsive buys and want it immediately, before they change their mind. Someone may have found your offer completely by accident but now they want your product or service immediately. Someone who can deliver the goods quickly offers a better and higher quality offer than those that can't. Did you know that $0.25 out of every $1 spent online goes through Amazon because of its Prime program?

Add More Value

There is no such thing as too much value. As Russell Brunson says, "Is it ok if I over-deliver?"

That is exactly what you need to do. Over-deliver every aspect of your offer. Remember, if everyone in your space is offering the same thing, then you need to offer more. Your customers must perceive your offer as superior to your competitors' offers. The only limitation to your VL is your imagination. There is *always* something bigger and better that you can offer.

Make Sure You Include A Continuity Plan

Having a continuity plan is essential to your business. It should be your top goal. At some point at or near the top of your VL, make sure you have a continuity plan in place. Strive to hit this continuity plan with every customer. The more customers you have on a continuity plan, the better off you will be.

There is no strategic advantage in being the second cheapest. Believe in yourself. Believe in your product. Hold your price and your head up high and go get those sales!

> ### A Gift For You
>
> Do you want to see what software I use to make passive income DAILY on autopilot? Visit www.getfriendorfoe.com and check it out now! You can start using it today for FREE!
>
> www.getfriendorfoe.com

Alan Dean is a husband and father of three. He has spent the past 20+ years learning everything there is to know about sales and marketing. He has been personally responsible for more than $20 million in sales.

Alan now focuses his time on creating courses and teaching other entrepreneurs how to achieve their dreams through his Facebook group, Digital ADgency.

CHAPTER TWO

Selling Your Digital Services

By Megan Flanagan

I currently coach entrepreneurs who are starting out. I have discovered that entrepreneurs who don't have sales experience need to learn how to sell their own services or products.

While starting their entrepreneurial journey, entrepreneurs learn to craft an offer, start being a social media manager, or become a digital marketer but they do not think about learning to sell their offer. Much of my coaching is dedicated to these new marketers and helping them master selling themselves.

In The Beginning

I started my retail sales career at 14 and continued it all through college. After I graduated from college, I decided I wanted to travel and I ended up using retail as a vehicle to pay my way.

I knew I could get a job anywhere in the world selling. What I didn't anticipate were the challenges of selling in different cultures. I quickly learned that I had to adapt my selling to the culture in which I was working.

For example, in London, people do not want to buy from *shop people*. But when working for The Gap, an American company that excels at selling, the expectation is sell a pair of jeans, add on a few t-shirts, a pair of socks, and a sweater. We had Units Per Transaction (UPT) requirements that salespeople had to hit every day. We had to figure out how to work with the London culture, which is has existed longer than the US sales culture, to reach our daily goals. Not only did we have to work with the different customer culture, we had many different cultures represented by our salespeople.

When I returned to New York City, where everyone sells on overdrive and it is exhausting to sell, we had to reign salespeople in and infuse more personality in the way they approached customers.

After NYC, I moved to Hawaii, where the culture and lifestyle is very laid-back, and worked for Converse Shoes. Again, I faced the challenge of culture smashing up against the demands of corporate sales goals. I was solving the same problem over and over again. My store in Hawaii received store of the year two years in a row and for five years straight was always at the top of all retail stores for overall sales.

My last job was at QVC, which is an $11 billion TV/Internet/streaming retailer who has perfected the art of selling on TV, mobile, and the Internet. Their approach to selling was avoid pressure sales and to always act as if you were talking to your neighbor over the backyard fence.

Selling should be as conversational as a recommendation from someone you like, know, and trust. People trust a friend's recommendation and often buy a product because of what you tell them. Using stories, we sold the product very successfully.

The Six-Step Framework For Selling Yourself

1. Frame The Call

About an hour before you make a call to somebody, do some detective work: Find out who you're talking to.

Use social media and LinkedIn to get a snapshot of who you're talking to and have a point of reference for what they might need. Take notes on what they may need help with. Don't assume you know what they need without doing research.

About ten minutes before the call, make sure your space is clear. Ensure your desk or wherever you're sitting is tidy and clear, have your notes handy, review them, be prepared. Have a pen and notepad to write notes during your call.

The next part is important to practice and perfect. When they pick up the phone and say hello, be sure you are in the driver's seat of the call. You need to frame your call by crafting a statement, a sentence, that states the intent and length of the call. You must control the call.

For example: I like to start with, "HI, Mr Smith. This is Megan from 609 Media. Thanks for taking the time to speak with me regarding your need for social media. I have approximately 30 minutes to chat with you today. Does this time work for you?" Nine times out of ten, the client says,"Yes."

I won't go deep into the psychology, but getting your first *yes* is important.

2. Ask About Them

Once *yes* is uttered, most people think the next step is talking about themselves and how they can help the person on the phone. But I recommend you first ask about them, just as you would when talking to a friend.

I like to ask them to tell me a bit about themselves, their business, their goals, and share with what they need my help. I listen carefully to try and find a connection I can make with them further down in the framework. The client should be doing 90% of the talking at this point.

3. Share Yourself

Based on what the client has told you, share something about yourself. Pull out any relevant experience to illustrate how you can solve their problem or help them based on the information they have shared.

4. The Connection

Create the thread that ties you together. It can connect you for a moment or forever. You never know when talking to somebody for the first time to where it's going to lead.

Find a commonality to make that connection. It is the shared that makes them like, know, and trust you. You have to be very attentive in listening to them in the previous steps to find a way to connect with the client. It's important to remember that you are still not pitching your services here.

In a study done by Stanford Business School, one group of students were told that time equals money so don't waste time, go negotiate a deal and make that sale. The second group was told to get to know each other; share one personal thing about themself and look for a similarity between themselves and the customer.

The first group had a 55% success rate on closing full sales while the second group had a 90% success rate with sales worth 18% more than the first group's full sales.

Note that the connection must be made before you talk about business. You must build trust before trying to sell yourself to them.

5. **Engage,**

Now you can talk about business. Paint a picture for the client and repeat why you called:

- They reached out to you first; and,
- They want your expertise.

Your picture must demonstrate why you are their only choice: Restate their problem and state the solution you'll provide.

Be bold and mention your prices in this step. If the client balks at this point, they are not a good fit and you can state that and end the call and save yourself hours of work writing up your proposal.

When I started mentioning my prices all the fear, anxiety, and the feelings we attach to conversations regarding money disappeared. When you state your prices, you carry that confidence through the remainder of the call. The client is listening, looking, and trying to get a feeling whether you are confident in your abilities and they are going to decide on this call if they can trust their business with you.

6. **Restate And Close The Call**

After you outline your prices, restate the solution you are providing and ask if they are interested in changing their current situation and if they interested in your services?

If they want to hire you, tell them the next steps (for example, you will schedule another call to get more details from them and submit a proposal afterwhich more meetings may be required). Remember you stated you had 30 minutes; you need to keep it at 30 minutes.

Thank them for their time and follow up when you say you will. If you say,"I will reschedule another call." Do it. If you say, "I'll send you a proposal in 48 hours." Do it. If you can't meet your deadline, you must tell them why before the deadline. Be an ethical business owner.

Moving Forward

Selling yourself takes preparation. Not to convince the client to work with you but to get to know them as much as possible before telling them what you can do for them. Listen carefully and be confident, open, and honest. Don't be afraid to end the call gracefully if you feel the prospect is not a good fit and don't be offended if they feel you aren't a good fit. You can't please all the people all of the time.

A Gift For You

To get my FREE Six-Step Framework For Selling Yourself Guide, go to www.609media.com and check our resource page.

About Megan Flanagan

Megan Flanagan has used her retail career to travel and live all over the world. Her experiences working for *The Gap*, *Converse Sho*es, QVC, and in the outdoor industry, prepared her perfectly for her entrepreneurial journey.

She is passionate about tech, travel, fashion, music, and connecting with people. She has been interviewed by a national magazine about turning a lay-off from a corporate job into a six-figure business.

Megan is the owner of 609 Media, a digital marketing company that helps businesses connect and engage with their online customers. She also coaches female entrepreneurs in Business, Mindset, and Sales.

CHAPTER THREE

Media Secrets

By Lori McNeil

Entrepreneurship is an amazing journey of ups and downs with unlimited opportunities to impact the world. The power of one's story is critical to brand identity.

As more entrepreneurs realize that being themselves and sharing their lives and stories with their target audience lead to stronger business relationships and increased cash flow, they look for new ways to use platforms to share their message and conduct business. It's no secret that technology is always evolving. Social platforms like Facebook, Instagram, LinkedIn, and Twitter are a few places entrepreneurs navigate daily to reach and attract more clients.

It is easier than ever today to use national media to extend reach. In the past, getting published and being seen on TV were opportunities only a few lucky ones experienced. Those opportunities were rare and out of reach for most. Media is a powerful tool. When used correctly, it can catapult a brand, build credibility, and reach a more targeted clientele faster and more effectively.

The toughest concept for entrepreneurs to understand about media is that strategies are unique to each business and vision. Entrepreneurs get stuck thinking that what worked well for one business is the strategy they need to use to have success with their business. This type of thinking leaves many frustrated, exhausted, and feeling defeated.

Choosing Your Media Platform

Understanding the media's workings is the first step in creating the best strategies for your business. Well-known outlets such as *The Today Show* or *Entrepreneurial Magazine* are popular for many to gravitate toward in search of success. However, looking more closely at each outlet's target audience is critical to getting your desired results. In other words, identify your target audience before you decide what media platforms you need to use. Certainly, big named logos are nice to use on a website and in personalized marketing efforts, however, they may mean nothing to your target audience and they are extremely difficult to sustain. Approaching media simply to display logos on your website and marketing material is self-serving and doesn't leverage the media's power.

Here are five elements many entrepreneurs miss in understanding the media world and in leveraging media for growth. It is not enough to get booked on TV or become published; full spectrum understanding is essential.

Pre-Planning

Before publishing anything on media, delve deep into your messaging and personal brand identity to ensure continuity across all social media platforms, websites, and published information. This phase contains two vital components.

1. **Research.**

Research every possible outlet that aligns with you and your business. Choosing outlets that are in alignment will automatically result in reaching the right target audience. This takes time; however, the results are exponential.

2. **Brand Continuity.**

Media outlets to do their own research so invest the time to ensure all your branding, photos, messaging, content, and goals are clear.

The Pitch

The Pitch process has two avenues proven to be the most successful, although many exist: email (text only) or media sheet (single sheet, professionally produced)

Each avenue includes the same four elements:

- An Introduction
- A Value
- A Problem Solution
- The closing

Email

This is the most common way entrepreneurs pitch themselves, especially those trying to book themselves with a PR firm. When using this pitch, lead with your value at the top and thread it throughout your pitch.

When creating the Introduction, do not present an exhaustive list of accomplishments; That is a rookie mistake and your pitch may not be read thoroughly as a result. Communicate value. Part of that value is leveraging the white space; in other words, have a lot of it. Short, sweet, clear pitches get read. Those white spaces create a relaxing break for busy media professionals who read thousands of pitches.

Demonstrate benefits received rather than benefits given. Identify the problem and provide the solution (which is the time to personally shine – yet be brief). Include local or national statistics if possible.

Finally, close with a short, positive note that includes NLP[1] language. This is important as it automatically communicates added value and expectations of a reply. In the close, include your contact information and appropriate links to make the outlet's research simple. If everything a media outlet needs to make a decision , and information is easily i\available to them, the selection process becomes easy.

---

[1] Neurolinguistic Programming.

Media Sheet

If you are creative and have the time, you can create a one-page PDF or you can hire a professional.

This option allows for more graphics, branding, and overall personality than an email does. Media sheets are very effective if designed correctly, that is why it may be best to hire a professional. When using this option place the four elements strategically to follow the reader's natural eye movements: the most important information should be located in the upper left corner and the bottom right corner (a professional designer will know this).

Interview Preparation

Assuming success with your pitch, the next step is preparing for the interview.

Focus on the work you did during the pre-planning and the pitch and practice, practice, practice to reduce nervousness and be thoroughly prepared.

In most cases, TV interviews are three to five minutes, podcasts are 30-60 minutes, and most Facebook Lives are 20-60 minutes. Print media interviews are about 30 minutes and are completed via email or a phone call. Multiple outlets mean multiple policies, so follow the process closely. Don't go in blindly, even as an expert, practice timing, breathing, and not assuming.

The Performance

Your performance of the interview is vital; it determines whether an outlet will foster a relationship with you. Play the part. Get into character but don't be fake. Smile, show character, be naturally pleasant, be respectful of everyone you meet, and leave a great impression. The presentation is the shortest of the steps yet carries the biggest weight.

Post-Planning

Post-Planning is vital for building and maintaining relationships, which increases the chance for future interviews. It is also vital to building credibility and overall brand attractiveness.

Most people know to make social media posts after an interview or media opportunity and hopefully tag the outlet. Most are so excited they post before the interviewing announcing the opportunity and follow up with photos or videos afterward. Great steps to take; keep doing them but don't stop there.

Consider strategies to build relationships with outlets and individuals you met or connected with during the process. Relationship building is crucial. People conduct business with those they know, like, and trust. Amazing opportunities will arise from taking time to invest in others. Remain genuine and *always* lead with value.

Add a personal touch, for example, write a personal thank you card and mail it. Send a thank you email with photos that can be used to cross-promote their social media sites. Remember, make everything easy for them.

Moving Forward

There is more to media than most realize. Taking the time to learn and understand all aspects of media will prove mutually beneficial. Following these basic steps creates stronger paths to successful pitches and more experiences with media.

A Gift For You

To learn more about how to navigate each of these steps as well as other tips and tricks for brand building and more reach, please visit https://mediasecrets.net and register for a FREE tool to help you avoid the top three mistakes entrepreneurs make in media and a special program designed for success.

About Lori McNeil, M.B.A, M.Ed, CEME, CGSP

Lori is a 20-year International Educator, Speaker, and Business Coach, who focuses on the missing foundational tools needed for long-term success. Lori's experience is vast in helping new businesses grow and more established companies re-strategize. She has successfully grown countless organizations organically, including her own international company that includes Legacy Builders, Media Secrets, and Driven Mastery; all brands that help entrepreneurs build a true, long-lasting purpose.

Lori is featured on ABC, NBC, CBS & FOX as well as 500 other media outlets per year. She is an official speaker for the Think & Grow Rich Legacy World Tour and co-host of the National TV Talk Show *The Business Doctor*. www.LoriMcNeil.com also features special global support programs for literacy, cancer research, young entrepreneurship, and military support programs. She was recently awarded the Lifetime Presidential Service Award for her long-term success in working with communities nationally.

CHAPTER FOUR

The Essentials of Starting a Business

By Matt Rodak

Being an entrepreneur and starting a business is exciting; whether it's your first company or your fifteenth, it's always a thrill to fine-tune your ideas, plan your approach, set goals, and get started.

In recent years, becoming an entrepreneur and working for oneself has become popular. We watch shows like Shark Tank and the Profit or read stories about people making $5 million overnight running a website that sells used socks. Watching these shows and reading the overnight success stories gives entrepreneurs hope that we, too, can accomplish the same thing. What none of these shows or news feeds mention are the essential steps needed for a business to run and operate successfully.

In The Beginning

My business journey did not start off after college or growing up in a well-to-do family. I started off in the streets as a member of a criminal organization.

I have started or assisted clients start businesses 18 times. I have seen countless clients get so wrapped up in the idea of launching a business that they overlook the essential steps needed for success.

Starting a business is quite simple as long as you follow the essential steps in this chapter. More is required than clicking on a Facebook Ad, signing up, watching a 37-minute course, and starting a business.

Five Benefits Of The Essential Steps

Here are five benefits of following my essential steps:

- You will gain a deeper knowledge of your goals and dreams.
- You will discover what type of business you should to start.
- You will learn which business structure is best for you.
- You will learn the steps to make your business official.
- You will have a clear outlook and precise vision for your business.

The Five Essential Steps

These are my five essential steps to follow when starting a business:

1. **Sit down and give some serious thought to why you want to be an entrepreneur.**

This may seem simple, but you need to write down your goal(s). If you want to live a certain lifestyle, are you ready to work for it?

It's easy to get frustrated with a job and say, "I just want to work for myself!" but the question is, do you have what it takes to do that? Being an entrepreneur isn't easy. You must spend a lot of unpaid time setting up, promoting, and growing your business. There are benefits but don't get blinded and see only the benefits; a lot of the hard work goes into starting and running a business and there are no guarantees that you'll make money or break-even.

On my website you will find tools and worksheets to download that will help with all of these steps. Two of the most useful are the Goal Mapping and the Seven Levels Deep worksheets. These will help you set your goals and understand, deep down, why you want to be a successful entrepreneur. Along with the worksheets, I have included videos for you in which I walk through the worksheets with you to ensure your success.

2. **Determine the type of business you want to start.**

Make sure you follow your heart as well as your passion and start a business you care about. If you choose a business you don't care about, running it will become the same drudgery that your 9-to-5 job was. It's the journey you must think about most, not the result you hope will come about.

I have my clients fill out a worksheet that breaks down their top five hobbies, passions, and skills to determine the best business to start.

If you have not done so already, go to my website now and download the free worksheets there.

3. **Decide how your business will be structured.**

Various types of business structures exist in the US, including sole proprietorship, partnership, corporation, s-corporation, or a Limited Liability Company (LLC). The most popular is the LLC; it is cost-effective and the most protective for you and your business when starting but it may not be the best structure for you in the long run. Do your homework and make sure you understand the different structures for your location.

Each business structure has pros and cons that affect taxes, income, and profits. So, take your time and carefully decide which best fits your business. If unclear about any of the structures or which is right for you, seek professional legal advice to ensure the right choice.

4. **Obtain your Employee Identification Number (EIN) from the IRS for tax purposes.**

Go to www.irs.gov to apply for the EIN, this step is very easy and takes only a few minutes to complete. After you get your EIN you will need to register with your state to get your business license and any permits you may need.

Go to your state's Secretary of State website and search for 'filing a new business.' Follow the directions and also see if your state has any other requirements that you may need to complete. Doing this yourself can save you a lot of money compared to some of the online legal services.

Once you have all your documents from the IRS and your state, head to the bank. Check to see what is needed to open a business account. You will need a business account to keep personal and business monies separate for accounting and tax purposes.

5. **Create a business plan.**

I'm not talking about a traditional business plan, that can be hundreds of pages; I am talking about a personal plan for you or you and your business partners.

Check my website for the sample business plan with directions. It will keep you focused on the key points of your business: marketing, branding, mission, values, and more. Creating your business plan will help you think of questions that may not have already arisen. It will help you improve your business and help you be prepared for any obstacles that may come your way.

Moving Forward

Use this book as you write your business plan. Use each chapter to build on your business. Remember to use all the tools given to you to make your chances of success better.

Follow the Five Essential Steps to create a strong foundation for your business. Properly completing the Five Essential steps will set you on the best path for success You will not only save time, money, and stress but you will also be prepared for the future growth of your business as well.

About Matt Rodak

"You are worthless and will never amount to anything!"

Those were the words yelled at Matt by his teacher in school that would change his entire life and set him on a crazy journey. Matt started his entrepreneur journey as a member in a criminal organization. He owned several businesses legal and illegal.

Eventually, life caught up and Matt was under investigation. His friends had turned on him and he hit rock bottom. Matt eventually gave it all to God and decided to change his life. Luckily, for Matt, charges were never brought up against him due to lack of evidence. That was over 20 years ago and

A Gift For You

Since you have already shown your desire to succeed, you should go to my site wwww.gutter2glory.com and get all of your free worksheets! There is a special The Entrepreneurs' Guidebook link on my site just for you!

Your free worksheets!

1. **7 levels deep worksheet**
2. **Massive Goals**
3. **Passion, Knowledge, Skills worksheet**
4. **New Age Business Plan**

As well as the free worksheets, I am offering a crazy package deal that will literally change your life! Go now and check out your special offer at www.gutter2glory.com

he has since changed his entire life by giving back and starting over 18 businesses across various markets and industries. He used all his knowledge from both the street and traditional business practices to build his empire. His passion to help others is like no other!

CHAPTER FIVE

Cold Email Marketing/Big Data

By Robert Raff

You've probably never heard of me, but you've probably heard from me and my clients.

How would I know that?

I'm the founder and CEO of *Direct Aim Media*. We've been building the world's most effective cold email marketing solution at scale for the past 15 years.

Email marketing is worth talking about for every business looking to make more money, every marketing pro trying to run better campaigns, and every entrepreneur looking to build a brand and acquire new customers.

Email is still one of the best ways to reach people and convert customers.

Even in 2019, email marketing provided an average Return on Investment (ROI) of $44 for every $1 invested.[2] You wanna stick to social? Good luck with that. You're 40 times more likely to gain a new customer from email marketing than you are from Facebook or Twitter activity.

Let's back up for a minute, so I can better explain myself and what I do.

When I say "cold email," I'm not talking about some cute Gmail plugins that let you send a hundred emails a day before Google throttles or blocks you.

Direct Aim helps our clients deliver more than a billion emails every month, to lists of contacts that have never subscribed or opted in. We've run campaigns for lists of more than 10 million verified contacts many times. This is truly cold email, at scale.

We help some of the world's largest businesses and most recognizable brands get their message in front of millions of prospective customers.

That automaker you've been eyeing for a new convertible? They've probably sent you an email through *Direct Aim*'s systems. The software developer that keeps your company's back office humming probably uses us to reach out to huge lists of Business-to-Business (B2B) decision-makers.

I actually ran the numbers and, odds are, you've gotten a few emails from *Direct Aim*'s systems.

There are almost four billion email users in the world, so there's a 97% chance you'll get one of our emails over the course of a year.[3] I'm sure that number's higher in our target markets, since we focus on emailing North American and European contacts.

---

[2] Carter, E. (May 9, 2020). *9 Tips for Improving Your Email Marketing ROI*. Retrieved on July 24, 2019 from https://www.webfx.com/blog/marketing/9-tips-improving-email-marketing-roi/

[3] Cumulative probability of 1 billion emails a month to approximately 3.89 billion people over 12 months

In The Beginning

I needed a system like *Direct Aim*'s 15 years ago when I transitioned from the mortgage industry into online marketing. You think it's hard to run digital marketing campaigns today? Try doing it in 2004. No Facebook ads, no paid search, and no viral social tweets. Heck, Facebook only launched in 2004.

If you wanted to promote something online in 2004, you had email, and basically that was it.

In 2004, every service or app for email marketing was either a low-volume answer to a high-volume problem or super expensive and not ready to handle cold lists in the first place.

I tried some email marketing services available then, but I was banned real fast. Mailchimp does not like you sending thousands of emails to a list you uploaded five minutes ago.

No one had a service or an app capable of effectively sending cold emails at scale. No one. In fact, as far as I can tell, that's still true today, with the exception of *Direct Aim*.

I figured I couldn't be the only one with that problem. Since no one else had a usable solution, I went all-in to solve it myself.

Once I had a development team in place, we had to learn – on the fly – how to get past early spam filters. Developing our system at the same time email providers were figuring out how to filter and block spam gave us a huge leg up in that arms race. We're still staying ahead of your inbox filters 15 years later.

Advantages Of Email Marketing

Do you use email marketing? If you don't, you should. 89% of digital marketers use email as their primary channel for lead generation.[4]

Here are some of the best reasons to use email marketing:

- Email marketing has an average ROI of $44 for every $1 invested.
- You're 40 times more likely to gain a new customer from email marketing than from Facebook or Twitter activity.
- Transactional (sales) emails are opened eight times more often than other emails.[5]
- 61% of consumers prefer to be contacted by brands via email.[6]
- 63% of business professionals prefer communicating via email.[7]

Cold Email and List-Building

Cold email marketing is a bit different from list-based marketing.

---

4 Selder, S. 26 Noteworthy Email Marketing Statistics for 2019.

5 Harbin, L. (July 24, 2019). 70 Email Marketing Stats Every Marketer Should Know. Retrieved on July 24, 2019 from https://www.campaignmonitor.com/blog/email-marketing/2018/12/70-email-marketing-stats-you-need-to-know/

6 Harbin. L. 10 Email Marketing Stats Every Marketer Should Know.

7 Sands, V. March 19, 2020. 19 Fascinating Email Facts. Retrieved on July 24, 2019 from https://www.lifewire.com/how-many-emails-are-sent-every-day-1171210

Everyone starts from zero when they build a subscriber list. Some of us are better at list-building than others, but it still takes time, effort, creativity, and money to get people to click *Subscribe* so you can start sending sales pitches.

Lots of people try cold email marketing because they think it'll let them skip the list-building process and start generating leads and sales right away. Most of the time, they fail, because they don't really know what they're doing. They don't know how to hit the inbox instead of the spam folder, or how to keep from being blacklisted by email providers.

That last point is why most email marketing services won't let you use cold lists.

When you send emails from Mailchimp or Constant Contact, it only **looks** like it's coming from you@yourbrand.com. It's really coming from a Mailchimp or Constant Contact server.

If you look at marketing emails, you'll often see a *via* tag next to the sender's address, at least in Gmail. You can also look at an email's source code to see where it really came from. An email might show your address in the reply field, but that *via* or the source code shows which server really sent it.

If you use Mailchimp to send cold emails to a big list, and lots of people start flagging you, that hurts Mailchimp's sender reputation (i.e., deliverability rating). Email marketing providers are **very** protective of their sender reputations and will kick you off fast if it looks like you might damage it.

We avoid that problem by creating new domains and spinning up new servers for every client. If you wreck your sender reputation sending emails with Direct Aim, it only hurts the reputation of the domain and servers used to help you to run your campaign.

This is one of the keys to running a successful cold email marketing campaign: never use your primary domain to send cold emails at scale.[8]

You can always migrate anyone who responds positively over to the real you@yourbrand.com list, or even ask them to subscribe to the real list after they've responded to your cold email.

When you use a new domain to send cold emails, you'll need to verify the technical settings on your email servers. Direct Aim handles this during the setup process for every client, but do-it-yourselfers have a lot of extra work to do before starting a cold email campaign.

Cleaning Your Lists

Before you start, however, you really should clean any list of cold emails you want to use. Cleaning a list involves running it through verification services, which check every email against a number of qualifying factors[9]:

- Is its address unique (duplicates are removed)?
- Is its syntax correct (an address might be mistyped or formatted incorrectly?
- Is its server accessible (servers are pinged to see if they respond)?
- Is its role valid (domain-wide addresses like info or postmaster are removed)?

---

[8] Jones, C. (April 26, 2018). *The Ultimate Cold Email Checklist.* Retrieved on July 24, 2019 from https://blog.leadcandy.io/the-ultimate-cold-email-checklist-fcc87be84ced

[9] Vaghasia, R. (July 14, 2020). *Top 10 Email Verification and Validation Services Compared.* Retrieved on July 16, 2020 from https://www.accuwebhosting.com/blog/top-10-bulk-email-list-verification-validation-services-compared/

- Is it a honeypot or spam trap (these emails are added to lists to catch spammers)?
- Is the email itself accessible (the address is pinged without sending an email)?

The process of validating a list is actually more complicated than this, but the important thing to understand is that you need to clean your email list to avoid wrecking your deliverability by sending thousands of emails that bounce back, fail to deliver, or add your domain to lists of known spammers.

I've had clients come to me with more than a million emails and wind up with only a few thousand valid contacts after cleaning their lists through a verification service. Not only can cleaning a list save your deliverability, it also saves you money. Email marketing services like Direct Aim bill you on a per-send or per-contact basis.

Warm Up Your List And Mail Server

Once you've got your system in place and your list cleaned, you still shouldn't jump right in and email everyone on the list all at once. We highly recommend warming up your list and mail server by starting with small batches of emails and increasing your daily sending volume over the course of days or even weeks, to avoid getting blacklisted by being too visible too soon.

Remember how a subscription list always starts from zero? Email providers remember. A brand new domain sending thousands of emails a day as soon as it's registered will make a provider suspicious.

Create A Compelling Message

As with any email campaign, it's critical to create a compelling message for every email. If anything, this is *more* important in cold email marketing.

Your recipients won't know who you are, because they didn't sign up for your emails. If you don't give them a good reason to click and read, or if your pitch is disconcerting or amateurish, they might just flag your email as spam.

Anyone can send an email. Lots of people can send a million emails. Anyone who can actually write emails that **sell** are the ones who win with cold email campaigns.

Direct Aim helps its clients take care of these critical steps, which is why we've built so many successful long-term relationships. There is a reason most of our business now comes through word-of-mouth.

Moving Forward

You can look for alternatives, and you can try going it alone or by yourself, but in the end, there's no substitute for experience and infrastructure. I'm proud to say that nobody else can match Direct Aim on either count.

About Robert Raff

Robert Raff is the founder and CEO of Direct Aim Media (https://exactprospect.com/), the world's leading cold email marketing solutions provider at scale. He has created, built, and exited successful ventures in a wide range of industries, many of which he's grown primarily through high-volume cold email marketing campaigns.

Robert enjoys working with entrepreneurs and executives with businesses in need of creative marketing approaches to power the next stage of their growth. He's worked with some of the world's largest and most successful companies to create marketing campaigns that really work.

Interested in working with Robert and Direct Aim Media? Visit https://exactprospect.com or send Robert an email directly at Robert@exactprospect.com.

CHAPTER SIX

The Three Principles Of E-Commerce Success

By Earnest Epps

If you master the principles in this chapter, you will be able to build freedom, success, and joy into your business no matter what type of business you currently own or want to own.

$1.2 million

Yes, 1.2 million. Once I fully understood the three principles I'm going to share with you, I went from $498,000 to $1.2 million the next year. I know if you follow these principles, you'll be able to do the same.

In The Beginning

I am a full-time digital e-Commerce entrepreneur, but I didn't start that way. While working at several different 9-to-5 jobs from 2009 to 2015, I was always pursuing entrepreneurship outside of the traditional corporate arena because I knew the goals I wanted to achieve in my life would require more revenue than I could make working in a cubicle or for someone else.

During that time, I attempted to start several different types of businesses. I tried Multi-Level Marketing, an e-Commerce store, a remodeling company, another MLM program, I tried, I tried, I tried, and I tried. But nothing was working. To add to that disappointment, I had some ups and downs in the corporate world.

When I was 20, I was hired as the marketing director of a remodeling company. While there, I was able to help my company make an additional seven-figures in revenue in less than six months

Then, in April 2011, I was laid-off.

In 2012, I started working as a sales associate for a marketing firm. I set a record in launch day sales for a multi-billion-dollar telecommunications company. I was consistently one of the top five sales associates in the company and was first in individual sales for several months.

While working for that company, I was promoted four times in less than a year to become a district sales manager. I started with three employees for the project I managed. My project grew quickly, and I hired more than 250 employees. The team I built was consistently in the top three in sales and revenue, generating millions in revenue for the company.

Can you guess what happened after I helped them grow so rapidly? I was fired during a company restructuring.

This practically broke me, and I fell into a depression for two years. I had given that company so much of myself and they just let me go as if I was worthless. I knew I needed to do something more self-fulfilling to provide for my family. That's when I really started to study e-Commerce.

I fell in love with the business model because I could maximize three things:

1. I didn't need large startup capital.
2. I could build a business that made money while I slept.
3. I didn't need any employees.

In September 2015, I made a 30-day promise to myself: I would make a serious, dedicated effort to make e-Commerce work for me while continuing to work at a full-time job.

In the first few months, I made an extra $150,000; I quit my job to focus on e-Commerce full-time.

The two skills I've mastered through my career are how to market and sell products and services. As a result, I've been able to achieve success with my e-Commerce endeavors and I'm considered to be in the top e-Commerce income earners! I know first-hand what it takes to launch a product or service into the marketplace, how to start driving sales for that product or service, and how to scale a product and service from zero- to seven-figures.

Three Principles Of E-Commerce

The literal definition of e-Commerce is *electronic commerce*, which can be either buying or selling goods and/or services online. It has grown quickly over the last few years and e-Commerce sales are now in the trillions of dollars annually.

Creating success in e-Commerce, in my opinion, boils down to these three principles:

1. Market Research – Identifying the demand
2. Understanding Your Audience – Getting to know your target demographic
3. Riches Are in Niches – Finding your niche

Market Research

The most critical thing in any business is understanding and knowing the level of demand for the product or service you want to sell. This is also something many people forget to do before moving forward with their business idea.

You don't have to pay a big data company to do this for you because you can leverage online tools that give you information. For example, *Keywords Everywhere* (keywordseverywhere.com) you can see how many people search on Google for what you want to sell. This number is an indication of your market demand. You can also use *Keywords Everywhere* to research products or services that are already available. Thus, you can learn whether there is a demand for your product/service and determine if other vendors are already meeting the demand or if the market is under-saturated with sellers. I like to see a demand of over 20,000 searches per month to feel confident about what I'm planning to sell.

Understanding Your Audience

One of the main reasons people fail at marketing is that they don't know and understand who exactly their customer is. Your audience is a critical factor when it comes to everything you do in your business: branding, advertising, marketing, copywriting, creative, etc. Are your customers mainly male or female? Are they younger or older? Are they single or married? And, so on.

When you discover all the core attributes of your customer, it makes everything much easier to do. Once again, there are free tools on the Internet that will give you this information. The primary tool to use is Facebook Audience Insights: After plugging your product or service into the interest section, Audience Insights will give you a lot of details of who your target audience is.

In marketing and advertising, you don't ever play guessing games with your strategies. Get the data and the insight so you are sure your marketing, branding, and advertising are on-point before launch.

Riches Are In Niches

You must be niche specific with whatever you want to sell. Successful e-Commerce entrepreneurs understand this principle.

A niche is a small, specialized section of the population. In a nutshell, don't go too broad with what you want to sell, focus intently on your niche market and don't worry about selling to everyone.

People who want to sell physical products online always ask me, "Earnest, how can I be successful with Amazon, Wal-Mart, and so many other retailers online?"

The answer is easy: Focus on a niche part of the market that they're not serving and build a business and brand around that.

For example, if you chose to sell electric fireplaces (rather than all types of fireplaces), and create a website called electricfireplacesusadirect.com, the site is solely targeted at selling to people that are specifically looking for electric fireplaces. By doing this, you separate yourself from other fireplace retailers because your branding is focused on electric fireplaces, you come across as an expert in that field, and it's easier to stand out.

Moving Forward

Focusing on the three principles of e-Commerce will provide a clear path to follow for long-term success with an e-Commerce business.

About Earnest Epps

Earnest Epps is an international speaker, digital marketing entrepreneur, and CEO of High Ticket eCom Secrets. Earnest has ten years of marketing and sales experience and helps people use offline and online strategies to become marketing powerhouses for their e-Commerce businesses.

A Gift For You

If you'd like some additional support on how to use the tools I mentioned in this chapter, I have some great bonuses:

Bonus #1 The Entrepreneurs' Guidebook Resource Guide ($97 value)

Bonus #2 The Entrepreneurs' Guidebook Video Training for eCom Success ($497 value)

Total Value = $594

Your Price = FREE

Just go to https://www.earnestepps.com/free-stuff

CHAPTER SEVEN

Emotional Intelligence In Digital Marketing

By Page Nielson

motional intelligence is not usually addressed in books dedicated to digital marketing, but it is key to resonating with an audience, increasing engagement, and attracting a loyal following, which – in turn – leads to an increased client base and increased sales and profits.

The Internet allows us to reach so many more people that we think we should be able to work a few years and retire but we have a tendency to forget that on the other side of the screen are living, breathing human beings with their own fascinating, intricate lives, hopes and dreams, fears and everyday stresses. When we choose to recognize this, take the time to understand the real-life experience of those to whom we're marketing, we create an authentic connection that has a real impact on our bottom line.

Usually, we start trying to understand our customers with an Avatar that gives us a snapshot of our ideal client: age, education, relationship status, etc.

It's a good start, but relying on an Avatar too heavily leads you to talk *at* your audience instead of talking *with* them. Speaking at them reduces them to a commodity rather than recognizing them as a valuable person who is supporting us and our endeavors.

> **What Is an Avatar?**
>
> An embodiment (as of a concept or philosophy) often in a person.
>
> In the case of business, a person who represents an ideal customer (or group of ideal customers).

In The Beginning

I've had the honor of working intimately with thousands of people over the last several decades and witnessed digital marketing's birth. I've seen the success and joy of both marketers and customers when the marketing is congruent with both the values of the business and the customers. When Emotional Intelligence (EI) is used phenomenal growth happens and creates successful thriving businesses with raving loyal fans!

An example of exceptional EI in digital marketing, social media, strategy, and real life is Honeycomb Salon in Oregon, USA. The owner and facilitator, Alicia Brown, is a natural empath and has increased her team from one to over 40 and opened four locations in less than four years!

Alicia's success is attributed to her high EI as well as her entrepreneurial skills and intelligence. She continually improves her self-awareness and teaches those skills to her team. In turn, she and her team understand their customers' needs better and are ready to meet those needs positively.

EI has allowed Alicia and her team to resonate with their present and future customers because the team truly understands what the customers are feeling and what they need; these are true relationships and conversations. The team navigates, problem-solves, and speaks the customers' vocabulary. Honeycomb Salon's raving fans feel seen, understood, and sincerely cared for.

It is EI that makes people *want to* throw their credit card in your face and say, "Take my money!"

Five Elements Of Emotional Intelligence

When a person feels a real connection there is trust. Trust is vital for successful business. Success expands as our awareness of self and others expand. The higher our EI, the more we can understand how our audience feels about themselves.

The brilliant Daniel Goleman laid out the five elements of emotional intelligence in 1995's *Emotional Intelligence* and those five elements are still true today. While we're going to address them individually, please observe how their interdependence enhances the entire EI concept.

Self-Awareness

It is important to understand the role emotions play in our lives. Particularly in Western culture, we've developed a tendency to judge our emotions as good or bad when they are neither but are simply messengers attempting to tell us what's going on at a deeper level.

For example, anger in the heat of a moment may be the body's attempt to show us there's something wrong that needs correcting immediately to protect others or us. If we look at the deeper motivation, can we still say the emotion is bad?

Learning to see beneath the surface of our own emotions allows us to see how our audience may be having similar experiences and we become empathetic.

Self-Regulation

Self-regulation has to do with our reactions and keeping our behavior in check. When we learn to reduce or eliminate our impulsive reactions, we can learn how to use that energy to our advantage.

Self-regulation stops us from snapping-back at others who need our compassion (like cranky customers) and allows us to honor both ourselves and the other person. Demonstrating poise under pressure does wonders for both your messaging and your brand and invites our audience to raise themselves to their highest potential, as well.

To practice this idea, think about your content before you share it with these following questions:

- Is it authentic and sincere?
- Does it serve the greater good (and your brand)?
- Will it help or harm you when you share it?

This practice alone could revolutionize your entire business and help you create a stronger bond with your audience.

Motivation

Do you see people or dollars first, and which do you value more? Getting this out of order can potentially limit how much of either show up in your life. From my own experience, it's beyond worth it to put people first and treat them with empathy. The money will naturally follow the value created for them.

Empathy

It's my firm opinion that connecting with people on an authentic level, meeting them where they are, is how we can greatly enrich the lives of everyone around us. Perhaps it's selfish to want to feel good inside, but isn't that what we're all seeking?

Empathy, which only comes once the first three elements are addressed, is what allows us to make a profit while helping people solve their problems. The money becomes a natural byproduct of the service we provide, creating a win/win scenario for all.

Social Skills

The first four elements translate to how we conduct ourselves. I'm not suggesting you make these internal changes to make it easier to manipulate others. What I am suggesting is that, as we learn to like ourselves more, we naturally like others more. When you operate from a place of self-love rather than one of self-doubt or self-hatred, it overflows to others and they like and love themselves more, too. As you prioritize relationships and understanding over profits, it naturally flows with genuine validation for both you and others.

As you learn to speak to the individual, the bigger your circle of followers becomes. Your ability to lead increases as does your ability to influence. You'll become a better communicator, more able to problem solve, and will have positive interactions with others.

Moving Forward

EI is the key to personal and professional success. The only time self-awareness, self-regulation, motivation, empathy, and social skills are useless is when you don't have a clear sense of your values. Digital marketing is getting people to the end-stage to buy something. If your values are congruent with your EI then you're going to be a success! You may be able to work a few years and then retire, but you will likely find that you don't want to because of the relationships you develop with your customers.

A Gift For You

Send a DM to Page on Instagram @page_nielson the words: "Style My Brand!" and receive your gift: The Anatomy Of A Great Personal Brand.

About Page Nielson

Page Nielson is a multi-passionate, digital marketer with a prolific career in the beauty and fashion industry. Having wore many entrepreneurial hats, she is an art director, stylist, and personal branding expert. Her biggest love is helping entrepreneurs increase their cash flow and impact through creative visual story telling and digital marketing campaigns.

She is the author of *Houses With Names* the soon to be released book about coming of age despite an offbeat, sometimes lawless, family. She vividly and with welcome humor, portrays being raised surrounded by a backdrop of poverty, drugs, child abduction, and small town high fashion. Page is based in Oregon, USA.

Connect with her on Instagram @page_nielson and at: www.pagenielson.com

CHAPTER EIGHT

Promotion Through Signature Stories

By Pierre-Francois Rio

The essence of being an entrepreneur involves taking action and promoting your business. The term *taking action* has been overused in the past and can be ambiguous. I believe the definition of taking action entrepreneurs should use is Richard Branson's:

> *Do something that improves people's lives, don't try to do everything yourself, use yourself to promote your business and put it on the map, and have fun.*

Many new entrepreneurs focus on what they are selling and take lots of courses to learn how to run their business. They do this before they have made any money because they are afraid of making errors. But spending time learning skills like bookkeeping, different types of marketing, and sales does not allow the time to do anything productive! The key is to take action rather than trying to learn everything before you start.

Successful entrepreneurs spend a lot of time promoting themselves – making themselves useful to their customers -- the only thing that matters, the ultimate role of the entrepreneur, is to leverage yourself to promote your business. An excellent way to do that is through signature stories.

In The Beginning

Ten months ago, I never thought I would be writing this chapter. On a sunny afternoon, I was standing in my kitchen, with my phone in hand. Most days, I would be calmly settling into my day with a short espresso. But this day was different. As I spoke on the phone, my heart was beating fast, really fast, and I hadn't even had an espresso yet. I was pacing the kitchen, excited by the prospect of what I had just done. The adrenalin was coursing through my veins and I felt like I could do *anything* right at that moment.

But that euphoria didn't last long. As soon as I hung up the phone, the transaction went through: I had just taken a bet I couldn't afford to lose.

A few minutes earlier, I had a couple of thousand dollars in my bank account and a line of credit at $9,251. Not a great situation. Now, with just one call, I had an additional $20,000 in credit card debt.

What the *heck* had I done?

A few months before that sunny day, I made a pact with myself that I wouldn't settle for anything less than an extraordinary life.

Yes, I had moved to Canada (from France, years before), but each time I went back to visit my family in France -- as my parents' shiny eyes constantly, tearfully, questioned why I was leaving again -- I felt like I hadn't done enough with my life. I was just leaving them for a normal life that I could have had in France without being an eight-hour flight away. I kept thinking, "If I'm going do this, it's got to be for an incredible life and nothing else."

And so, my obsession with building an incredible life began.

Like many entrepreneurs, I took courses, went to events, and chased fake opportunities. I spent money I didn't have and was deep in debt. Something had to change. In other words, I had to take action and start promoting my business and me.

Your Signature Story

Storytelling is one of the most effective methods of promoting and selling because it stimulates more areas of your brain than any other.[10] People connect with stories emotionally and emotions can have a great impact on perceived value. Stories are not a pitch, but they do sell.

It is important to take action and promote your business by creating a signature story. Your signature story is your promotional message; it is storytelling and story selling. If people buy into your signature story, they will likely buy into your product(s) or service(s) as well.

Story selling is both an art and a science; there is a method for writing a solid signature story that can be broken down into four parts that follow.

Follow The Specific Structure

A good signature story appeals to people's emotions but it must also make logical sense for them to buy. People often feel they need to justify their spend to themselves and others.

The structure of your signature story must follow a specific approach:

1. Begin with the Context – Appealing to Emotion

You must appeal to the emotions around your ideal customer's need. Describe the problem this customer is having and call upon the emotions they face each time they deal with the problem. Tell them you had that problem, too, and tell them how it made you feel.

2. Introduce your idea – Appealing to Emotion

Tell them how you've solved the problem. Be excited about your solution. Show them how great your life is now that you found the solution.

3. Project *their* future – Appealing to Emotion

Tell your customers how they are going to feel and what they will be able to do once they have or use your solution. List all the benefits of your solution and exaggerate the relief they will have once they have purchased your solution.

4. Results – Appealing to Logic

---

[10] n.a. (July 1, 2019). *7 Powerfully Effective Ways to Market a Product*. Retrieved from https://www.wordstream.com/blog/ws/2017/04/06/how-to-market-a-product on September 16, 2019.

Share the actual results you and others have seen or experienced. Use data and numbers whenever possible to support your claims.

5. **Present a Case Study or Example – Appealing to Logic**

This is the proof or testimonial from real customers that your solution works. You can provide one detailed case study and then shorter examples or testimonials from real customers who have used your solutions and are happy.

Using this structure builds up both the emotional and logical attachment your customers have for your solution. At this point, your prospects should be curious and want to know more about how they can get the same results as your examples.

Make It Relatable And Specific

People have things going on in their lives; they have problems. Your signature story must relate to them and their problems. It must be specific and tell details about a specific moment, a turning point, in your life or situation; a turning point that they want to reach and experience,

Here are a few questions you should answer to help create your story:

- What was the turning point in your life that got you to change?
- When did this turning point happen?
- Where did it happen?

Don't Just Sell, Show What Your Solution Can Do

One thought in your prospect's mind is, "You're just trying to sell me something because you want to make money."

You must address this thought or people will stop listening to you. You must tell them why you're telling them this story. How you want to help them with their problems, not how you want to make money.

Your Story versus Your Product's Story

As I started creating my stories, there was one difficult point for me; I thought the story had to be about *my* origins and *my* results.

The story isn't my origin story; it is the origin story of my product through me.

There are two approaches to talk about your product/service:

1. **The Expert's Story**
2. **The Product Evolution Story**

The expert story is exactly that: If you are an expert in your field, talk about your own experience with the problem, how you solved it, and the results of the solution.

The product evolution story tells the story of the product/service directly. Again, you can talk about the problem, but the solution is a product or service so talk about how it solves the problem and the results it obtains.

Russell Brunson of Clickfunnels uses the product evolution approach to market his sales funnels.

In his signature story (about the potato gun), Russell portrays sales funnels as the evolution of websites. Although he wrapped it up in a story that is his own, the positioning of the product has nothing to do with him.

It goes like this: Before, people drove traffic to their website using ads and it worked. Then, it became more expensive to advertise online and driving traffic to websites wasn't profitable anymore. Sales funnels add up-sells and draw traffic to your site, which makes more money on average, and sales are profitable again.

Essentially, the product evolution story could be told by anyone; only an expert can tell the expert story. Think of your market and your role in relation to the market; that helps determine which story approach to use.

Moving Forward

Once you've created your signature story, it can be used in many ways: videos, podcasts, Facebook Live, blogs, email campaigns, webinars, advertising, etc.

Use yourself to promote your business. Doing so makes your business real for you as well as your prospects. Once you get the promotion aspect rolling, it tends to have a snowball effect.

A Gift For You

At the time of writing, Pierre-Francois took the challenge to grow a business (SaaS product) focused on helping retailers count their inventory and building better business practices.

You can follow the journey on Instagram and Facebook:

Instagram	@pierrefrio
Facebook	@pierrefriohq

About Pierre-Francois Rio

Pierre-Francois is an entrepreneur and marketer with an obsession to understand and create lucrative campaigns to help grow businesses.

At 21 years old, he started his first venture, while studying as an undergrad. It was a clothing business that wholesaled to big box retailers in France, which he left to the next generation of students to take over when he decided to move to Canada to take on new projects.

CHAPTER NINE

Five Shifts To Successful Selling

By Allie Bjerk

If you want to sell digital products and make passive income, without a gigantic email list, special influencer status, or Internet-famous friends, you can start right now. I discovered this strategy after failing many, many, times.

There were five shifts that I had to make (not only mentally but in my business model as well) to launch and scale a system that made me over $392,000 in just six months.

In The Beginning

I was focusing on Done-For-You services, but I wasn't making the impact that I wanted. I was doing OK, but I wasn't feeling elevated by my work. I wanted more; more freedom and more money, but that wasn't going to happen without taking on more clients while I was already chained to my laptop while being smothered by my dreams.

The shifts began when I had a horrible client experience that finally broke me. I was laying with my son as he was falling asleep one evening when I had a notification from Stripe that $6,000 was going to be debited from my bank account the next morning.

A client had sent through a chargeback for work that had been delivered months prior. It had been the worst client experience I'd ever had, and I was completely helpless; that money had already been spent. I had a contract, and I could still take legal action, but that takes time and energy. That's a lot of money to have pulled out of your business when you're living client to client.

I was scared, but I took action immediately. I had many doubts; I was afraid of failing. What if I put all of my time into creating something and no one bought it? What if I should be spending my time on something else?

I understood launches inside and out and I knew that with typical launch methods, there's too much room for error, and I needed money now. I didn't have a big list. I didn't have a lot of confidence in my ability to make money with my brain or with digital products, but I didn't have a choice.

I didn't have time for the traditional launch method. It can take weeks to build enough trust for people to buy a high-end product.

I knew that my best chance for success would be designing a new method to speed-up the process and get me selling a product to a new, cold audience because I didn't have a list or time to waste.

Five Shifts To Successful Digital Sales

I made several shifts in my attitude and business model in a short time to solve my problems, the top five of which are listed here.

Some involved a mental shift from offering a service to offering a product and some involved working with a cold audience rather than building trust over time. I knew I couldn't rely on my social media followers to buy what I was offering; it would take too long to build the trust necessary to entice my followers to buy. I decided that the one thing that motivated cold prospects to buy was price and value, so I focused on those and relied on advertising to find my buyers.

Here are the shifts in thinking and approach that I made:

1. Your Social Status Doesn't Equal Profits

Guess what? You can't cash-in followers at the bank. Shocking, I know. Social media followers do not equal dollars in your bank account – even though many people tell you it's all about the followers – it's simply not true.

The first time I heard that you should never focus on building your social media following without a selling system in place, it almost crushed me, because that was everything I had been doing: The followers, the likes, the shares. Yet, I could see the painful truth firsthand, many of those followers weren't buying from me.

The people who bought my product went from ad to sales page to email list. They didn't look at any of my social media, they didn't go read my blogs or listen to my podcast. They took immediate action on an offer suite that was directly in front of them. Remember, your perceived social media status has nothing to do with revenue.

2. Stop Giving It All Away

People spend an average of 6.7 hours online every day.[11] They are hooked to their devices much of the day, flipping between Instagram, Facebook, Instagram Messages, Stories, Facebook Messenger, email, YouTube and seeing over 10,000 ads every single day.

To get customers, you need to give something of value away but not everything (then you just get followers). You can either live chained to your social media or you can launch a product that attracts the right audience.

If you are giving away all your information freely, stop right now! Instead, build a small front-end offer on which you can run limitless advertising. Make it a too-good-to-be-true price, and it's not necessary to build trust with your audience first. Instead, super-pack the value in a $27 product and collect contact information for a list of people willing to invest in themselves and you.

People who pay, pay attention, and that's on whom you should focus your energy and time.

3. Build It And They Won't Come

Most people start by building solo products, presenting them somehow, and wait for them to sell, which they rarely do. You need a product suite or a bundle. A product suite is a set of products that complement each other. This works better than a single product because it harnesses the power of (psychological) buying triggers.

---

[11] Salim, S. (February 4, 2019). *More Than 6 Hours of our Day is Spent Online – Digital 2019 Reports*. Retrieved on May 22, 2020 from https://www.digitalinformationworld.com/2019/02/internet-users-spend-more-than-a-quarter-of-their-lives-online.html.

Buying triggers are usually visual cues that you don't even realize are there, like when you're at a restaurant and the most expensive item on the menu is bold or has a circle around it. Or, when you're at a department store and all of the things you need to redecorate your bathroom in a particular style - the perfect soap dispenser, the towels, the shower curtain – are displayed conveniently at the end of an aisle.

A product suite is designed to meet your customers where *they* are. It's designed to solve their problems or relieve their pain points before they even realize the problem/pain exists. It is not manipulation; it is using marketing to help drive desire for a product that helps them get results they've been seeking. In this way, you are serving your customers better.

The challenge is figuring out what your audience thinks they need the most. As an expert, you know more than your audience. There's often a disconnect between what people think they need and what they actually need, so your mission as the business owner is to meet them where they are not where you think they should be.

4. The Four Specific Triggers Every Product Suite Needs

Your product suite needs to do four very specific things; this is the secret formula!

- It needs to save time.
- It needs to provide control.
- It needs to teach something new.
- It needs to inspire bigger thinking.

The product suite presentation must be choreographed and presented in a specific order so that you can create a *solve and agitate* cycle. As you solve one pain point with your product, you're agitating a new problem. Solve. Agitate. Repeat.

Start tiny and get bigger. When creating the tiny offer, think about the final result you have in mind for the client and then brainstorm every step they need to take to get that result. The key is finding the sweet spots and themes throughout the essential steps for the customer. Try looking at the content you're already using for existing clients and package it up into a minimal viable product quickly.

5. Enact The System

A lot of small businesses fear advertising. Most feel they don't have the money to waste on advertising. By using the system I'm about to explain, you will see whether your ads will be profitable or not on the first day of a campaign

Begin by advertising a $27 product – that re-captures any advertising and other costs – to a cold audience, with a $37 order bump, and a $77 upsell.

When I started my ads, I spent $30 on the first day. That was hard for me to do. I told myself, "If I sell one of these things, I'll be fine (because my ad cost will be re-captured). I sold two or three on the first day.

I spent $75 the next day and doubled it again. And then, $150, and $300, and then $600 a day. You can see how quickly this scaled for me. I never once second-guessed if I should be paying that much for ads because I knew it was gas in the tank. I wouldn't expect my car to drive without gasoline, so don't expect your business to grow quickly without well-done advertising.

Using this method, you see if your ads are going to be profitable on the first day. No waiting out the ten-day launch period and crossing your fingers. If the ads aren't profitable right away, shut them off, tweak a few things, and try again.

Moving Forward

I spent thousands of dollars on courses and coaching and this is the first thing that worked for me. It helped give me confidence and reach a level of self-efficacy that I'd never experienced. I've seen this strategy work to transform my students' lives as well. I know it can work for you, too.

A Gift For You

If you would like me to show you how I went from a burned-out service provider to CEO of a 7-figure empire, register for my free Masterclass here: https://www.tinyofferlab.com/

About Allie Bjerk

Allie Bjerk is a visibility strategist, coach, and consultant. She has helped hundreds of business owners create the visibility strategies and marketing plans behind growing super-profitable businesses for balanced and prosperous lives. Allie has taken her marketing agency experience and used it to lead entrepreneurs towards their goals through her transformational programs.

Allie's mission is to help entrepreneurs be authentic, own their expertise, and not shrink from their dreams. Her focus on inner-work, confidence, consistency, captivation, and clarity has set her work apart from other marketers and strategists, who focus on tactics and algorithms over relationships.

Before launching her business, Allie spent four years working for corporate web development and Internet marketing agencies. She managed the SEO and Social Media departments, teaching marketing, and training new agency employees. Allie left her corporate career after the birth of her first baby and a battle with debilitating postpartum anxiety that served as the catalyst for her to transform her life and never look back. She now lives an adventure and travel-filled life based in Northern Minnesota with her husband and three young children. https://www.tinyofferlab.com/

CHAPTER TEN

How to Write a Client-Attracting Book to Use as a Marketing Tool

By Suzanne Doyle-Ingram

If you are an entrepreneur, it's my belief that you need to become a published author as quickly as possible. Your book will be the only lead generation tool that you will ever need. What's great is that because you're writing your book based on your expertise and your experience, you will be able to write it very quickly. It will not take you five years to write a book; it pains me when I hear people say they've been writing a book for years! You can get it done in as quickly as a few weeks and I am going to show you how.

In the Beginning

Let's back up a second here and get real. Even though I have written and co-written 20 books in the last ten years, I must confess something to you. I do not enjoy writing. That's the truth.

Back in 2008, when the economy crashed, I limped along for two years running my marketing agency but by 2010 I had to face the truth and pull the plug. No one was spending money on marketing and my income was dropping drastically every month no matter what I tried. I was embarrassed and ashamed; I had no one to talk to and I thought it was just me. I felt like a failure.

I knew I had to change something so I decided to take advantage of Amazon's newly positioned self-publishing arm and write a book. I needed money desperately so I researched what I thought would be a trending topic and decided to write a gluten-free cookbook. I was so depressed, I wrote it under a fake name because I thought it would totally fail and I did not want anyone to know that it was me. I couldn't bear for people to know I had failed yet again.

Lo and behold, the book became a bestseller on Amazon! So I systematized the process and wrote six more books that year. Amazon was sending me $1000+ checks. People started coming to me and asking me to teach them how to write books. I will never forget the first time I put on a course in my little local town. I charged $100 per person and 20 people signed up. I stood in front of a group of people and talked about what came easily to me and made $2000 in one day. I was thrilled! That encouraged me to put my course online and now I have taught over 1,000 people from all over the world how to write a book.

Why a Book Matters

My motto is, ***it's not about the book sales.*** Instead of trying to sell books, use the book to sell you.

If you only learn one thing from this chapter, let this be it: **The money is not in the book sales.** The money is in the clients that you attract because you are a published author. How do I know this? Because when I first started writing books and Amazon was sending me fat checks, I thought it was great, but I had to work so hard to keep my books selling. I was tweeting and posting and blogging and basically begging people to buy my book. Quite frankly, it was exhausting. When I made $2000 in **one day** teaching my workshop, it finally hit me - ***It's not about the book sales!***

Think of your book as a tool. Just as every business has a website, a social media presence, and a telephone, every business owner also needs a book. People need to be able to find you online (on highly credible websites like Amazon), and learn who you are and what you stand for before they will even speak with you. Then they will come to you pre-sold on who you are and what you do.

I'll say it again. Always remember: You are NOT writing a book to generate sales on Amazon. The majority of the money that you make from your book will not be from the book sales. It will be from the clients that you get as a result of the book.

The truth is that the average business book only sells about 200 copies. You are going make money from the clients that you attract because you have become a published author, not from book sales. (Notice that I've said this three times now!)

By the way, I am talking about a real paperback book that you can literally print for about $3 or $4 apiece and either give to potential clients or sell at events. If your potential clients are trying to decide between doing business with you or your competitor, they'll pick you – the published author – who gave them a copy of their book.

You might be thinking:

- *"I don't know how to write a book..."*
- *"I have no time to write a book..."*
- *"I'm actually kind of dumb and I don't know all that much..."*

It's natural to have these thoughts! That's your brain trying to protect you.

If I have managed to write and co-write 20 books, I know that you can write one measly book. I am a single parent of three children and I own a business. I'm busy too! No excuses.

You will not believe how many doors will suddenly open for you once you become a published author. It is literally unimaginable because there are opportunities out there right now that you don't even know exist. The juicy stuff all happens after you write your book. Make a commitment and get it done and then you can have fun with what comes after.

Some of my clients have gone on to create online courses that go along with their book, they've done workshops, Tedx Talks, podcast interviews, and even TV shows. One of my clients is in talks with Netflix right now for a documentary based on her book.

Do You Want a Competitive Edge?

Let me ask you a question: How many of your competitors are published authors? Does it even matter? What matters is that right now, *you are not*. I don't mean to beat you up here but we're going to change that when I show you my simple method you can use to write your book.

Once you are a published author, you will have a massive competitive edge over your competitors. You probably already know that there are people in your industry who have doubled their business as a result of becoming a published author. That's what I want for *you*.

If all things are equal, the published author will always get the sale over the non-author because they will be seen as a credible authority and they will always have the competitive edge.

Lead Generation is really what my book writing philosophy is all about. Giving your book away for free as a lead generation tool is ideal because when you really think about it, what is one new client worth to you? If you don't know, I want you to stop reading right now and figure it out.

Every legitimate business owner needs to know their Average Customer Value. If you are a real estate agent, one new client over the lifetime of doing business with you could be worth $10,000 - $20,000, or more, depending on the real estate market where you live. If you're a business coach or consultant, look at the average lifetime – the average length of time that your client works with you – and the average amount of money that they spend with you over their lifetime. That is the value of one client to you.

Once you know the average lifetime value of one new customer, you can determine how much money you'd be willing to spend to land a new client. Don't tell me that you can't spend $4 to get a new client. That's about how much it costs to print your book.

As we have already established, once you give them a copy of your book, they see you as a credible, trustworthy authority figure and expert in your industry.

Here's how to write a book quickly

In my programs, I teach several methods of how to write books. Some methods take longer and are more indepth than others. Today, I am going to share with you how to write a simple book quickly so you can get it finished, listed on Amazon, and set up for Print-on-Demand.

The Foundational Pieces

Before you start writing your book, there are a few key things to think about. Don't just start writing whatever comes to mind. Take a notebook and answer the following questions:

1. **Why are you writing this book?**
2. **Who are you writing it for?**
3. **What do you want the book to do for you?**
4. **What's in it for the reader?**

Here's something most people don't want to hear: *Your book is not about you.* If you write a book all about you, your reader will think, "What's in it for me? Why should I spend hours of my time reading this book?"

The Outline

You MUST have an outline for your book. Otherwise, not only will your reader be totally confused as to what on earth you're blathering on about, it will also be very difficult to write. When you have an outline, you'll never have writer's block because each time you sit down at your computer to write, you'll already know what you're going to be working on.

The simplest method of writing a book quickly is to write a Tips book. You simply think of a specific topic that you are knowledgeable about, then write a list of things that you can teach your reader. Aim for 25-30 tips. After you've compiled your list, expand on each tip by writing the following:

- **What it is**
- **Why it matters**
- **How to do it**

For example, if I were to write a book about how to write a book, I might call it *27 Things You Need to Know to Write a Simple Client-Attracting Book.* I'd write a list of tips, then expand on each one. Here's an example:

1. Don't Make It About You
    a. What it is: Make the reader the focus of your book.
    b. Why it matters: You want your reader to feel like you're talking right to them.
    c. How to do it: Give examples of how to focus on the reader.
2. Always Have an Outline
    a. What it is: Your outline is your blueprint for your book.
    b. Why it matters: If you don't have a plan, it's almost impossible to write your book.
    c. How to do it: Give examples of outlines and step-by-step instructions.
3. Begin With the End in Mind
    a. What it is: You need to know what you want your book to do for you.
    b. Why it matters: When you know what you want, you can subtly *seed* that into your book.
    c. How to do it: Give instructions on how to do the tip here.

That's pretty clear, right? If you want to write a book quickly, you can use this example and start writing today. Always keep your reader in mind. Ask yourself, what do I want my reader to feel? To think? To do?

Moving Forward

As you can see, a book is the best way to establish yourself as an authority and stand out in your industry. Not only does it position you as a leader, it also helps to educate your ideal clients (your readers) on who you are and what you do. When they read your examples and stories and Tips, they can imagine themselves having those same results, then they come to you, ready to buy.

A Gift For You

If you are interested in writing a book and need someone to guide you, join my FREE Facebook group here: https://www.facebook.com/groups/bookwritingandpublishing

If you are serious about writing a book, you can apply for a strategy call to discuss your book ideas and get feedback from Suzanne here: http://prominence-strategy.youcanbook.me

About Suzanne Doyle-Ingram

Suzanne Doyle-Ingram, CEO of Prominence Publishing, is a best-selling author and co-author of 20 books. She has helped over 1,000 business professionals write books and get published.

Suzanne coaches and trains coaches, consultants and entrepreneurs on how to write and publish a business book, and how to use that book as leverage to increase visibility, open doors for speaking engagements, increase revenue, attract new clients and much more. If you are serious about writing a book, you can apply for a strategy call to discuss your book ideas and get feedback from Suzanne here: http://prominence-strategy.youcanbook.me

Contact: http://prominencepublishing.com

LinkedIn: https://www.linkedin.com/in/suzannedoyleingram/

Facebook: http://facebook.com/SuzanneDoyleIngramBiz

CHAPTER ELEVEN

Relationship Building In The Digital Age

By Andrew Izumi

I had just spent $15,000 online and did not have a physical product to show for it. This was the biggest one-time purchase I had made in my life and I was freaking out. It was a calm, sunny day outside but my heart was beating a million miles a minute: What had I gotten myself into?

In The Beginning

It was 2018 and, for the previous decade, I had been selling high-ticket products for several companies, including Emerson. If there was one thing I knew how to do, it was building strong relationships and selling expensive products. It was so much fun! $20,000 sale, $50,000 sale, $250,000 sale, $2,000 sales came in like hotcakes. Although the money was rolling in, something was missing from my corporate career. I was working for someone else's dream, rather than my own.

One day, as I dreamed about my next fishing vacation and browsed through YouTube videos, I saw a make-money-online ad:

Make money online, even from the comfort of your own home or laptop computer on the beach! How I made millions of dollars without even getting dressed or putting on a suit and tie.

I had to click and check it out. "Affiliate marketing! Sell other's products and earn a commission," is what the ad said. I was intrigued, so I dug deeper and did my research. It seemed legitimate, but I was uneducated and needed training on how this format worked. $15,000 later I was in!

I entered a new world. My previous customer sales calls disappeared and I dug myself into Facebook Ads, YouTube Marketing, Multi-Level Marketing, and more. As intrigued as I was, I wasn't making a dime. I went from a six-figure income to zero – I realized I needed help.

I reached out to an acquaintance, who suggested I go to a particular conference. She told me conferences are where entrepreneurs meet and learn from each other. Finally, this was something with which I was familiar: Relationship building, talking in person, pitching products, and just having a good time was what I knew very well.

At the conference, I spoke with over 100 people and made over 50 new connections that I still have today. I also gained clarity and purpose for my business. As I sat on the airplane traveling back home, I realized that, even though we live in the digital age, relationships and personal connection can't be given up. I thought I could do everything myself and have great success, but that was far from the truth.

Speaking with others and building relationships at the conference did more than just help me launch my High Ticket Momentum product. I've met people like Kevin Steven, who have gone above and beyond the call of duty to show me how to navigate around the digital market landmines. Others have pointed me in the correct direction and offered Joint Venture partnerships. None of these would have happened if I hadn't built relationships.

Key Relationships

I'm going to write about two types of important relationships in the digital market: Shared Knowledge Relationships and Business Partnerships.

Shared Knowledge Relationships

Sharing what you know with others and receiving knowledge back is integral to both parties' success. It's impossible to be a master and expert at everything. But, if we leverage other people's skillsets and allow them to leverage ours, a win-win relationship is created. Nothing can replace one-on-one sharing between colleagues. I encourage you to learn from others, build relationships, and learn from other people's mistakes. This is a huge shortcut to success and much faster than trying to overcome every hurdle by yourself. There is no need to blaze a new trail when someone has already done so. You have to build a connection and trust with others to take advantage of this.

The most critical thing to remember about knowledge sharing is to always pay it forward and reciprocate. I live by the rule: Give before trying to receive. Everybody has an expert skillset they can share. Be proactive in helping others and you will find knowledge and assistance come back to you in droves.

Business Partnerships

A step beyond a knowledge sharing relationship is a business partnership in which each partner is responsible for his or her area of expertise. Great partnerships create great companies. Not every employee in a company needs to be a profit-sharing partner, but every business does need to have top of the line talent in different positions. A business partnership is an agreement between two or more individuals, with different talents or skillsets, who receive money for their work within the company. Knowledge sharing does not involve the exchange of money for knowledge, while a business partnership does.

For example, my business is *eboomz LLC*, and my flagship product is High Ticket Momentum. I am an expert in high-ticket sales. I am comfortable with selling and building relationships. On the other hand, when it comes to Facebook ads, website design, chatbot marketing, mobile app development, affiliate marketing, virtual events, and more in the digital marketing sector, I am no expert. Thus, I have partnered with experts who are passionate about those areas and do that work for eboomz for a portion of its revenues.

Moving Forward

In the digital world, relationship building cannot be ignored. It has not only allowed me to succeed in sales both now and in the past, but it is the one thing that helped me launch my business, eboomz, and create my product, High Ticket Momentum www.highticketmomentum.com. Building relationships with others is a fantastic experience and results in both knowledge sharing and business partnerships, as well. Relationships are key to entrepreneurial success.

Sales drive every company and without customer and collegial relationships, sales will not happen. Often, we can get lost in the computer or on our phones, but remember they are only the tools we use to connect with others around the globe. Use these tools to build better relationships and create more wealth for your business.

A Gift For You

If you would like me to show you how to:

- Create win-win relationships.
- Sell and close 40% more high-ticket deals.
- Overcome any customer or partner objections.

I invite you to watch a short, free training video and claim your complementary consultation call with me. To get started, contact me at www.conversionpublishing.com .

About Andrew Izumi

Andrew Izumi is an active, independent thinker, and a leader in high-ticket sales strategies. He loves to help small- and medium-sized businesses attract more high-ticket clients, command higher prices, and scale their bottom line revenues. This is achieved without hardselling clients, using up-to-date sales strategies, or building complicated sales funnels.

Andrew has been a leading sales manager for over a decade having achieved certificates like Leading at Emerson, a Fortune 500 company. Some of his past customers include Miller Coors, Disney Animations, Edwards Air force Base, Port of Long Beach, MGM Grand, and more. When working with these companies, a Return on Investment (ROI) is always achieved and may be as high as multiple $100,000s per year.

Andrew enjoys working with business owners who are looking to solve their customer's problems and serve them at the highest level. His customer's high-ticket solutions are the driving force behind his service. Outside of work, Andrew enjoys outdoor hobbies, fishing, rock climbing, and skiing. He looks forward to connecting and building a great relationship with you.

CHAPTER TWELVE

Why Do Most Businesses Fail and Only A Few Succeed?

By Mike Lasswell

There is a common belief that starting a business is EXTREMELY RISKY because the odds are stacked against you. But it's not true! At least not completely...

See, this belief is based on statements like this one: "According to the SBA 89.88% of businesses close each year." For all intents and purposes.. THAT'S A 90% FAIL rate!

Here is the actual stat from the SBA: 627,000 new businesses open each year. At the same time, about 595,000 businesses close each year.

That's a huge number of business owners who are shutting their doors never to open them again. That's a lot of hopes dashed. That's a lot of people returning to the grind.

But ....WHY?! Well, maybe it's because there are simply not very many people buying products...

Here's the thing, we know that people are buying products. Lots of products actually. For example, Amazon averaged 306 transactions per second at their peak in 2012. That's 26.5M transactions per day. And it's not just corporate giants. Startups are launching and succeeding too!

So, why do 90% of businesses close? Well According to the SBA, the # 1 reason businesses fail is because of "not investigating the market." But if 90% of businesses are closing... that means that 10% aren't.

So the more important question is: what ARE the 10% doing to succeed, and how can you do what they did?

If you want to know how to stack the deck in your favor and dramatically increase the odds of your success, the answer starts with Market Research. And that's what this chapter is all about.

How to do Market Research So You Succeed

To exponentially increase your chances for success, here are the questions we need to answer:

- How do the top 10% build products that people want?
- How do they get people willing to buy?
- How do they promote?
- How do they build anticipation for their products?

- In a world where convenience is king, how do they get people to wait in line for their products?
- How do they advertise?
- How do they get leads?
- How do they talk about their products?

Ultimately what we NEED to know is: "How do they get sales?"

As you can imagine, it's a combination of things and they aren't likely to tell you flat out. But the strategy behind all of it is created from the info they gathered from doing market research.

Literally everyone from Grant Cardone & Gary V, to Russell Brunson and Warren Buffet will tell you the same thing. Do your market research! (and if an "expert" doesn't tell you that... unsubscribe!)

But that doesn't quite cut it does it? Just saying "Do market research" falls a bit short, right? If you tell 2 people to do market research they will come back with very different results from each other.

If the whole point is to get information you can use, then it's important to understand what you're looking for.

To be able to look at a market and evaluate it in a way that will allow anyone to extract useful and actionable info has been the driving force behind why I personally have bought every book on the topic, taken every course on the subject, and attended seminars and conferences. After all that, I can tell you 2 things:

1. Who to turn to for the best processes and frameworks for researching markets
    - Steven Larsen is a personal favorite; he has a great training series on how to evaluate markets. Search Youtube for "Sales Funnel Radio" (Seriously it's legit.)
    - Pat Flynn has a book called "Will it Fly?" that will help you get started.
    - Ryan Levesque is another success story who has literally written the book on how to choose your market called "Choose." In it he helps you define your market, define who your ideal customer is and where they are in that market so you can reach them.
2. The second thing I learned is that there are 7 main advantages that your research should produce which you can apply to your products & marketing so you can proceed with confidence!

The 7 Main Advantages Are

1. Knowing Your Avatar: Understanding the Product-Market fit
2. Determining Your Positioning
3. Identifying Beliefs: Conversations that Create Compelling Campaigns
4. Understand your Competition: Their Features vs Your Benefits
5. Price Wars: Sell the thing that sells the thing to leave your competition in the dust
6. KPI's : Key Performance Indicators
7. Skip the line! How to identify industry influencers that will promote for you!

First, and most importantly, you have to know who you are selling to. Here is the recipe to make selling EXTREMELY difficult and costly. If you think "everyone" is your ideal customer you'll end up using words that are so generic they end up actually only connecting with a small percentage of people...

So to sell it, you'll have to over-hype it or discount like crazy it to get someone excited about your product. Which puts the numbers against you and you'll have to talk to hundreds of people just to get one sale. Ugh! It's no wonder so many people go back to a job. Doing all that means you're grinding either way. So most businesses fail because their sales message falls flat. And it falls flat because it's generic.

Here's why it doesn't work. When you have a product it may solve things for a large group of people, but all those people are in wildly different situations from each other and as human beings, we usually see differences easier than similarities. So if one person buys your product and has success, it's actually VERY RARE for a another person (in a different situation) to think that your product will also work for them. They will literally say, "Sure... it only worked for them BECAUSE they are in a different situation from mine. My circumstances include this other aspect so it won't work for me." Seriously we all do that!

However, when you do your research, you can identify people in different parts of one market (or different situations) and evaluate how big those parts are.

For example, if you look at almost any market, the labor force usually makes up the majority of the market, then management, then Directors, then C-level types. Once you understand this, you can create messaging that speaks to each slice of the market, and show them how your product authentically helps them in their unique situation. That's how you put the numbers in your favor and increase your success rate!

Why Positioning Matters

One of the worst ways to present yourself to the market is "Hey everyone! Look! We made a cool thing! Here's how you can buy it!" Seriously don't do it... It's the worst.

WHY? Because only your mom cares about something you made enough to buy it!

Which means that understanding how to position yourself in the market is a key differentiating factor that the top 10% do and the 90% don't do very well.

If you want to understand the basics, here is what you need to know: Most every marketer will tell you that to find your ideal customer you need to understand which of the three main markets your customer is in: Health, Wealth, or Relationships. And that's true to an extent. Those people ARE buying products related to those things. But to really understand them, we have to ask why are they buying products related to those 3 markets?

The reason we decide to learn about stock trading, or get in shape, or work on our relationships, isn't because we love those things. What's really going on is that we all have issues related to those things that we are trying to solve. They actually want out of those things.

Let me explain...

Each of the markets isn't a place people go to buy things they want. It's the place people go to find the solution to a problem they want resolved.

People want wealth so they don't have to worry about money anymore! This means they can finally focus on their health or focus on their relationships which they have been neglecting!

That's why when you ask someone why they want to start a business there are several levels to their answer.

The first is to get money, the second is to get freedom, the third is usually to get more time, and the fourth is usually to be able to spend time with the ones they love.

But they can't because they have to trade time for money.

For the VAST majority of people, this is what is going on in each of the markets. Are there exceptions? Yes of course. There are those who love trading stocks so much that they would do it even if they were financially set for life.

But even then, they are usually in that career because it solves another deeper need. And if you pay attention to them in interviews, you'll hear them say something like: "I really love it because I love challenges and putting things in order and this allows me to do that on a grand scale."

So the truth is that these markets aren't the destination! They are the means to a different destination.

So now, when you do your market research, you will be able to look at indicators with this lens. Why are people spending a billion dollars a day (cumulatively) in this industry?

When you position your product as the destination, it's a MUCH harder sell. But when you position the products as the vehicle that people need to get them to their destination, it naturally aligns with their desires and becomes attractive. However, this means that if you are positioning your product in line with their desire (vs just dropping your product into the market.) You are setting yourself up for success.

For more advantages check out the free training at MarketResearchMastery.com.

A Gift For You

For more market research factors, check out my FREE training at MarketResearchMastery.com.

About Mike Lasswell

Mike went from a dream job in the commercial broadcast industry to helping local business owners take advantage of online marketing.

Like many, Mike believed that advertising and sales only worked for big corporations. But, since 2012, Mike has studied marketing, influence, and behavioral psychology to learn what it takes to create promotions and campaigns that have increased revenue by up to 400% for his clients, who are big corporations.

Mike learned that all powerful strategies come down to getting one thing right, which will actually tilt the playing field to your advantage.

That one thing is Market Research.

CHAPTER THIRTEEN

Masterful Messaging

By Christa Nichols

It's only five words, but this short five-word question is the most important in your business: *Who is your target audience?*

The answer to that question is the key to everything: Engagement, interaction, advertising, and – most of all – sales.

I cringe when I ask this five-word question and get answers like, "Oh, sure! That's easy. It's women. Or men. Or moms. Or ..." I've even had clients tell me, "Well, everyone. Everyone needs my offer."

Yikes.

Describing your target audience requires more than just a quick one-word response, and here's why: Copy that tries to appeal to huge audiences ends up appealing to nobody.

The main reason campaigns fail is because of a disconnect between the message and the audience. Misconceptions about who your audience is and the idea that your messaging should appeal to everyone can cost you your business.

I'm going to breakdown the truth behind messaging and why trying to appeal to everyone with your copy hurts your business. Then I'll show you what to do instead so you can reach the kind of people who will be your diehard customers for life!

Paging Sherlock Holmes

I should have been a detective. As a copywriter, I ask my clients what probably seems like a ridiculous number of questions. They may walk away from a call with me feeling like they're still squinting from the bright lights of an interrogator's interview room.

I ask clients all the usual questions about their business, their goals, and their offers. But I spend the most time asking them about their target audience. I need to know who the audience is, what they want, what they're thinking, and what they need. Until I have that information - and more - I can't write copy that addresses the specific problems, questions, and objections the audience has. I can't know what needs to be communicated to help my client's audience know, like, and trust their business.

Stay Connected

How is it possible for an entrepreneur to become disconnected from their target audience? It's your job to know, right? Yes, but it's so easy to get caught up in the what and the how of serving them that we forget the who behind it. In other words, your offer takes over.

It's not your fault. Building a good offer takes an immense amount of time and energy. As entrepreneurs, we pour our hearts and souls into what we're putting out into the world because we care about the people we're serving. When you've put that kind of concentrated time and focus into one thing, stepping back and separating yourself from your offer is almost physically painful. Soon, you're seeing everything through the rose-colored glasses of your amazing offer. It's so awesome everyone will want it, right?

Sadly, that's just not true. Not everyone will want your offer, but the right people will. It's hard to put yourself in the shoes of the target audience because you've already seen the results your offer produces but that is exactly what you have to do to have success – stay connected to your audience without focusing too broadly, and losing them.

Resonate With Your Audience

Have you ever read something that resonated so deeply you almost jumped out of your skin? Perhaps it spoke so clearly to what you were thinking and feeling you wondered how the writer had crawled into your brain and read your mind?

That is the power of messaging to a specific target audience. When you pinpoint exactly what your audience wants and needs and address it in your copy, your message comes through in an authentic, memorable way. Setting yourself up with solid target audience research gives you the information you need to write copy that:

- Validates.

When you write with a specific audience in mind, you see and hear them. Mirroring back the feelings and desires they have validates them, and they believe they matter to you. This is so powerful.

- Connects.

Your audience is bombarded with countless messages every day. It's easy for them to just keep scrolling or click away. By knowing your target audience, you can reach in and communicate with them in a familiar way that makes them stop and read more. The "Oh yeah! That's just like me!" connection reassures them that they're not alone.

- Motivates.

Sometimes all you need is permission to act. When you know exactly what your audience wants and why you can address the exact reasons for action that will deeply resonate with them. Just try to hold them back from the Buy Now button!

- Builds Trust.

People trust people they feel safe with. When your copy makes them feel validated, connected, and motivated to act, you'll be a trusted expert in your field. They'll feel like they know you because they can tell you care.

Four Tips For Audience Research

Whether you work with a professional copywriter or not, you're going to have to know your audience. Get started building your target audience research right now with these four basic questions that dig deeper and help you reach your audience more effectively.

1. **What do they want?**

Sorry, but the correct answer isn't, "My offer!" They're not aware of your offer yet, so you have to think further out than that. What result do they want that your offer can give them?

For example, a car sales rep who primarily sells Subaru Outbacks rarely has a customer come in and say, "I want a Subaru Outback." If the rep hit them with that right out of the gate, it wouldn't resonate. What the customers know is that they want a vehicle that seats at least five, is all-wheel drive, gets good gas mileage, and will be dependable for years to come. Those are the things they want, and the Subaru Outback is the way they can have all that. The rep asks what they are looking for before suggesting the car model that fulfills their needs.

Settling what they want right away ensures you'll be able to communicate in a way that makes them feel seen and heard.

2. **Why do they want it?**

Why questions are my favorites. If you can speak their reasons for wanting something back to them, there's an instant connection and trust is encouraged.

Why do they want a vehicle like the Outback? Well, they've got three kids and they live in the mountains where the weather can be dicey, and the roads get icy (see what I did there?). They have to get everyone to school and soccer and debate team, so they spend a lot of hours on the road and don't want to end up calling AAA because of a breakdown. They also need plenty of room for all the stuff they regularly cart around – backpacks, groceries, and sports equipment.

The *whys* are your attention-getters. If you create copy that includes elements of their whys, they will feel connected with you as someone who understands.

3. **What's holding them back from already having it?**

Anybody out there a safe shopper? I am. I'll stroll around putting things in my cart, then stroll back around taking them all back out again. I'm great at talking myself out of things, and your audience is, too.

If you can anticipate their objections, you can avoid them before they crop up. In the case of our car buyer, price is probably a big one as well as decision-overwhelm and feeling pressured to buy.

List the objections. Ask yourself how your offer can solve those objections, then make sure your copy addresses that.

4. **How is your offer the best fit?**

When you really know your target audience, you have an advantage. You can get very specific in the way you promote your offer because you already know exactly what they're thinking, feeling, and wanting.

There's more than one Outback sales rep on the planet, even in one city. The audience is going to want to know about the warranty, how soon you can get one in their favorite color, what your interest rates are, and where they can test drive one. You can make the answers to these questions and more available before they even ask if you've done your audience research.

Don't Leave Money On The Table

The power of really knowing your target audience means the difference between a lackluster campaign and massive success.

Here's one final truth bomb for you, and it's not what you'd expect to hear from someone who makes a living writing high-ticket sales copy: Copy is not king.

Good copy can yield amazing results and ROI, but the best copy in the world will not accomplish anything if it's not part of a messaging system that's created specifically with your target audience in mind. The audience is king. Without doing the work to determine exactly who your audience is, what they want, and why, your copy won't capture the attention of the people who could be your raving fans and hot buyers, leaving serious money on the table.

A Gift For You

Want to steal my framework for yourself?

Grab my FREE quick guide on the *8 Questions You Must Ask For No-Fail Copy That Connects And Converts* at https://go.christanicholsmessaging.com/8-questions.

About Christa Nichols

Christa Nichols is a messaging expert and high-ticket sales copywriter. She's developed a no-fail framework for creating messaging that converts by dialing in on who the target audience is deep down; what they want, and what they need to hear to connect and convert.

She's a popular writer in the digital marketing space and you can see her copy in funnels, ads, and email sequences for some of the most prevalent names in the industry. Putting her framework to use has led clients to achieve sold out beta launches within 48 hours, record-setting high-ticket program sign-ups, and absolute clarity and confidence in messaging.

Christa and her husband and two teenagers live on an acreage in Iowa, where they enjoy bonfires, games night, and all things outdoors.

CHAPTER FOURTEEN

How To Spark Life Into A New Or Dying Business

By Anton Gray

"The secret of getting ahead is getting started."
~ Mark Twain

I hate to be the bearer of bad news but, before we get started, I have to let you know that a high percentage of businesses fail in their first year. And, in many cases, businesses die before they even get started.

However, you've picked up this book and within its pages are secrets to surviving online. In this chapter, you'll learn four secrets to spark LIFE into your business to build the momentum needed to survive.

In The Beginning

What kind of guy walks away from a $150,000 salary with the notion that he can make a living and support his family just by helping people? I did it and it was one of the scariest things I've ever done.

L – Learn And Leverage

Often when we start a new business or look to expand our current one, we focus on all the things we lack. In most cases, the focus is on a lack of knowledge or skills.

We convince ourselves that we can't do something because we don't know this or aren't sure how to do that. We then set out on a quest to obtain the knowledge we feel we need to move forward. In doing so, we inadvertently open the door to the entrepreneur rabbit hole and get caught up in all of the how-to videos and courses, only to discover that there is much more to learn. The next thing you know, you're weeks, months, maybe even years into your business and you haven't made any progress or money.

How do we prevent ourselves from going down the rabbit hole in the first place?

First, forget about focusing on all of the things that you think you need to know to get started. When you focus on all of the things you think you lack, it becomes overwhelming and discouraging. You really can't know what you don't know yet because you haven't even started. In the end, there's no way to know everything anyway.

Second, I encourage you to focus on one or two things that are critical to your business at a time. This will allow you to move forward and avoid being overwhelmed by trying to learn everything at once.

Third, when you come across something that you haven't learned yet use the power of leverage to solve the problem. Just as there is a ton of information available for any topic you can imagine, there are also resources, tools, and people with skills and expertise that can be leveraged in place of possessing the actual knowledge yourself. Use them wisely and use them to your advantage; don't feel you have to know and do everything yourself.

I – Implement Immediately, But Intelligently

The power of the knowledge you do have is in its implementation. You're finding information that can help you start and improve your business in this book and elsewhere. But just being more knowledgeable isn't enough. Knowledge alone won't add money to your bank account. The most important step -- and the key to your success -- lies in implementing the things you learn.

I've experienced this firsthand and – I suspect – you have as well. I had taken course after course, and read countless books. but, although I was learning, I wasn't getting results. Initially, I wanted to blame the courses and books and believe that they didn't work, but then it dawned on me: I had missed a step, and that was the implementation step.

As you learn, I encourage you to take the time to write down a plan of action for each thing that can help your business. Most importantly, be sure to implement those plans and do so immediately. Inaction is the killer of all success but fast, planned action has the power to catapult your business forward.

Understand that there is a ton of information and many useful strategies and each comes with advantages and drawbacks. As you lay out your plan, implement immediately but also implement intelligently. Ensure that the strategies that you choose align with your specific business goals and vision. In other words, don't do what everyone else is doing just because they are doing it; be sure that what you do supports your specific goals at the time.

F – Fail

Now, onto my one of my five favorite F words (if you're curious about the other 4, message me on Facebook or Instagram and I'll fill you in on them). The word I'm referring to is FAIL; one of the most dreaded F words in business.

I am sure that as you learn, leverage, and implement you'll wonder, "What if it doesn't work? Can I even do this?"

These questions are linked to your fear of failure. But I want to help you get over that fear. Because once you get over it, your path to success will be much smoother. Fear of failure keeps most people stuck because their attitude toward it is off. They view failure as something negative but, in reality, it can be one of the best things for you.

Failure is just a successful attempt at learning what doesn't work. Take something usually viewed as negative and flip it to something beneficial. The more you learn about what doesn't work, the closer you are to finding the things that do. One of those things can become your biggest breakthrough. Don't be afraid to fail: Fail fast, fail frequently, and fail forward toward your success.

Now that we've learned how to deal with fear and failure, we're ready to use it to our advantage. But before I tell you how, I want to affirm that we are on the same page and agree that failure can be a good thing. Agreed? *(Hint: that was your cue to nod yes.)*

E – Experience, Evaluate, and Elevate

I want to emphasize that every failure provides a learning experience. A good thing about the experience is that it leaves an impression. Take the time to evaluate what went wrong, what went right, and what could have been done differently (without judging yourself harshly). You'll now always have that experience and impression as a reference point whenever faced with similar situations.

Most people miss this evaluation step and get caught up in the fact that things didn't go as planned. They completely miss the chance to develop an elevated level of thinking about what went wrong.

The only difference between someone that is a master and someone who isn't is that the master has failed and evaluated so much that they have a higher understanding than everyone else of what works and what doesn't.

Live LIFE

There you have it! You are now ready to spark LIFE into your business. Using these four secrets, you are ready to maximize your productivity: You understand to both learn and leverage, to plan, and intelligently implement immediately without the fear of failure, because you know how to evaluate experiences and elevate your business growth.

Moving Forward

I am confident that the secrets I just shared with you will help you build the momentum that you need to launch a new business, scale an existing one, or spark LIFE into a dying one. I am also confident in you! And know that you have everything that it takes to make your business dreams a reality. After all, you picked up this book, which is a huge step in the right direction. I am a firm believer that with the right mindset, discipline, and business strategy your dreams are within reach!

A Gift For You

I want to help you along your LIFE journey, and give you access to some addition FREE resources:

- An Entrepreneurs' Guide: The Top 10 Pitfalls To Avoid To Keep Your Business From Dying.
- Three-Part Video Series: Building Your Business On A Foundation Of Success.
- FREE Business Strategy Call (limited availability).
- $100 (no kidding!) just for taking advantages of the other three bonuses!

Go to: www.antongray.com/EPBonus

About Anton Gray

Anton Gray truly believes that everyone has greatness within them, but sometimes needs a little help finding it, and a little friendly nudge to bring it out. He also believes anyone crazy enough to take a run at entrepreneurship has a six- or seven-figure business within them, and just needs the right strategy and guidance to reach it.

As a former Business and Technology consultant for 16 years, he advised large tech companies and government agencies how to grow departments, implement solutions, and get results. Anton also served a combined 15 years in the United States Army and Air Force.

As a Business Coach and Strategist, Anton is dedicated to getting results for his students and clients! His mission is to help 100,000 individuals shift from employees to entrepreneurs, live the life they've always imagined, and have more time and freedom to do what they really love. All while making a true impact on this world.

CHAPTER FIFTEEN

Strategic Consultancy: The Creation Of Blue Oceans

By Trevor Wood

I am often asked 'How Do I Create A Blue Ocean?'

For Modern Strategic Consultants, there is a framework to follow which makes it easy; here are a few tips and tricks to guide you through the pathway to allow you to operate in a 'new space' or 'Blue Ocean'.

First of all, let's set out a clear understanding that there are two keys to unlocking success in a Blue Ocean, namely lowering costs and introducing innovation, (or differentiation). Costs must be reduced, even if volumes increase and innovation should be included, ideally but not necessarily technological innovation, if, at all possible. Your new space can be competitive or complimentary to your existing Red Ocean. It does not have to be outside your core business.

You need to 'stand out' in the market. It isn't enough to stand out from your competition, you must be 'remarkable' in your sector as well as in areas outside of your sector, i.e. in adjoining or converging spaces. It is not about creating new customers. It is about exploring those that are non-customers.

This is where the 'creativity' starts. Instead of consistently chasing your competitors. Competing on price, adding new features (because they have), or obsessing over what they do. Simply stop. Look around the market and see where the new opportunities lie.

Don't set out to create a new market, as such, try to create a new 'space' on the edge of an existing market. A space where you can shine. A space where you can be the star, the Category King, the expert, the guru.

Creating a 'Blue Ocean' is not new. The term was popularised by W. Chan and Renee Mauborgne back in 2005 in their bestselling book Blue Ocean Strategy. Since then, it has been adopted more and more, especially by leading practitioners in the Digital Marketing space and certainly by the more effective and successful Strategic Consultants.

But, let's discuss, for a moment, what a Blue Ocean is not. It isn't a minor change to an existing product, or range. It isn't making a minor tweak to something you already sell into a Red Ocean. It must be something that draws your client or prospect out of an existing highly contested, highly competitive space, to a place where you are the primary, if not the sole choice.

If you don't know if you are currently operating in a Red Ocean, here is a quick test. Name 5 competitors. Name your market leader. List the main features and the pricing of their products/services. Are you obsessed with what others are doing? Is there a real pressure on your costs or selling prices? If any of this strikes a chord, then you are almost certainly operating in a Red Ocean.

Review any of the Blue Ocean pioneers, even from recent times, such as Dyson, Tesla or Apple and they all followed a different strategic logic to the main market. They all created their own 'space'. They became the only company, product or service within that space. They were uncontested within the space and they were all technological innovators. Additionally, they all reduced costs of production or distribution. Allowing them to become Category King.

They then all went on to retain their positions for some considerable time, by continuing to innovate and add Value Innovation to keep ahead of the competition.

This is important, because value creation, without innovation is not usually enough to make you stand out from the market, or at least not for long, as others can more readily catch up, or imitate. On the flip side, technological innovation on its' own isn't enough either, as it can leave you in a space so alien to the existing market where no one dares to join you. Or worse, needs educating on how, or why, to buy into your concept.

To create a Blue Ocean though you don't need to be 'bleeding edge', nor the first into a space. You simply need to be the one that captures the imagination, or makes the right offer, or makes it irresistible to the current users in the Red Ocean.

But what about Strategic Consultants?

Well, if they are of the right mindset, i.e. not one of the old school, traditional, accountancy focussed consultants, they will perform all the reviews and orchestrate all the right meetings to enable your business to comprehend your current realities and to open up the Blue Ocean opportunities that are available to you.

They will let you define your space and be recognised as the solution to the problems within that space. A space you have created, defined and now own. If you can add in some IP (Intellectual Property) to it, then it will further assist your differentiation. Being 'Googleable' also helps (do you come up in google when you type in this word or phrase, e.g. Dyson, Tesla, Apple, etc.)

It is at this point that they will truly earn their fees. They will help you to discover how to lower your costs, create more value and stand out as the 'only' option to your target audience. The 'Offer' must work for your specific target, be it users, buyers, supply chain partners, etc. as each will likely have different pains, issues and aspirations and desired results.

So how do they do it?

Two of the major tools are the Strategy Canvas and the Value Curve.

A Strategy Canvas provides an overview of where you fit into your existing and adjoining markets.

Let's illustrate this with an example. Instead of simply being another 'luxury car maker', Tesla produced the P Series Electric cars. They are both a luxury car AND an electric car, thus falling outside of the core red ocean, yet associating itself with two key groups of buyers, luxury and electric. They not only had the first to market approach, they also provided novel ways to fund it (the deposit scheme), but also gained a huge competitive advantage with the Supply Chain sourcing of batteries for their vehicles.

They were in their own space. Had provided significant technological advantage. Had cost advantage too and yet still touched on the two key red oceans they were aiming to poach business from, the luxury car sector and the electric car sector. The Model 3 is now aiming to achieve the same success in a lower class of cars, competing head on with the BMW 3 Series, even daring to use the same number in it's name.

The Value Curve approaches this slightly differently. It aims to see where each and every one of your deliverables sits on your Value Curve. If all of your deliverables mirror your competitors, then you are truly operating in a Red Ocean. If this is the case and you are not Category King, then you need to take some action, be it with costs or innovation. The trouble is, it is unlikely that you will be able to change costs sufficiently to undercut your competitors and innovation on its' own may not be enough.

Review of the Value Curve is key to determining your current reality and your future path. It isn't a costly process to follow, yet it can yield significant benefits.

A Strategic Consultant will deliver cost advantage and differentiation as well as creating your 'tag line' to ensure it is adopted internally and externally and then create the pathway for implementation, or at least that is what they should do.

If you have got this far, then assuming you have an irresistible offer, (checked against utility, price, cost and ease of adoption), you must now implement. The potential hurdles typically faced are cognitive, political, motivational or resource based. Sounds complicated, but it is really about getting everyone that matters on side. The masses don't matter at this stage, it is just the influencers, positive and negative. They will carry the rest with them.

You will need to spend time on each of these elements, as well as the Value Proposition, the Profit Proposition and the People Proposition, but being able to recognise your new space is key. A Blue Ocean Strategy will align all three of these, with both differentiation AND low cost. A Red Ocean Strategy will only achieve one of these two goals.

Being able to find a way out of a Red Ocean is key.

It is not about creating a niche and then a sub niche. It is the reverse.

Being able to see and create a New Opportunity and create your own space, your Blue Ocean is not always easy, which is why Strategic Consultants exist. They can often talk to you for a ridiculously short period of time and see the issues and the solution.

That is why they don't 'charge by the hour'.

They will help you to discover your future path and help you discover and walk along the pathway to success. No mean feat.

About Trevor Wood

As a Strategic Consultant, Trevor continues to work with many leading corporate clients, as well as smaller growing businesses. His SaaS distribution company continues to consult for major corporates including Astra Zeneca, British Airways, Govia Thameslink, GWR, Southeastern Trains and Willmott Dixon.

His passion is to understand 'what makes a business work', then deploying strategies to enable growth.

This is often achieved via organic traffic, on platforms such as LinkedIn, but also through the creation of Blue Ocean Pipelines, including the use of 'High Ticket' sales and the opening up of new markets.

Create your Blue Ocean Pipeline and watch your business grow!

Trevor has 1 wife, 2 kids, 3 dogs, 4 donkeys, 5 cars, 6 offices ... and lives in rural Shropshire, England.

To book your strategy session, go to http://www.makingmarketingwork.co.uk/ss-application

If the form is not available, you can join our waiting list.

CHAPTER SIXTEEN

Parentpreneur

By Lisa Kuntze

Being an entrepreneur is like being on a roller coaster, and so is being a parent. So, being a parent and entrepreneur at the same time requires a special level of crazy, right? Not necessarily.

Parents can't risk everything. They must provide stability for their family and care for their home. The stability of regular income often means giving up entrepreneurial dreams, perhaps living on one income due to childcare costs associated with double-income arrangements, and finding ways to earn extra money on the side.

Many parent entrepreneurs give up because they don't know how to manage a family and a business. In this chapter, we'll look at how to maximize your time and minimize your mental load with my Parentpreneur lifestyle hacks.

Parentpreneur Hacks

1. Balance is Key

We think of successful entrepreneurs like Bill Gates, Steve Jobs, and Elon Musk and believe we can't be successful if we aren't working all the time. When I started my business, I worked myself to exhaustion and neglected my family and home. I've learned that being an entrepreneur with a family doesn't have to feel like chaos.

Create a schedule for your business and your family. Get a wall calendar, an organizer, or a whiteboard (or, all three) and organize your life. Write a business plan outlining your business goals, key performance indicators, and budget projections and work those into a balanced schedule that includes time for your family and home. Stick to the schedule to stay the course and avoid distraction.

Don't forget to schedule time for self-care. Find whatever relaxes you and keeps you healthy -- meditate, pray, get a massage, exercise, cook – and add those activities to your schedule. Taking care of your physical and mental health, is non-negotiable for optimal performance.

Remember that quality family time can be found in routines such as family meals, bedtime, game nights, and other regularly scheduled activities aside from special occasions. A schedule holds you accountable and fosters healthy habits.

2. Create Win-Win Situations

A lot of time can be leveraged by creating win-win situations for business and family. For example, working in the evening while the kids sleep, instead of watching TV. Schedule conference calls while you're at the gym on a cardio machine or while you're at a kid-friendly work venue while the kids are entertained in a safe place. These are both win-win situations: in the first, you're achieving self-care while also working and, in the second, you're working while your kids are having fun and socializing.

You can schedule your kids screen-time or other activities as a distraction (TV, video games, arts and crafts, etc.) and take a call at home. Just be sure to let the other party know that your kids are around and mute your phone when the other party is speaking to minimize background noise. Use a Bluetooth headset to be hands-free.

Don't do unplanned multitasking. It is tempting to pick up one more call, email, chat, or comment notification but stick to your schedule. Delay responses for your scheduled work time so it doesn't conflict with family time. There's nothing more unprofessional than speaking to a CEO while changing diapers with kids screaming in the background. Be fully present for business and family by using the balance hack.

3. Leverage Teamwork

We have all heard the saying, "Teamwork makes the dream work" and it can work like a dream to make dreams work. Kids' play makes messes, so your kids clean it up. If both parents work, both can do chores. Set up a chore chart to assign chores evenly among all able family members. If you don't have a partner, ask your friends and community for support. Many hands make light work.

Get friendly with your children's classmates' parents and suggest a carpool. I save ten hours a week with the carpool hack! Just remember to do your share of driving or offer some gas money in exchange for their help. Maybe grandparents can babysit or maybe you can schedule play dates to free up time for work, too.

Finally, if you believe your company would benefit from partnering with someone whose strengths complement yours, do it. Consider different ways of partnering – perhaps rather than money, consider exchanging services or other non-monetary services or products that you both need.

4. Use Technology To Stay on Schedule

It's easy to be distracted when working from home. For me, Alexa helps! I set daily reminders for my business *and* family. Alexa keeps everyone accountable for chores, life, and work. Find a technical device or app that becomes your alarm, calendar reminder, and to-do list so you don't have to remember everything and stay on task.

If you work in teams, use shared Google Docs and time trackers to organize. Many apps can schedule a month of social media content at once. Google Ads, Facebook Ads, and Facebook Pages Apps on mobile help me manage business remotely. Engagement pods will increase your following and help grow your network. Zoom is for conferences across devices. DocuSign does digital contracts; no more printing and scanning. Canva makes content creation easy. Most platforms have integrations, plugins, or apps to streamline workflow. Tech will help you reach goals, so use it.

5. Outsource What You Can

When I first started, I didn't make progress because my time was eaten by errands. I couldn't scale until I learned to outsource. Errands don't make money! You cannot do everything in your business and successfully scale it. Save a lot of time and stress by outsourcing jobs you do for both your family and your business.

For your business, consider outsourcing customer service, order fulfillment, social media activities, accounting, web design, and/or anything that takes a significant amount of time away from scaling.

For your family, outsource jobs that don't need your personal touch: shop online, use grocery delivery, try a meal delivery system, have a cleaner come to your home once a week to streamline workflow in the home. Think of your family and home as a business.

Remember, not all outsourcing requires employees. Use automated email, flows, and funnels that allow you to "set and forget" whenever you can.

6. Keep Your Finances In Order

Entrepreneurs must separate business expenses from family expenses. Your business needs a separate line of credit and separate checking and savings accounts. You need to track bookkeeping and have a small business tax person. If you don't do this upfront, you'll end up spending extra money to sort it out during tax season. Be sure to keep your family and business finances separate.

If you don't have funds to start your business, and can't use business credit, find investors. Don't risk your family's financial stability -- don't use your child's college funds -- to fund your business. Yes, you have to take risks and spend money to make money, but don't risk your home or spend money your family needs now or in the future.

Cut out money-draining expenses; put money into needs, not wants. Watch your expenses and income to ensure you are continuing to make money rather than accumulating debt. Remember, sales do not indicate profit until all expenses are considered. Finally, don't forget about life and business insurance; it protects your business and your family.

7. Take Care of Your Legal Requirements

Make sure you have all the business licenses, permits, and/or patents required by your location, profession, industry, or market. You can obtain them using your laptop; you don't need an expensive attorney. Also, ensure all business and sales taxes are properly paid in a timely manner.

Don't rely on a handshake or verbal agreement when working with clients, partners, or outsourcing; get everything in writing. You can copy-and-paste policies and legal contracts from the web, just make sure they apply to your location and/or situation. Protect your Intellectual Property with Non-Disclosure Agreements and patents. File patents, copyrights, and register trademarks yourself. Don't be misleading or fraudulent or you, your business, and your family will be at risk.

Moving Forward

It has taken me years of experience to collect my favorite technology tools, resources, services, and platforms to be a successful Parentpreneur. You can use mine but you will also find your own. Struggle is normal. Wishing you the best of success in your entrepreneurial journey. Enjoy it!

A Gift For You

It's your lucky day! You can skip Google searches and get access to the best hack resources at MommEComm.com/Entrepreneur-Resources.

About Lisa Kuntze

Lisa Kuntze has always been a creative. She enjoys creating art, music, and growing ideas into businesses. Lisa's desire to work from home, travel, and be available to her family led her to entrepreneurship. Lisa is a self-taught Mompreneur (@Mom preneurMentor) who started in digital marketing and grew into e-Commerce. She has a voice to give underserved mompreneurs hope, help with coping, and a business model to reach success!Lisa hosts a Mompreneur Mentor YouTube Vlog and offers her digital course, MommEComm, for those who want to learn the step-by-step route to high-ticket dripshipping success. It covers tech, legal, product marketing, niche, scaling, and more. E-Commerce is a great way to get your start as an entrepreneur.

The Kuntze's enjoy traveling and want to share it with you. Follow their travels on Instagram @travelwiththefamily.

CHAPTER SEVENTEEN

The Power of Outsourcing

By Travis Linares

Any person that has access to the Internet has access to the most powerful way to create millionaires and billionaires: Outsourcing.

Outsourcing is quickly becoming the world's most powerful way to accumulate wealth, and is now more accessible than ever before. This evolution of entrepreneurial thought is a lifestyle that will leverage your time, and maximize what you can accomplish. Embrace these principles and reap the rewards. The truth is, even though most people have heard of it, very few set themselves up for success.

"You can lead a horse to water but you can't make him drink."

I'm passionate and happy to share with hungry entrepreneurs how to take their business and life to the next level. I will do so openly and freely, but the truth is, most people reading this chapter will not leverage what they learn about outsourcing. But, here's the great news... for those that do, you are going to win, and win big!

What Is Outsourcing?

You might have an idea of what outsourcing means, but let's define it:

Out·source /ˈoutˌsôrs/ ***verb***

obtain (goods or a service) from an outside or foreign supplier, especially in place of an internal source.

"**outsourcing** components **from** other countries" contract (work) out or abroad.

"you may choose to **outsource** this function **to** another company or do it yourself"

Outsourcing involves contracting work from another party and supplying the deliverable (ie: a product or service) to your client. Either with transparency or as a behind the scenes workforce, clients are happy when they receive value from a job well done.

In The Beginning

People frequently ask me these two questions: How did you start? How can you handle so much? My answer is simple, but I bet you can guess it; yes, it's outsourcing.

I was in business for years before I discovered this super power. Before outsourcing I was disorganized, burning the candles at both ends, and never took a day off ... I was miserable. Eventually my health took a hit and I was sidelined. During my recovery I had no other option and was FORCED to hire help just to retain the clients I had.

Surely this would be the end of my business.

But... it wasn't. In fact, even as I recovered, I decided to keep my new team member, and focus on growth. The GROWTH of my TEAM. With less stress, and more capacity, the light bulb went off in my mind and I became obsessed.

Today

Fast forward to today: Outsourcing has allowed me to build a team of 23, delivering over $6 million a year in services as a white-label agency to help scale other agencies and companies of all sizes (we've even been able to work with juggernauts such as Microsoft & Rackspace among others). Our team is laser focused on filling in the gaps to deliver huge results for our clients that help make them Rockstars to their own customers.

What do we do for them? You name it, we've done it. With outsourcing we deliver on SaaS software builds, Facebook Ads, Google Ads, websites, funnels, and much more. When we take on a contract, we typically handle everything from start to finish so our clients can focus on making *their* customers happy... this way, everybody wins.

Today, I look back at the early days of struggling to pay the bills (or get a good night's sleep) and have only one regret: Not building out my outsourcing infrastructure sooner!

*Gold*en Nuggets

Although simple, implementing these steps will help you on your way to leveraging the power of outsourcing. This will work to limit risk and reduce your workload, *while still growing your company and profits* aggressively.

First: Pick Your Passion

Outsourcing can impact any industry or niche, so if you haven't already, I want you to envision a business that you can see becoming an extension of you. You do not have to be an expert, but ideally your business will involve something you are passionate about.

Second: Take Swift Action

Build a landing page, outlining your business concept, and highlight your unique advantages so you can IMMEDIATELY focus on driving traffic to your page to generate leads. Don't know how to make a landing page, or run ads? Outsource it.

(Plug Alert: Even better, outsource it to an agency, *like ours*, who can help generate sales quickly)

Third: Get Organized

Think through each task that is needed to achieve the desired product or service for your client.
-Can you easily explain each task to an employee?

-Is each task broken down in a way that allows it to be repeated accurately?

Begin a Standard Operating Procedures (SOP) document, and outline each task to be delegated to your outsourced team. Make sure it's written in a way that allows your business to deliver a consistent, dependable result time and time again.

Finding Your Clients

"It all sounds simple, but how do I get my product or service in front of the right audience?"

Data is **key** to finding clients in a particular niche. Do you want to find chiropractors? Or maybe you want to find Real Estate Agents or Housewives who are into sewing. How do you do that?

The first thing that you should do is build your list. To do this, you must have a reliable data source where you can get your target audience lead information such as their email address, phone number, physical address, etc. By far the best tool I've found for this is AgencyLeads.io.

Pro Tips:

1. Go to MapDataPro.com, purchase a list of all US cities
2. Use the AgencyLeads.io chrome extension to build your lead database
3. Identify businesses that are under served, and could use your product or service the most
4. Execute an outreach campaign to targeted leads to build your sales pipeline
5. Demo / Pitch / Close new sales!

Outsource any and all steps if possible, and remember to build out clear SOP's!

Moving Forward

As you can see, outsourcing gives you the power to quickly scale your business to the next level.

Move forward with confidence, and realize that through outsourcing anything is possible. Unbelievable growth is possible, and the opportunity is yours for the taking. Outsourcing speeds up growth and allows you to focus on your strengths, while also leveraging the strengths of others. You CAN do this. But, if you'd like help, or a quicker path to success, we provide coaching and services to fast track building the business you've always wanted.

A Gift For You

Grab a free one-on-one consultation to see how we can help you outsource and automate your business!

Just Schedule here: https://replug.link/Free-Consultation

About Travis Linares

Travis Linares lives in San Antonio, Texas with his wife, family and two boxer pup's Rocky & Bullwinkle. As a serial entrepreneur Travis has built businesses from the ground up and is currently operating as the Co-Founder and CTO of a 7 figure Digital Marketing & Software Development Agency. His Agency operation has helped over 500 Agencies and Agency Clients scale their profits and grow their businesses.

Travis continues to mentor and help create the next generation of highly successful entrepreneurs.

CHAPTER EIGHTEEN

Beat Burnout

By Kelly Shockley

How often have you experienced burnout? Can you get through a campaign, launch, or Mastermind event without experiencing burnout afterward? There are strategies entrepreneurs can implement to keep their minds and bodies healthy while running their businesses.

My exclusive Health Optimization System allows you to measure and track your health statistics so you can optimize your health using lifestyle and nutrition recommendations customized to your needs.

Entrepreneurs can now supercharge their health, so they no longer suffer from various maladies including brain fog, poor memory, lack of focus and concentration, sleep disturbances, aches, and pains.

Entrepreneurs are the ultramarathon runners of the business world. Extreme burnout is not something to mess around with and is completely avoidable if you take simple action steps regularly.

In The Beginning

In 2015, I began training for my first 50-mile ultramarathon. I'd just been through a horrific divorce, was a full-time single mom of a three-year-old boy who had robbed me of sleep since his birth, and was working at my functional health clinic.

It was a beautiful Colorado morning on January 22nd, 2016; the snow was crunching beneath my feet as I ran through the woods on my favorite trail. I planted my foot wrong and found myself on the ground with an abrasion. One week later, I was in Emergency with a life-threatening septic infection.

I was in great shape. I ate perfectly 95% of the time. I took supplements. I was the least likely person to end up in the hospital but there I was.

The fact was, I was burnt out. I had been running on empty since completing my doctorate 14 years earlier without truly knowing the level of my health. When I ran my numbers, my entire body was working at suboptimal levels. My reserve tank was empty. There was nothing there to fight. Traditional medicine called this a fluke and stated I was sensitive to skin infections. Before this, I had never experienced a skin infection. Something had changed about my health. I needed to get back to how healthy I was years earlier.

Benefits Of The Health Optimization System

The strategies presented in this chapter work best when implemented in your everyday life. Create routines now, like you're training for a race, and you'll compete at a higher capacity every day without any burnout.

Benefits Of The Strategies:

- A strengthened immune system that ensures you stay healthy through stressful periods, which means you can enjoy your "downtime" instead of being sick in bed trying to recover.
- Improved brain function for mental sharpness that improves memory, focus, and concentration while working.
- Regular restorative sleep allowing you to wake up feeling refreshed and ready to take on the day and keeping you efficient and productive with your time.
- Renewed resistance to stress and anxiety allowing you to face daily challenges with grace and speed while easily reaching your goals without having to take time to cope.
- Follow your body's key indicators to supercharge your health and withstand the physical and emotional demands of the world, which means you won't be taken out of the game for days, weeks, months, or indefinitely.

Top Five Strategies To Avoid Burnout

Following the five strategies listed here will help you stay healthy day in and day out. Get started on them today!

Establish A Sleep Routine

Sleep is incredibly important for your health and it is recommended that adults get between seven and eight hours of restful sleep a night.

Quality of sleep is superior to quantity. If you are in bed for eight hours but toss and turn all night, you're getting less restorative sleep than someone who sleeps soundly for six hours because you're failing to have deeper levels of sleep; your mind and body will not recover or repair properly if this disrupted sleep continues.

Go to bed and wake up at the same time every day, even on days off. Sleep routines are not just for babies. Sticking to the same bedtime every night will help your body know it's time to sleep. To find the best time to go to bed, start from when you have to wake up. Count backward by 1.5 hours increments. For example, if you have to be up by 6 am, go to bed by 9 or 10:30 pm. Your sleep cycle is 90 minutes; waking up when a sleep cycle is ending instead of when you're in your deepest sleep will be easier.

Solid Nutrition

With all the diet trends these days, it can be difficult to know how to properly fuel your body. From the beginning, humans have lived on ample amounts of good fats, moderate amounts of protein, and low amounts of carbohydrates. Research shows these ratios produce the best results when looking at blood pressure, cholesterol, blood glucose, hemoglobin A_1C, inflammation, and body composition. These are the ground rules.

Eat whole foods. Stay away from any food with a label. If it's in a package or box, it has been processed in some way. With this in mind, shop around the perimeter of the grocery store and avoid the aisles. Avoid eating out as much as possible. You have no control over food quality.

Eat only one serving of fruit per day. Fruits contain a lot of carbohydrates. Steve Jobs was a lifelong on-and-off-again fruitarian. He died from pancreatic cancer. Ashton Kutcher became a fruitarian while prepping for his role as Steve Jobs and ended up in the hospital with pancreatitis. Too much of a good thing can be bad.

Sugars and grains are on the chopping block as well because they spike your blood sugar level and can keep it spiked for long periods. Grains of all types are worse for you than sugar. Spiking blood sugar levels is stressful on the body and causes inflammation in your system, like mini fires throughout it. This is the path towards disease.

Unplug Technology

Research suggests shutting down all technology two hours before bedtime! Blue light emitted from computers, tablets, smartphones and such is like caffeine to your brain. If you stimulate your brain up until it's time to go to bed, you may have sleep problems. So, make shutting down technology part of your sleep routine.

What you do in the 30 minutes before going to bed sets the tone for the type of sleep you'll experience. Shut down all technology and dim the lights to help your body know nighttime has arrived. This helps the body produce melatonin, a hormone necessary for inducing sleep.

Move!

You are a dynamic being. You were not meant to be sedentary. Sitting is worse for you than smoking, so movement is key to your survival. Exercise is crucial for health but that's not what this section is about. You need to negate the ill effects sitting has on your health.

If you're at your desk for hours, sit on an exercise ball, or alternate between sitting and standing options. Set up your workspace ergonomically to decrease stress on your body. However, do not waste money on an ergonomic chair: The chair braces your body and keeps it from slouching, which is helpful, but this is an outside source doing a job your muscles should be doing. In other words, the chair makes your muscles lazy and weakens them. Keeping your muscles engaged is key to improving posture while reducing the aches and pains that result from sitting at a desk. Using an exercise ball is the answer.

Follow Your Key Health Indicators

If you're not testing the level of your health, you're guessing. Did you know symptoms (headache, aches and pains, allergies, short-term memory issues, etc.) present only once your body has been struggling for a while?

When you are exposed to a germ and get sick, you didn't get sick as soon as you came in contact with the bug. The germ had to spread and challenge the immune system first for you to experience symptoms. Symptoms are your body's warning signs that it needs help. It's kind of like when your check engine light comes on in your car.

And, are you healthy when symptoms disappear? No. Symptoms are the last to show up and the first to go away while the cause may still exist. This is why doctors tell you to take your full prescription. You'll feel better after a couple of days, but the underlying infection is not gone yet. In the same way, you may feel better after a few days off having suffered burnout, but that does not mean you've completely recovered and are healthy again. Outward appearance and how you feel is not the best indicator of how healthy you are.

The only way to know if you are healthy through and through is to have testing – of your blood – done regularly and having annual physicals with your medical practitioner. All those things I learned after my septic infection were discovered through blood testing and each of those tests (and more) can be part of your annual physical. Or, you can simply request the tests at any time by visiting your doctor. If you do suffer burnout or any other illness or injury, have blood testing done after you feel better to be sure that you truly are. Your business depends on you.

Moving Forward

The ultimate key in avoiding burnout is making sure you're healthy before going into a campaign, launch, or Mastermind event. Don't wait to implement health strategies during high-stress. Remember, it's like you're training for a race. How well you train is how well you'll perform. It's during high-stress times you need your routines and strategies the most, yet that's when the temptation is to let them slide. Start setting up your strategies and routines today.

A Gift For You

It is my passion to serve you so you can be the best version of you!

Be sure to download the free ***Quick Start Guide to Combating Burnout*** at https://chlabs.link/playbook

The strategies in this chapter are just the tip of the iceberg. My complete customized program delves much deeper into each strategy, complete with checklists and easy action plans to help you be more successful.

About Kelly Shockley

Dr. Kelly has been helping entrepreneurs take the guesswork out of restoring their health since 2005. She understands the importance of staying healthy because missing work is not an option. As a fellow entrepreneur, she understands how important it is to have your body working at its highest capacity so you can perform your best.

With her Health Optimization System, you will experience improved focus, concentration, mental clarity, and energy levels. Her system provides you with a comprehensive health check through state-of-the-art lab analysis, which measures key indicators that identify nutrient imbalances, deficiencies, and toxicities. Her goal is to create science-based strategies that promote peak efficiency in your daily tasks and enhance your effectiveness.

If you're already experiencing burnout or are experiencing other symptoms, have a family history of illness/disease, or even if you feel great, there's no time better than now to know your numbers.

CHAPTER NINETEEN

Become A Successful Health And Wellness Entrepreneur

By Brittani Feinberg

Part of being a Health and Wellness expert involves being healthy and well but many people in this field are not – in business, at least, and in life, at worst. My strategy for business is applying a secret system that helps those in the Health and Wellness Industry – or any other niche – create the business of their dreams while freeing themselves up to enjoy life to its fullest. It's the L.O.V.V.V.E.™ system!

In The Beginning

I consider myself a serial entrepreneur. My passion for business started at the age of eight. From washing cars to manufacturing supplements, stripping, and real estate, the list goes on and on.

It wasn't until I met my beautiful wife who taught me a secret formula that I have applied to all areas of my life that I have become successful not just in business but also personally and spiritually as well.

After competing in a bodybuilding competition and being involved in several businesses, I decided to pursue my passion – the Health and Wellness Industry. The level of commitment, determination, and discipline I had to use both mentally and physically was one of the hardest things I had ever done. When the entire process was over, my breakthroughs weren't that I hit my goal, got on stage, and won the trophy; my breakthroughs were the moments I wanted to give up but didn't let myself.

My breakthrough was learning how to unblock myself from success, not only for the competition but in all areas of my life. My breakthrough was *L.O.V.V.V.E.* ™

The Secret System:

- Let Go
- Open Your Heart, Mind, and Spirit
- Visualize
- Voice
- Vibration
- Empower with the Power of I Am

Let Go

This is a very important step for a Health and Wellness entrepreneur and maybe the hardest one for many.

You must learn to let go of control. Thinking you can be and do everything, not asking for help, and not delegating projects is the fastest way to burnout. To get on the fast track to success, you must let go of ego, old thought patterns, and habits now. When you try to control everything, you enjoy nothing.

Breathe.

The easiest way to start letting go of control is delegation. To simplify your life, take focused action. Let go of victim mentality, simplify your life, and learn how to create more time.

Focused Action

Implement Stewardship Delegation in your personal or professional life, a method created by Stephen Covey and described in his book 7 Habits of Highly Effective People.

This delegation method requires you to create and inspire a team you trust and who is committed to your vision (so you must know your vision well). Once you communicate a clear, vivid vision and everyone agrees on the result to be achieved, you delegate certain tasks to each person but allow them to use whatever methods they see as fit to complete their tasks. You provide guidance and support when needed.

This gives you freedom and gives each team member invested responsibility to complete their tasks in a way that works for them, without feeling micromanaged.

The result will be more clients, a launched program, an organized house, etc.

Open Your Heart, Mind, And Spirit

The second step requires change and vulnerability. When you open your heart, mind, and spirit you contribute to Humanity and live with purpose, which fuels you to create.

Before working with me, Tony, a gym owner and master personal trainer, spent most of his days in the gym, he was the sales team, personal trainer, plumber, electrician, cashier, and Smoothie guy. He was constantly putting out fires and hustling to provide for his family. He was a slave to his own business.

When we started implementing the system, his major breakthrough was cracking open his heart to remember who he was and why he opened his gym. Once he reconnected to inspired living and fulfillment, we were able to create a master plan for his business that allowed him to have more time, money, and freedom.

We transformed his gym into a hub to generate different streams of income, created a winning, trustworthy team to work at the gym and launched a successful online weight loss challenge to build his community and improve the lifetime value for his customers.

Focused Action

Use this link for a L.O.V.V.V.E.™ meditation https://youtu.be/mA6GbzYf0U8

Visualize

This step is fun. It is time to visualize your success – whatever that means to you.

Remember that vivid vision we talked about in the letting go step? Well, it's back. Create a vivid vision of the life you want to live and what you want your Health and Wellness business to look like. The key here is don't be scared or nervous about dreaming big; you must be clear.

Focused Action

Answer the following questions and have fun with it.

- Who do you want to serve?
- Why is serving this community so important to you?
- What is it that you want to accomplish?

Voice

This step is empowering. Use your voice to confidently share your knowledge, message, and mission with your audience.

Many of my clients who are in the Health and Wellness Industry suffer from low self-esteem and fear what other people think. This paralyzes them and keeps them dreaming small. This is a huge block if you want to succeed as a Health and Wellness entrepreneur in the digital space. Plus, it's a disservice to your audience. Learn to use your voice with confidence and integrity and you will authentically attract a loyal following.

Focused Action

Publish, Publish, Publish. Figure out which platform(s) work(s) for you and start publishing (podcasts, video, blogs, etc.)

Vibration

This step is about keeping your vibration high with clean food, rest, and exercise. This should be obvious to those in the Health and Wellness Industry, but it is easy to get consumed with work and forget the basics of health. So, this is your reminder to be the product of the product. If you want to help people improve their health, you better authentically vibrate health and vitality. It's that simple. People want authenticity and transparency.

Focused Action

Take inventory. In the last 30 days,

- What have you been eating?
- How many hours of sleep do you average per night?
- How many days per week are you exercising?

Empower With The Power Of I AM.

I = Intention

A = Action

M = Mastery

Focused Action

Every morning set your *Intention* for the day.

Take focused *Action* with integrity.

Stand as a *Master* of your expertise.

Moving Forward

Being a Health and Wellness entrepreneur is all about providing value. Once you implement the L.O.V.V.V.E™ system and unblock yourself from success, use ClickFunnels. The ClickFunnels platform is worthless unless you know who you are and who you want to serve in your business. ClickFunnels are just the vehicle to help drive your ideal clients into your world.

You must be the master of your domain. Train yourself to be a better person with L.O.V.V.V.E.™ and let ClickFunnels help you attain the ultimate success that you envision.

About Brittani Feinberg

Brittani Feinberg is a serial entrepreneur who is a co-founder of Warrior Life Code and is obsessed with helping entrepreneurs around the world.

Growing up, Brittani was always motivated by education and she traveled an interesting path to get to her present life. Planning to enter medical school and become a pediatrician, she began studying radiology at the age of 16 at Keiser University, where she attained her Associates Degree in Science.

While in school, she waitressed, but at 17 she walked out of her shift and into the world of exotic dancing. For the next three years, she danced, was complimented on her body, and delved deeper into a taboo fantasy world. At 22, she knew she wanted to further explore the world of adult entertainment and opened a shop.

A Gift For You

To get a FREE Guide on how to implement my L.O.V.V.V.E.™ system with the use of ClickFunnels go to www.warriorlifecode.com

Despite the shop's success, Brittani decided she wanted to focus her attention on Health and Wellness and started selling supplements online. She has now broadened her expertise in the online world and is coaching entrepreneurs to help increase their revenue ten times without the stress and expense of classes.

CHAPTER TWENTY

The Unfair Advantage of Butterfly Marketing

By Mike Filsaime

Butterfly Marketing was a strategy and software that took the world by storm, creating more millionaires than any other product out there. I launched "The Butterfly Marketing Manuscript" back in August of 2006 outlining the strategy behind Butterfly Marketing and numerous individuals and influencers went on to make hundreds of thousands of dollars applying its tactics. Through the years, many have transformed their businesses using the unfair advantages of Butterfly Marketing.

Today, these Butterfly Marketing strategies are even more powerful because I have created an entire software solution tailor-made for marketers in mind.

Before I get into these unfair advantages of Butterfly Marketing, as well as how you can apply my exact steps I use in my own business, let me set the stage so you understand what butterflies have to do with marketing.

What Is The Butterfly Effect?

The 'Butterfly Effect' is something that has always intrigued me. Very simply, it is the understanding that small changes can have a dramatic effect, or outcome, over time.

One small change, word, waive of a hand, smile... can change history. One seemingly insignificant action can put into place, a connection of events that one day may drastically change the entire world (from what it would have been.)

In fact, the plot of the movie titled "The Butterfly Effect" was on the same premise. The main character would try to go back in time to make a relationship work, with the girl he loved. Every time he went back, he did one small thing that had drastic or a dramatic effect when he returned to present day.

This was also seen in other movies and books like "Back to the Future" and "The Time Machine" along with many others.

Here are some things to consider...

Do you remember Mark David Chapman? He was the person who assassinated John Lennon. What if his parents never met? Would John Lennon still be living today? He would not have been murdered on that December day. What would be different in the music world today? Or imagine "The Beatles" reunions had he lived.

What if Lee Harvey Oswald's bullet "missed"? John F. Kennedy would have remained president and perhaps he would have been reelected. Maybe there would've been no Vietnam War, or maybe there would've been World War III. Who Knows?

What if the Bullet that hit Ronald Reagan moved over ½ of an inch? He would have been killed by a bullet to the heart. How would that have changed the world? Would we have seen the fall of communism?

The bottom line is that these butterfly effects would have drastically changed the outcome of each of these scenarios. Can you imagine butterfly effects in your own life and how different your life would be today?

Here is the definition of "The Butterfly Effect" from a book by Ian Stewart: "The flapping of a single butterfly's wing today produces a tiny change in the state of the atmosphere. Over a period of time, what the atmosphere actually does diverges from what it would have done. So, in a month's time, a tornado that would have devastated the Indonesian coast doesn't happen...." (Ian Stewart, Does God Play Dice? The Mathematics of Chaos, pg. 141) For this very reason, you cannot measure the weather for more than 5-7 days ahead. There are just too many changes that affect the atmosphere at any given moment. It is not a simple mathematics numbers game.

So what does this 'Butterfly Effect' have to do with marketing...

Butterfly Marketing is understanding that certain **very small changes** that you make just one time early in your marketing can have a DRAMATIC effect on your results, your income and your business...good or bad.

These small changes, when put into a Viral Marketing Campaign, can mean the difference between: having a growing 200,000+ member database in a short amount of time and more money than you can shake a stick at, or site that is dead and will remain dead. It is possible for the 'dead site' to even be superior in many aspects (as far as service and value) than the 'successful site.' However, if it is not set up correctly to grow, it is destined to fail.

We need to determine if there are small changes we can make to our marketing, good or bad, which can have a dramatic effect on our success over time. This also goes into something called the Viral Exponent.

Butterfly Marketing's Biggest Unfair Advantage: Viral Marketing

The term Viral Marketing is actually fairly new. It was started around 1996 when the owner of 'Hotmail' coined the phrase. The Internet was relatively new, so before this, there was nothing that could spread around the world as fast. Email could go "FWD: FWD: FWD:" to millions of people all over the world in just days or in sometimes just a few hours. So the thought of a marketing campaign spreading like a virus was not even conceived until the Internet. Before that, it was called 'Word of Mouth' advertising.

It is called VIRAL because, as you can guess, it spreads like a virus. A virus duplicates itself with everything it comes in contact with. Every new contact becomes a 'HOST' and can start the process off on its own new leg.

You want to focus on the Butterfly Effect in your marketing. You need to make SMALL CHANGES that can have DRAMATIC EFFECTS.

Many people simply launch a site and do not understand the power of Butterfly Marketing. The Butterfly Effect, in your marketing, is what will allow you to go from a "One Hit Wonder" to passive income that can make you a millionaire like it has done for me.

What Does Being Viral Mean For Butterfly Marketing?

Many people build their sites and funnels ending the visit on a thank you page. What if, you can add a special component that will create huge daily passive income and a huge email marketing list?

You need to focus on viral in order to apply Butterfly Marketing in your business:

Step 1 - Offer A High-Quality Free Product: In this step, you need to provide a free offer that has incredible value that you give away for free. It should hurt to give it away and leave them feeling as if there must be a catch because it is almost too good to be true.

Step 2 - Upsell To A Quality Offer: Your offer should be correlated to the free offer or more of what the free offer was.

Step 3 - Make The Customer An Instant Affiliate: The key step is to instantly make the customer or free member an affiliate using automations. My software Groove is the only software on the planet where Butterfly Marketing tactics can be used including making instant affiliates.

Step 4 - Provide Pre-Made Promotion Tools: As soon as your customer becomes an automatic affiliate, they are immediately taken to a portal where pre-made affiliate assets are provided. With Groove, there are over 12 categories of affiliate assets, including their custom affiliate links they can begin sharing immediately.

Increase Upsell Conversions: While other marketers are ending their customer's journey on the thank-you page, you will be able to instantly increase upsell conversions because their journey hasn't ended yet. They are now inside your portal that showcases your upsell offer to those who didn't purchase the first time.

Step 6 – Wash, Rinse & Repeat: These steps with the special components will help you create huge daily passive income and a huge marketing list. As you know, the gold is in the list.

In fact, I have used these tactics for years. I grew the largest list in internet marketing history in the early 2000s and became the #1 affiliate for many big brands. Having the list was the key with a deep focus on giving stuff away for free and upselling them later.

Butterfly Marketing strategies have worked for decades and now coupled with Groove as the software, anyone on the planet can leverage the power of these 6 steps. And better yet, anyone can use my software for free, create a free offer, offer an upsell promotion, make your customers automatic affiliates, have pre-made promotional assets available to them, increase conversions and just keep the process going for years to come.

What Tools Must You Have To Do Butterfly Marketing?

- You need the concepts and training – the steps we just covered above
- You need the tools – http://getgroovecrm.com
- You need the technology - http://getgroovecrm.com
- You need the pages - http://getgroovecrm.com

Moving Forward

Butterfly Marketing offers you some unfair advantages in addition to viral marketing including giving value at no cost to the marketplace, expecting nothing in return, building a profitable list of buyers and leads on autopilot, creating an army of affiliates equipped and ready to promote your product, and so many more. It is my hope that you can also harness the power of Butterfly Marketing so you can enjoy the benefits of growing income streams online.

I built a game-changing all-in-one solution called Groove so that you too can apply Butterfly Marketing Strategies. With Groove, you can create your landing pages, funnels, brand website, ecommerce stores, host videos, email marketing, automations, run affiliate programs, sell products, capture leads, membership sites, stream live, webinars and so much more. In the launch of Groove in 2020, I used Butterfly Marketing to grow a userbase of well over 300,000 within the first months of the software's existence. Therefore, I am proof that Butterfly Marketing is not only back, but more powerful than ever.

A Gift For You

Leverage Butterfly Marketing strategies using the Groove software by grabbing it for free at http://getgroovecrm.com and be sure to pay attention to how you move from this page into an automatic affiliate.

Grab this free video to see Butterfly Marketing in action at http://butterflymarketing.io and get not only the blueprint I used to grow Groove to hundreds of thousands of users in a short period of time, but also a copy of the Butterfly Marketing Manuscript.

About Mike Filsaime

Mike Filsaime is known as the Michael Jordan of Internet Marketing. The over-the-top expert on funnels, in front of, and behind the scenes! Mike holds the distinction of doing more Million Dollar launches for more brands than any marketer.

After running one of the largest auto dealerships in the U.S.A, Mike decided to follow his vision and create software designed to eliminate the pain and frustration of running an online business. His visionary ideas coupled with talented developers and designers have delivered game-changing software for countless online businesses.

Following his passion, Mike Filsaime's companies have generated over $150 Million. Historically, Mike was responsible for a number of well known "classic" software platforms, such as WebinarJam, EverWebinar, Kartra, DealGuardian, Butterfly Marketing, EvergreenBusinessSystem, and PayDotCom. He has since sold many of these brands.

Mike is now the CEO and Co-Founder of GrooveDigital™, Inc. GrooveDigital™ is one of the fastest growing software platforms for digital and e-commerce marketers. With over 200,000 users adopting the platform within just 6 months, GrooveFunnels™ website and funnel builder is the No. 1 Landing Page and Marketing Funnel Builder on the planet!

You can visit http://mikefilsaime.com to find out more about Mike Filsaime.

CHAPTER TWENTY-ONE

Getting Business Credit Funding

By Joe Lawrence

New digital start-ups and well-established digital companies have one thing in common: they both need money.

I learned in college that businesses are created to make money. You can create a company with a great mission statement, or you may have a desire to change the world, but businesses are different from non-profit organizations (NPOs) because they make a profit. Unfortunately, most businesses fail in their first few years due to a lack of money.

Businesses need startup capital and they need capital during slow months to stay afloat. Whether your business is seasonal or not, some quarters are going to be more profitable than others. You must plan for these slow times by applying for business credit.

In The Beginning

Between 2004 and 2007, US banks were careless with their underwriting (lending) guidelines. They would lend to almost anyone. This subprime lending period led many banks to go bankrupt. Today, it is much harder for small business owners to get business credit cards, lines of credit, and Small Business Administration (SBA) loans from big banks.

However, many community banks and credit unions are still eager to lend to small businesses. They remained vigilant about screening loan applicants when national banks were giving credit to anyone. As a result, these lenders are still financially healthy and need to lend money to raise money to pay interest to their investors and make a profit.

Credit Bureau Scores

Just like personal credit scores, good business credit scores are important for obtaining business credit cards, loans, and lines of credit. The advantages of using business credit are:

- It does not show on your personal credit report(s) or affect personal credit eligibility.
- It allows you to separate business debts/expenses from personal debts/expenses.
- You can have unlimited business credit profiles (one for each entity you own) while personal credit is limited to one social security number.

It is recommended that you do not use personal credit to fund a business; if you do, your personal credit score will drop any time you have business debt and you won't be able to use credit to live (e.g., get a mortgage or car loan).

Three main business credit bureaus monitor and track business credit reports: Dun & Bradstreet, Experian Small Business, and Equifax Small Business. If you already have some form of business credit, you already have a profile with these three bureaus. If you do not have any business credit yet, it's time to get registered with them to build a credit score.

Getting Business Credit

Think of credit as a three-leg stool. The three legs represent the Personal Credit Profile of the business owner, the Business Assets, and Business Revenues. The seat of the stool is your Business Credit Profile. Before approaching a bank for credit, be sure you have a least one leg of the stool in place.

Make an appointment with the bank manager. Choose someone who has been at the bank a long time, has approved a lot of loans recently, and is ready to help you be approved. Some branch managers will tell you to apply and see what happens; this is not the ideal banker to work with.

Business Credit Options

There are three types of business credit.

Business Credit Cards

- Most only require a two-page application.
- Cards are unsecured and require the applicant to have both good business credit and personal credit.
- Do not show on your personal credit report, provided you always pay on time.

Lines of Credit

- Most require a personal financial statement and additional documents.
- It can be secured or unsecured and requires the applicant to have a good business credit profile.
- Personal credit scores are not as important.
- Will not show up on your personal credit report unless you default, although a Universal Commercial Code (UCC) filing may be made that limits how many lines of credit you can have per company.

Small Business Administration (SBA) Loans

- Requires business and personal tax returns, personal financial statements, and possibly other documents.
- It can be secured or unsecured. The personal credit score of the applicant is checked, but a strong personal credit score is not always required.
- Does not usually show up on personal credit report (provided you pay on time).
- If you get an SBA Loan, the loan is backed by the SBA and the bank is risking less money, so you get more.

- The only disadvantage of SBA Loans is that they are paperwork heavy.

Seven Steps To Prepare For Getting Credit

Here are seven steps to follow when applying for credit in the US. It may take some time to complete but it is worth it.

1. **Form Your Business**

You must create a company (entity) separate from yourself to get business credit. Create either a Limited Liability Company (LLC) or a Corporation (S-Corp or C-Corp). The type you choose doesn't matter but be sure you get your Employer Identification Number (EIN) from the Internal Revenue Service (IRS) after creating the company.

Choose an equivocal name and use an ambiguous type of business. For example, the name *Legacy Management, LLC* is better than *Legacy Real Estate, LLC* and register your company as a *Business Services Company* or *Business Management Company* rather than a *Real Estate Company.*

2. **Get Business Credit Ready.**

Before taking your company to business lenders, complete a few compliance matters to avoid getting declined for trivial reasons:

- Make sure your company has a landline that is dedicated for business use. The number you get should be in the area code where you are doing business. List the phone number with the yellow pages and 411 directories.
- Create at least a basic online presence for your company. Ideally, purchase the .com for your company (e.g., mycompany.com). Also, create an email account for the business.
- Prepare your articles/certificate of formation, EIN letter, and operating agreement. A business plan is helpful but not always required.

3. **Network With Local Banks.**

Choose small banks and credit unions over large ones. Determine the bank's lending mood. Some banks are very conservative, and some are eager to lend to small businesses.

4. **Setup Your Business Credit Profiles.**

Dun and Bradstreet specifically monitors business credit profiles. Visit their website or give them a call to request a Data Universal Numbering System(DUNS) Number, which is a nine-digit business social security number. The two other bureaus, Experian Small Business and Equifax Small Business, will create profiles once you have been granted business credit.

5. **Build Trade Lines of Credit.**

This process will increase your business credit score.

Reach out to companies from which you buy supplies (paper/office supplies, gas, technology, and other suppliers) and ask them to offer your company business credit terms. Start small (as low as $10, as high as $2,000) and ask to be billed on NET30 terms: When you buy supplies from the company, you will receive the product in a few days, but you'll pay for it, in full, within 30 days. Essentially, you'll be buying supplies on short-term credit in your company name. Aim to establish at least five trade lines of credit to boost your business credit profile.

6. **Optimize your Business Credit Rankings.**

After purchasing products on NET30 terms, you will get some positive credit history reporting. Your business credit profile will start to get ranked within a system called PAYDEX. Your goal is to get a PAYDEX Score high enough that banks and lenders will lend to you. PAYDEX scores range from zero to 100, aim for a score of 80 or higher.

Start getting and using store and gas credit cards to create profiles with Experian Small Business and Equifax Small Business. A favorite of mine is the Commercial Account or Commercial Revolving Account with Home Depot for Business. Once you use the card, Home Depot reports to all three credit bureaus.

7. **Get Business Credit.**

Start with small business credit cards. Apply for SBA Loans, Business Loans, and Business Lines of Credit based on your needs.

Speak to your branch manager about the approval process and their requirements before applying to make sure your company is ready and will be approved. If you are declined, always have your branch manager take a second look and make a recommendation to the underwriter to approve the application.

If You Have Poor Personal Credit

If you do not have good personal credit, you can still get approved for business credit. Follow these three steps right away:

Request a credit analyzer

Request this from either your mortgage broker or an online service. The credit analyzer looks at your credit report and determines any possible adjustments to increase your credit score. Scores can increase from 30 to 100 points. Then request rapid rescoring from the credit bureau, which allows you to update your credit score in as little as 48 hours, instead of waiting the normal 30days.

1. **Enroll with a credit repair company.**

Many companies repair credit; simply choose your favorite or ask around for a good referral.

2. **Recruit a credit partner.**

Reach out to someone that has good credit. Build a relationship with them. Offer them an incentive for being your credit partner. The incentive can be money, a percentage of the credit they help you get, or partnership percentage in the business. Properly disclose the risks, the terms of the arrangement, and the exit strategy. Sign documents allowing you and the partner to apply for business credit.

Many credit partners are family members or friends. When applying for a business credit card, they complete the section for a guarantor. The guarantor needs to have good personal credit but does not have to be the primary business owner. If the business defaults on the credit, then both the guarantor and the business are liable. The business credit card will not show on the guarantor's personal credit report assuming it doesn't go into default.

Be sure to have a business attorney draft a credit partner agreement, letter of understanding, and a Chief Financial Officer (CFO) Resolution. Keep it simple. This doesn't need to be complicated.

After you get business credit, consider paying off your personal debt. You will look debt-free and your personal credit score will dramatically improve.

Moving Forward

Once you obtain business credit, use it wisely. Make payments regularly and on time to avoid penalties. Focus on keeping both your personal and business credit ratings strong to stay financially healthy.

A Gift For You

Want to dive deeper into this topic? Get access to our advanced training with video modules, audio interviews with lenders, and a full list of current lenders!

How to get $100K in Unsecured Business Lines of Credit…Without having to show tax returns: https://www.businesscreditworkshop.net/

About Joe Lawrence

Joe Lawrence is an author and Business Credit Coach from New Jersey who helps small business owners obtain large lines of business credit. Working in real estate, he discovered methods to line up cash quickly as a means to fund his business. He takes pride in correcting the myth that only "older, large companies can obtain lines of credit." His company, Business Credit Workshop, teaches methods to develop a rock-solid business credit profile as well as the little-known techniques on how and where to obtain unsecured business loans in today's market.

Website: www.businesscreditworkshop.me

CHAPTER TWENTY-TWO

Tax Hacks

By Carlotta Thompson

The key to paying the least tax legally possible is understanding that our tax code is designed to help entrepreneurs; it is not your enemy. 98% of the tax code is written to explain all of the deductions and credits available for entrepreneurs. The fact the tax code helps is a well-kept secret because these benefits are only available to entrepreneurs and investors, not employees.

In a debate with Hillary Clinton, Donald Trump once said the fact that he paid no taxes made him smart. I couldn't agree more. It is our duty as entrepreneurs to pay as little tax as possible, so we can help the economy by employing others and change the world. I am going to give you three secrets that every entrepreneur should know and implement to ensure they are paying the least tax legally possible.

In The Beginning

One day, I was sitting across from Mr. Rodgers* as he struggled to recover from the report I had just given him. He had been in business for a few years and his business was doing well but the news I just delivered could put him out of business instantly.

"Mr. Rodgers, your tax bill for the three years I audited, after penalties and interest, is $65,452."

As the tears welled up in his eyes, he asked, "How am I ever going to pay this? My business after expenses makes only $90,000. All of that is required for my family to live. We don't have money just sitting around. I was not trying to do anything wrong. I had a CPA that I worked with and they were supposed to help me. Why doesn't the IRS make you take a course before you start a business?"

As I sat there, I thought to myself, "I came to the IRS to help people and to educate them and now I am ruining their lives. I came to make a difference in this organization that is known for being harsh and not caring about people. I spent countless hours educating taxpayers and showing them items they may have missed on their taxes."

But, as I was sitting with Mr. Rodgers, I realized it was too little too late. He was grateful for all of my help but if I had come into his life three years earlier his current situation would never have happened.

---

* Names have been changed to protect privacy.

I realized that day that I had to get ahead of this instead of trying to help when it was too late. In September of 2017, I left the IRS. It had been my dream job since I was 14 years old, and I was leaving it behind for a bigger mission to save small businesses across the US.

Three Tax Secrets for Entrepreneurs

The IRS does not look for tax savings you may have missed. You and/or your tax specialist must look for deductions and savings yourselves. How does a busy entrepreneur do this?

1. Tax Strategy Mindset: How Can I Make This A Tax Deduction?

In business, we are always thinking strategically. After all, that is what sets us apart from the employees of the world. Yet, when it comes to taxes, we bomb.

One of the easiest ways to save taxes is to start asking yourself," How can I make this a tax deduction?" rather than, "Is this a tax deduction?"

The first thing I teach is how to have a tax strategy mindset. That is a term I coined when trying to explain how to save taxes on autopilot. Let me give you an example of what it means to have a tax strategy mindset:

When I started my business, I was driving 60 miles to and from my office, which cost $30 a day. I would go straight to my office every morning. The IRS considers this commuting, which is non-deductible. By changing my mindset, I started asking how to make my travel into a LEGAL tax deduction.

I went to the post office and bank every day, but I usually went at lunchtime. By going to the post office before work and the bank after work the entire trip becomes a tax deduction because it is no longer considered commuting. This is now a $10,000 (60 miles x 300 days/yr x $0.58/mile = $10,440/yr)[12] tax deduction where before it was zero!

Likewise, when I plan to go on vacation, I try to do some business on the trip so that I can write some of it off. I also do this with every purchase I make. Of course, I don't write off everything I buy, but I have trained myself to always ask the question, "How can I make this into a tax deduction?"

2. Create A Tax Strategy Plan

As I already said, 98% of the tax code consists of deductions and credits. Tax strategy is figuring out which of these plans makes sense for you and your situation. It also includes structuring your company to pay less and applying the strategies so they work together instead of independent of each other. After all, the goal is for you to pay the least tax possible.

A tax strategist creates tax strategy plans. These tax strategy plans can save you several thousand dollars in taxes. I would suggest getting one of these no matter how big or small your business is. These strategy plans are custom, so they meet you where you are and show you the next few steps in front of you. Once you have a tax strategy plan, you will want to get it updated annually.

3. Use A Tax Strategy Team

As an entrepreneur, I understand the desire to do everything yourself. I have built websites, funnels, and created ads. I like doing things myself, so I understand what I am dealing with before I outsource

[12] Based on 2019 IRS standard mileage rate, which changes annually.

it. Tax software such as *Turbo Tax* will teach you a lot and, if your business earns less than $20,000 after expenses, I understand using it. Yes, you might miss something, but you will learn a lot and you will likely find more expenses than an accountant who just throws what you bring them on a tax return as fast as possible.

As a business owner, you need to have a basic understanding of taxes. Once you have a viable business, you need to hire a tax strategy team that is solely focused on tax strategy. Any accountant can do your books; any tax preparer can prepare taxes. But you need someone for whom saving you money is their number one focus. They should take your tax strategy plan and infuse it into your bookkeeping, taxes, and financial strategy. Remember, when hiring an accountant, it is not how much they charge you but how much they cost you that matters.

What should you look for in a tax strategy team?

- A team that infuses strategy into your books, taxes, and financial planning. Your tax strategist, bookkeeper, and tax preparer should all be the same person. They should also be a part of a team in which their work is reviewed by another tax strategist.
- A team that is always learning new strategies because tax laws change quickly.
- A team that is not scared of the IRS. They can't be afraid to implement strategies.
- A team that will go above and beyond. Look for someone who truly cares about you and your business.
- A team that is focused on saving you money. If every time you ask a question or bring up a strategy, they are super conservative and say that it is a red flag, they are not right for you.
- A team that is available and practices ongoing communication. You should have regular communication with them, and you should be doing tax planning all year. Most of the companies I work with are growing super fast. If they don't talk to their strategist until it is time to file their taxes, they are going to over-pay the IRS.
- A team that is also focused on compliance. Legal is the critical word in everything I have mentioned in this chapter.

Moving Forward

Practicing skills in this book will help your income skyrocket faster than you ever imagined. Instantly, you will be faced with a new problem: The government wanting a big chunk of your money. I want you to be prepared so you pay the least tax legally possible. I don't want you to feel like a thief came in the night and stole half of everything you worked hard to make.

The culture of your business is so important. Implement a culture of tax savings and you will always pay less.

A Gift For You

Find out if you are overpaying taxes by taking the short quiz at www.irsquiz.com.

Contact me and my team at:

- www.carlottathompson.com
- support@carlottathompson.com
- www.facebook.com/CoachCarlottaT

About Carlotta Thompson

Carlotta Thompson is the CEO of Carlotta Thompson and Associates. She left the IRS to help businesses nationwide pay the least tax legally possible! She remembers sitting across from taxpayers who were in tears trying to figure out how they would ever pay the tax she was showing on their audit report. It broke her heart and she knew she had to leave and make a positive difference for entrepreneurs. From there, her mission was born to help entrepreneurs pay the least tax legally possible.

Carlotta Thompson created her national tax strategy firm to be different from every accounting firm in the US.

There are so many things that makes her firm different but, first and foremost, they care about your tax bill as much as they do their own. Further, they are experts in tax strategy and they create and implement a custom strategy plan for you and infuse that strategy into your bookkeeping, CFO services, and tax preparation. Carlotta and her team of tax strategists, CPAs, and EAs are focused on saving you money so you can put your focus on making money.

"Carlotta saved me at least 75 grand this year."
- Jake Randolph

CHAPTER TWENTY-THREE

Patenting Your Ideas Without an Attorney

By Laurel Bloomfield

Logic will get you from A to B. Imagination will take you everywhere.
~ Albert Einstein

When you see a new product on a retail shelf, TV, or in a Facebook ad, do you ever think, "Hey! That was my idea?"

Lots of people have ideas, but the ones who act on their ideas are the only people who have a chance of monetizing them. People who offer their ideas to the world in the form of products and/or services often make money. When you have a unique idea, one that no one else has had, it's prudent to protect it from being stolen or copied by securing a patent for it. You can then build a business around the patented Intellectual Property (IP).

I am a patented inventor and I going to share how to secure Patent Protection for your unique idea(s) without spending any money on attorney fees.

We live in the most incredible time. If you don't know how to do something, you can search the Internet and learn how within minutes. This is the age of information and the age of self-education.

Some ideas can be executed and don't require or qualify for Patent Protection; some ideas are unique enough that they warrant Patent Protection. Obtaining a patent takes time but – should your idea take off and sell – there are important benefits to having applied for and secured a patent.

For example, a patent is a tangible asset, one that can – and should – be listed in your company financial records. Your IP is a bargaining chip when negotiating with investors and investors always like to see the security of a patent. Also, the only thing that can protect your idea from being stolen or made by someone else is a patent.

Building a unique product that has never been in the marketplace is like starting from the cellular level. It is going to take more care, extra steps, and more time to grow your little seed into a business. But it seems like in today's fast-paced information age, you don't have the luxury of time. Ideas are being produced at an exponential rate and you may see someone else execute your idea if you don't act on it quickly. Still, a brilliant idea could change the world for the better, which is why you should move by first securing your IP rights and then building a business.

In The Beginning

Since childhood, I have had tons of ideas for products and businesses. For many years, I just let my ideas go, thinking the obstacles to getting a patent would be overwhelming.

As a small child, when I couldn't sleep, I would watch John Wayne movies to calm down and feel safe. That little girl wanted to marry John Wayne. As an adult, I found the real-life version of Wayne: a cowboy, not a movie star. I wanted to get married and live in the middle of nowhere and raise cows and babies and be happy. But the babies didn't happen for us. One year, two years, seven years of heartbreaking losses went by. A fortune spent on medical treatments and we had nothing to show for it.

That struggle is what gave birth to my entrepreneurial spirit, it was born out of necessity and desperation. Not being able to become a mother nearly killed me. I had to find a way to create to survive.

I am happy to report that after seven years and a series of true miracles, we adopted a perfect baby boy. I cannot put into words how wonderful our lives have become. I would redo those seven years of hell a million times over for one moment with him!

I have learned to focus on and remind myself daily that everything we are going through or have gone through is preparing us for exactly what we have asked.

I had been building up my entrepreneurial muscles working side-by-side with my husband in our construction company. But now, when the baby was napping, I found myself considering all the opportunities to build businesses online. I started a clothing company with one of my best friends and then, like a lightning bolt, we had one of those brilliant ideas and knew we had to protect it.

Applying For A Patent

You have an idea, or a whole journal full of them, but they are not helping you build the life of your dreams and not changing the world because you are overwhelmed by the thought of activating them and protecting them. Most people never take their ideas anywhere because they don't know that they can file for and write their patents themselves.

In just a few steps you can write and file for USPTO Patent Protection. You don't need an attorney to gain provisional patent protection. You only need a little determination, some time, the ability to do an Internet search and a USPTO search, and a few hundred dollars for the filing fee and you can be Patent Pending in 24 hours!

Here are the basic steps:

1. **Search the Internet For Your Idea**

Make a list of any keywords and phrases related to your idea. Search each one on the Internet to see what, if anything, exists. I recommend using all large search engines and databases: Google, Amazon, Alibaba, etc.

Tip: Even if there is something similar, it doesn't mean your idea isn't patentable. However, if you don't find it on the internet that also doesn't mean it doesn't exist. You must dive deeper into your search.

2. **Conduct a United States Patent and Trademark Office Database Search (uspto.gov)**

This search is more technical and in-depth but there are tools on uspto.gov to help you with this. You must use engineering related keywords when searching here; use words that describe the use, the mechanics, the manufacturing processes, etc.

This search will tell you if anyone already holds a patent for your idea or has applied for one. Clearly, if someone already has the patent for the same idea you have, you are too late and must move on to another idea.

3. **Download A Provisional Patent Application and Examples**

After you have searched out any competing intellectual property in the USPTO database, download some examples of patent applications for products in the same classification as yours will be.

4. **Complete the Application**

Study the application examples you downloaded and use them as a template to write your own provisional patent.

Write each section and add labeled images and drawings.

5. **File**

File online or via regular mail (all instructions are on the uspto.gov website) be sure to include the filing fee and the downloadable cover sheet.

6. **You Are Patent Pending**

As soon as that envelope is postmarked or the application is submitted online with the fee, you are Patent Pending.

Patent Pending" gives you 12 months of full protection under the USPTO. 12 months is plenty of time to build a prototype, test your market, write your full Non-Provisional Patent Application (you can do this without an attorney too) And launch your product out to the world and generate a whole ton of cash.

Moving Forward

Sometimes, all it takes to open up a whole new world of possibilities is somebody else taking us by the hand and saying, "Hey, this is simple. Let me show you."

I cannot encourage you enough to act on your unique ideas, apply for a patent, implement the steps you learn in this book, and find the path your heart is urging you follow.

I am so excited to see how your ideas help to make the world a better place!

A Gift For You

For more detailed instructions, download my FREE Quick Start Guide at https://laurelbloomfield.com

About Laurel Bloomfield

Laurel Bloomfield is the founder of Dreamers Makers Doers Inc. and DMD Digital LLC.

She has successfully started, scaled, and sold several companies. She has built many products from idea to reality and is a patented inventor.

Her down to earth, simple and successful lifestyle makes her a relatable and engaging speaker, author, and coach whose mission is to help as many people as possible get ideas out of their heads and turned into profitable businesses.

CHAPTER TWENTY-FOUR

Understanding Google's Marketing Platform

By Petra Manos

Using online analytics involves looking at data to understand how people are using your website, which pages attract the most traffic, and which convert the most visitors to buyers. The most popular suite of tools for online analytics is Google's Analytics and Marketing Platform, which includes Google Analytics, Google Tag Manager, and Google Data Studio.

These free tools allow you to track the behavior of users of your website, measure the effectiveness of your marketing, and report data back to you, your marketers, managers, other stakeholders, or whomever you want to see the data.

In The Beginning

Before I became a Google data specialist, I worked with top-secret data automating cyber-graph security. I loved what I did but didn't like the hour-long commute and complete lock-down at our office. We had thick bars on all the windows. It wasn't clear whether they were to keep terrorists out or to keep data scientists in!

Others might have found another job, but I did what sensible people rarely do when faced similar circumstances, I decided to create a business that used data to solve marketing challenges.

I've implemented conversion tracking across large websites, simplified data so that it can be used in marketing and reporting platforms, and set up automatic reporting. My clients include e-Commerce businesses, hotels, information entrepreneurs, lead-generation businesses, and marketing agencies. They all want to simplify digital marketing management to make strategic decisions.

Why Use Google's Analytics And Marketing Platform

Data is the easiest and most precise way the evaluate the effectiveness of your online marketing efforts. And, Google has one of the best suites of tools for gathering and analyzing data.

To improve your site's conversion rates (and increase sales revenue), you can track users' behaviors by looking at:

- Which pages they view and spend the most time on and those they do not view or abandon quickly.

- Specific actions (or lack of action) they take on pages.
- Their purchases and how much revenue you made.

To measure the effectiveness of your site, look at:

- How many people took action and what actions they took.
- The Return on Investment (ROI).
- Where people come from.
- How many people come from your sales funnel(s), and if they need fine-tuning.
- How effective each Call to Action (CTA) is.

Reporting data can be as simple as reporting single numbers as Key Performance Indicators (KPIs) or including any of a myriad of charts and tables. Reports can be tailored to filter down to only the information you need and can automatically update based on any date range you select.

Google Analytics has been around since 2005, whereas Google Tag Manager and Google Data Studio are still fairly new. Using Google's Analytics and Marketing Platform effectively will have a significant impact on your ability to create winning strategies for online marketing and selling.

Tracking conversions and micro-conversions (basically what people do) across your website identifies ideas that are working and your best sales funnels. You can collect data as people progress from cold traffic to being interested to buyers and then you can double-down on what works and delete what doesn't. You can also feed those conversions into your marketing platforms to ask Google to optimize for other audience members who are likely to act similarly on your site.

Google Analytics

I started with Google Analytics because it was free and almost everyone had it on their websites. It is simple to add Google Analytics to WordPress, Shopify or any other website builder. Most of these have a space to add your Google Analytics ID already built into them.

Google Analytics data helps you understand how users find and use your website. Its main purpose is generating statistics about your website.[13] It allows you to track information like page-views, bounce rate, session duration, and referrals, etc.

It also allows you to segment engagement and revenue by more personal characteristics such as demographics, interests, devices, and other visitor details, which can help you learn about the types of people most likely to convert on your website and, therefore, you can double-down on finding more of these types of people while reducing your marketing spend on the wrong types of people, which can have a profound effect on advertising profitability.

Google Analytics is immensely helpful, but it cannot provide detailed information about sales, how people use features on your site, and other specifics until its data is fed through data collection apps such as Google Tag Manager.

---

[13] Fedorovicius, J. (August 22, 2018). *Google Tag Manager vs Google Analytics: What's the difference?* Retrieved from https://www.analyticsmania.com/post/google-tag-manager-vs-google-analytics/ on October 9, 2019.

Google Tag Manager

Google Tag Manager is free software that allows you to capture all of the actions people take on your website and track revenue. Tracking actions using Google Tag Manager allows you to tag users' behaviors on your website and to send this information to many of your social media platforms such as Google, Facebook, Instagram, email, and many more. It allows you to generate lists of warm users from your website to whom you can send personalized campaign messages and who have much higher click-through and conversion rates than cold prospects.

Tracking revenue accurately lets you optimize your digital marketing efforts towards higher revenue opportunities and, therefore, helps you make more money, faster.

Google Data Studio

Google Data Studio uses the data gathered by Google Analytics and Google Tag Manager to create reports and dashboards that provide the information to you and others you choose to see the information.

Powerful abilities to filter, modify, and create data using Google Analytics and Google Tag Manager let you simplify the information you have so that you can easily visualize it in a custom report or dashboard for ease of management and finding strategic opportunities.

Case Studies

Case One – Multiple Domains

A client managed 30 different websites and had separate Google Analytics and Google Ad accounts for each. Some websites linked to others. Each website had a separate payment processing website, so there were 60 domains in total. The data was impossible to read. The client needed to know how to spend their advertising budget.

I designed a single Google Tag Manager account that recorded which domain was associated with each transaction. The data was sent to a unique per-domain Google Data Studio view and simultaneously was available under a combined view that collected data from all the domains. So, the client could see the data for each website separately or all the data in aggregate, as they wished.

The client was now able to do what was previously impossible; they were able to see how changes to their advertising impacted their whole system. They could now make significant changes and know with confidence whether it had improved profitability overall.

Case Two

A client had an e-Commerce site and I added Google Analytics tracking to her site. The data indicated that women of all ages were visiting her website, which did not come as a surprise to her, but she also discovered that men aged 24-34 spent a much higher revenue per user than women even though men in other age demographics were highly disengaged and not profitable.

We split her marketing campaigns into men and women and only targeted the profitable age group for men. Her campaign budgets were adjusted to the actual revenue results these two groups brought in. The results were astounding: Competition was low for all men because her competition didn't bid on them, but she bid on the 24-34 age group, where the ROI was up to 20-times higher than the women.

Moving Forward

Five tips for how to use Google's Analytics and Marketing tools:

1. **Don't leave Google Analytics the way it installs on your site.**

By default, Google Analytics has no filtering, no demographics, no remarketing audiences, no goals, no e-Commerce tracking, and no Google Ads linking. Unless you turn all these things on, you are missing out on a wealth of valuable information. Filters and Goals are a bit tricky to set up but are crucial to your success; some others are a matter of simply selecting a checkbox.

2. **Track conversions and engagement with Google Tag Manager and pass them to Google Analytics as *Events*. Create goals in Google Analytics based on events.**

3. **Send your Events to Google Ads, Google Display, and YouTube based on your Google Analytics goals.**

Use Google Tag Manager to send the same Events to your Facebook Pixel (also used by Instagram). Sending the Events to other marketing platforms such as email is also possible, but you might want a data specialist to help do that.

4. **Turn on e-Commerce tracking to make sure that revenue is coming through.**

If you have a traditional e-Commerce store with integration built-in (e.g., Shopify or WooCommerce) this means clicking a few checkboxes. If you have a custom-built website or your shopping cart doesn't have e-Commerce built-in, e-Commerce tracking can still be implemented using Google Tag Manager manually.

5. **Once you determine the data you want to see, forget about playing with Google Analytics each time you check your data.**

Instead, pull in your data exactly the way you want to see it as a Google Data Studio report. You only need to design and format it once. You can then pull up your report or dashboard and pick your dates to see your data concisely and accurately.

I hope you have found this chapter helpful and are excited about using Google Analytics and Marketing Platform. Once you do, you will be amazed at what data can tell you!

A Gift For You

Want to know more? Get the free book I created just for readers of this book:

Visit thequantifiedweb.com/playbook for my free book called How To Unlock More Profit From Your Website Without Just Guessing.

I also have an extensive series of free videos and online courses available at https://thequantifiedweb.com/playbook .

About Petra Manos

Petra, also known as *The Google Data Nerd*, lives in Adelaide, Australia with her two children, partner, and cat. Her first website was created in 1994 at the age of 12.

Before starting The Quantified Web, Petra spent a decade writing software, particularly for the Defense sector.

CHAPTER TWENTY-FIVE

SEO: Search Engine Optimization

By Lisa Gaal

Search Engine Optimization (SEO) is the art and science of increasing the quality and quantity of website traffic for your business, products, or services as well as awareness to your brand, through organic search results.

Despite its name, SEO isn't just about constructing your website for search engines, but also determining what people are searching for, how they are searching, the words they are using, and what type of content they are consuming. Doing so will help you connect to your target audience.

In The Beginning

I've always been fascinated with technology and puzzles. That's why I find SEO so intriguing. I first discovered the magic of SEO in 2002. I was working for a small financial firm that needed a website. I worked with a website designer to build a beautiful and informative website aimed at potential clients.

When the website went live, we had a launch party, and there was much fanfare for this magnificent thing we'd built. We thought we'd have leads coming in droves. But, one week with no leads turned into months with no new leads. And, so began my journey with SEO.

Many people have this same misconception: If you build a website, you will automatically get customers and the search engines will find you. That's just simply not the case. You have to do things to attract search engines and draw people to your site.

Why SEO Is Important?

The majority of website traffic is driven by search engines. Paid advertising, social media, and other platforms can help generate traffic, but organic search results develop credibility and trust among organic prospects. Searchers look at the first two pages of results at the most. Landing on the first page is incredible and SEO leads to ranking higher on search engine result pages (SERPs), which is a way for your business to build credibility and respect.

When set up correctly, SEO continues to provide ongoing value and conversions over time. Developing a piece of content that ranks in SERPs for certain keywords can continue to provide traffic over time while paid advertising only delivers traffic for as long as it is being funded.

Improving Your SERP Rankings

Search engines and search algorithms are always changing, but still need help to identify relevant results to a searcher's queries. Optimizing your landing pages, websites and other online properties will help search engines accurately index and display your content in relevant search results. Here are some basic things you can do that can have a huge impact on your search rankings.

1. Optimize for People, Not Robots

Search engines are evolving all the time. Search engines do not publish or release what they are specifically looking for to rank pages. There is no magic when it comes to SEO. Things that work today may not work tomorrow and could even decrease your ranking. Thus, when optimizing your site, web properties, or producing content *always* optimize with the end-user in mind. Thoughtfully and carefully planning your content and properties based on how your target audience will use your content will send you in the right direction when it comes to ranking.

2. Tracking, Analytics & Goals

Set up analytics and tracking tools right from the beginning will help you understand and track user behavior and will provide a virtual plan of how to maintain your web properties using best SEO practices.

You will define what to measure. In terms of SEO, what metrics will determine your success? Keep the general flow of a sales funnel in mind when identifying your metrics. For example:

> *Awareness/need > keyword search query > your website ranking in search results > clicks from search > landing page > user behavior > sales lead or sale*

Your metrics should take measurements at any of the action points in the sales funnel process to help you identify what's working and what isn't. For example, you might not rank in search at all. Or you might rank, but not get the click because your page title and meta description are not enticing enough. Or, maybe you get the click but not the conversion because your landing page content isn't compelling enough. Only analytics can tell you these things.

I would recommend setting up Google Analytics, Google Search Console as well as the Bing Webmaster Toolbox. All of these are free tools that can help you to track and test your progress when it comes to SEO.

Google Analytics: https://analytics.google.com/analytics/
Google Search Console: https://search.google.com/search-console/welcome
Bing Webmaster Toolbox: https://www.bing.com/toolbox/webmaster/

3. Select Keywords Carefully And Thoughtfully

Identifying a customer-centric keyword list is the foundation of effective SEO and the list should be used throughout your pages. If you already have a website and have never done keyword research, do it now.

The first step is to determine the keyword SERPs in which you want to rank to attract the best traffic to your website.

A more-focused keyword targets a high-quality visitor and has a higher conversion rate, but also has a lower number of searches. For example, there are thousands of *real estate* searches each month but many fewer searches for *real estate marketing coach*. Ranking on the first SERP for the search term *real estate* will be very difficult. Ranking for *real estate marketing coach* may be easier but will also be searched less frequently than *real estate*. If you want larger numbers of high-quality traffic coming to your site each month, you'll have to optimize for a lot of focused keywords.

While you're planning and building out your keyword list for each landing page, keep in mind you don't want to rank for "real estate" if you're selling "real estate marketing coach" services. As you go through your keyword list, ask yourself, "What does the person want when they type this in?"

There are many free and paid tools available on the web for keyword research. Some of my favorite tools are aHrefs.com Keywords Explorer, Moz Keyword Explorer, and Wordstream.

4. Avoid Tricks To Rank Better

Don't try to take the easy way out. SEO takes patience and hard work. Don't try to speed things up by stuffing pages with keywords or buying links back to your content. Instead of trying to figure out how to manipulate search engines to get better ranking, just create landing pages and content that are useful to your potential customer and market them thoughtfully. Provide valuable content so people start talking about, sharing, and visiting your site. That is the best way to get the attention of search engines. Trying to trick your way to the top of SERPs will only result in search engines penalizing your landing pages and possibly get them removed from search results altogether.

5. Broken Links

"Check for broken links and correct HTML."

~ Google

One of the biggest errors that a website owner can make is failing to monitor broken parts of their site. Over time, most sites change, restructure, move, or disappear, if you link to one of these sites, the link of your site may become broken. It is your responsibility to be sure all links from your site are active and go to where they should. To fail to do so makes your site look bad. People remember things like that and it may affect their opinion of you, your business, and/or your offering.

You can use Google Search Console and Bing Webmaster Toolbox to monitor for broken links. Correct all the broken links and you might receive a small bump in rankings for some of your pages.

Moving Forward

Many things about SEO aren't mentioned here, like link building, social media, brand reputation, and more. These are all important aspects of SEO. This chapter provides a broad overview of SEO. Essentially, however, developing valuable content for your target audience is what search engines look for. Focusing on how your potential customer behaves and what their needs are while developing your landing pages will help to increase your ranking on SERPs.

A Gift For You

Get a FREE SEO Checklist and begin your journey to better search engine results!
Visit: http://bit.ly/SEO_AF

About Lisa Gaal

Lisa Gaal is an SEO/digital marketing professional and owner of Beauty & Brains, LLC. She's on a mission to educate others on the ins and outs of strategic digital marketing. Above all else, she has a deep-rooted passion for helping people and their businesses thrive by ensuring they generate substantial organic search engine presence and traffic to their websites.

With a career spanning two decades in the sales and online marketing space, she has achieved hundreds of number one rankings. She has consulted with small mom & pop businesses to large global news & media brands clients on SEO and web monetization.

Lisa was born in Baltimore, Maryland and grew up in the small town of Augusta, West Virginia. She currently lives in Florida with her husband and two rescue dogs.

CHAPTER TWENTY-SIX

Planning Your Strategic Marketing Schedule

By Laurie Shields

This is not the sexiest chapter in this book, but it is important and simple. So simple that the process often gets overlooked for the fun and excitement that other aspects of running a business bring.

But, once the fun and excitement wear off, you may be left uncertain in your path and have confusion in your messaging. To avoid languishing, let's set your business up for success with a Strategic Marketing Schedule (SMS).

Planning your SMS involves looking at your business, your core offers, your goals, and your timelines to develop a comprehensive marketing strategy that ties it all together.

I often see incredibly talented business owners with wonderful goals, but they are loaded with overshadowing ideas. They jump from one promotion to the next, move from offering a course to an unrelated webinar and back again. They have no cohesive strategy to tie everything together.

SMSs ensure that your messaging is clear and always ties back to what you are focused on (course, launch, product, etc.).

In The Beginning

I didn't originally set out to work with SMSs. It just sort of happened. I worked with entrepreneurs to help them create, launch, and fill small events. What I noticed, however, was that almost every single client I worked with did not have a clear and solid marketing strategy to successfully support these events. They needed a clear action plan to get their message to their audience.

I started working with my clients – looking at their business and their goals – to create a strategic marketing plan aimed at increasing their business in a variety of avenues that would lead to an event.

No matter where you are in your business it is not too late to ensure that your messaging and marketing are strategic and consistent. There are many benefits to creating an SMS.

Benefits Of A Strategic Marketing Schedule

- Building an SMS provides clarity.

Defining your goals and a plan to reach those goals helps you determine what you need to do each day and get it done.

- Developing an SMS will give you focus.

Do you have shiny object syndrome? Maybe you are a course junkie? I know, I've been there, too. Having a strategic plan will allow you to stay focused and moving forward.

- Having an SMS provides consistency.

Can you imagine knowing what you want to post on social media each day? Or, knowing what blog post you need to write? Planning your year of social media posts removes the guesswork and ensures you know where you've been, where you are, and where you're going so your audience finds it easy to follow you.

Six Steps To Create Your SMS

To get you going planning, we're are going to answer five Ws and one H.

1. **What?**

What do you want to accomplish? Do you want to host an event? Do you want to launch a course? Do you want to secure a certain number of new clients? What is it that you want to accomplish in the next year?

2. **Why?**

Why do you want to host this event, launch this course, or offer this product? My clients often want to host an event to get more one-on-one time with existing clients, to build influence and authority, or to beta test a course. If there is a goal you are trying to achieve with your business, ask yourself why?

3. **Who?**

Who do you want to serve? I'm sure you already have an ideal client or a target audience for your business, but I want you to dive a little deeper.

Who is the specific person in your audience that this specific event is going to serve? Have they already been working with you for a while and need to level up? Are they active in your Facebook community but haven't opted in to any of your offers? What are their pain points? What are their objections? Figure out exactly who you want to be serving with the specific event and tailor your messaging to them.

4. **When?**

By when do you want to secure a certain number of clients? By when you do you want to host a retreat? By when do you want to launch a course? Three months from now? Six months from now?

Once you know when, reverse engineer what needs to be done for your goal to happen on time. Create a schedule that outlines what needs to be done when to meet that date. Break it down into weeks and set specific goals for each week and month. Do you want to increase your email list by 500 to have a warm audience for your event? By when do you have to do that? How many subscribers do you need to have each week and each month to reach that goal? How many months do you want to spend building your email list or adding qualified leads to your Facebook group?

5. **Where?**

Where are you going to be focusing your marketing efforts? On which social media channels are you already active? Which channels does your audience use? Are you there? Look at the channels you are currently using to market your business and determine if you have an engaged and warm audience? Do they need more love? Do you need to spread your love elsewhere because that is where your audience is spending their time?

6. **How?**

How are you going to pull all of this together? What kind of messaging do you need to do, down what channels, and when? How many months before your event, product, service, or course launch do you need to start warming up your audience? What is the messaging for each month of the plan? What are the pain points that you will need to alleviate? Look at what you wrote down for When and then go back through your schedule and think about your messaging. Look at the Who you wrote about and determine what information they'll want to know and what objections they may have and tailor the messaging to those wants and concerns. Schedule the tailored messaging into the days, weeks, and months leading up to your launch date.

Moving Forward

I know SMS is not sexy but it's the solid foundation that leads to those sexy business dreams, faster.

I sat down with a client recently who was overwhelmed with ideas he wanted to implement to grow his business. When I asked him what he wanted to accomplish, he listed off about ten different events and courses he wanted to hold over the next year, but he had no strategy behind it.

We took a look at everything he wanted to accomplish, broke it down into months, created a calendar to ensure he knew what we were focusing on each month, and created messaging around each event. In the process, he went from feeling overwhelmed with ideas to feeling focused and in control because he had a clear and cohesive strategy to follow.

I hope this chapter helps you in the same way. By following the five Ws and one H, you can narrow your focus, prepare great messaging for your audience, create an SMS, and follow it through to successful launches for the year ahead.

A Gift For You

Please take advantage of my FREE offer for readers of this book.

Make sure you download my Free *Worksheet and Planning Calendar* to get started on creating your Strategic Marketing Schedule.

www.laurieshieldsmedia.com/freebie

About Laurie Shields

Laurie Shields is a Digital Marketing Strategist who specializes in helping entrepreneurs uplevel their business with strategic marketing and events. Laurie lives in the Pacific Northwest with her incredibly patient husband, two rambunctious little boys, one dog, six chickens, and two goats. When she is not building strategies and creating epic events, she enjoys rereading Harry Potter, perfecting the art of Pinterest fails, and providing the world with sarcastic commentary.

CHAPTER TWENTY-SEVEN

Masterminding

By Jenny Hansen Lane

Masterminding has been around for close to 100 years. It's actually older than that but was only defined in 1928 by Napoleon Hill in his self-help tome, *The Law of Success*. He studied what made millionaires different and laid out what he believed were the fundamental lessons of successful entrepreneurs and over-achievers. Sixteen principles of success were included, and the first chapter was titled "The Master Mind."

In *Think and Grow Rich*, Hill describes a Mastermind Alliance as,

> *... the coordination of knowledge and effort between two or more people who work towards a definite purpose in a spirit of harmony...no two minds ever come together without thereby creating a third, invisible intangible force, which may be likened to a third mind also known as The Master Mind.*[14]

The theory is entrepreneurs experience a great paradigm shift when they mastermind with other, like-minded, people. Andrew Carniege had a mastermind group and Henry Ford had one with Thomas Edison.

All three of these multi-millionaires believed that a mastermind group added focus to one's success. Tuning into the synergy of the group produces more positive energy than any other type of brainstorming. It's because it takes isolation out of the equation. By using the power of proximity and determination, mastermind meetings can be on fire!

In The Beginning

I've always been inspired and pumped when I walk away from my mastermind meetings. But my life was not always this rich and I'm sure some of you can relate. I can remember times in my personal and business life that I felt isolated and stuck. A lot of my friends and colleagues worked 9-to-5 jobs or primarily stayed at home to rear children full-time. I needed to find a community of people who were also excited about being entrepreneurs.

---

[14] n.a. (n.d.). *What is a Mastermind Group?* (Napoleon Hill, Think and Grow Rich). Retrieved from https://projectlifemastery.com/what-is-a-mastermind-group-napoleon-hill-think-and-grow-rich/ on September 8, 2019.

I attended traditional networking events and made few to any genuine connections and rarely experienced sparks of inspiration, but I was always looking for like-minded individuals who believed paradigm shifts would result in the life of their dreams. I didn't give up my search because I knew there had to be others looking to build massive momentum in their lives.

Paradigm Shift (noun):

an important change that happens when the usual way of thinking about or doing something is replaced by a new and different way.

And then it happened: Through the power of an algorithm, a like-minded entrepreneur targeted a Facebook Ad, which popped up on my newsfeed. It spoke to my reasons for needing a mastermind group. I had big goals, founded on standards that required me to be accountable.

I joined that mastermind group for added support and energy from the like-minded entrepreneurs there. Within eight months, I became the breadwinner for my household and I credit a lot of that success to the support and pure intelligence that blossomed in my mastermind group.

I experienced other small wins as well. When I decided to launch a podcast, I knew I could get it to rank in News and Noteworthy on Apple Podcasts because of those I had around me who had gone before me. They gave me tips and tricks to skip what doesn't work and created a clear path for me to follow. My first podcast hit number two in two days even though I did not have a large social media following.

Why Mastermind?

I need a mastermind group because surrounding myself with those who believe in the power of having a growth mindset is a game-changer. Sharing principles of paradigm shifts, marketing, and basic creativity that can give others massive results is what the world needs.

Paradigm Shifters Academy is a mastermind program that addresses the foundational life-changing principles of entrepreneurial success.

An important aspect of masterminding is to be the dumbest person in the room. Why? Because, as Jim Rohn says, *"You are the average of the five people you spend the most time with."*

Wouldn't you want the other four people to be at least a few chapters ahead of you financially and intellectually? Try to surround yourself with others who can bridge and shorten gaps in your journey. Sometimes simply asking someone you admire to join your mastermind group is all it takes. Other times, your goals may be very specific, and you may wish to create an agenda-driven mastermind group or find one to join. An ideal mastermind group would include people outside your field. We are already experts in our industries, so the different perspectives brought to a topic will create a more dynamic synergy.

Is Masterminding For You?

Here are some characteristics of good Masterminders. You are ready to join a mastermind group if:

- You're reading this book.
- You want to become the most confident version of yourself.
- You have big dreams and don't mind sharing them.

- You enjoy brainstorming, sharing ideas and resources, problem-solving, making deep connections with others.
- You are open to and embrace paradigm shifts brought about by listening to others' experiences and expertise.
- You are prepared to be vulnerable. Paradigm shifts require you to examine things you believe to be true and think about them differently.
- You are prepared to contribute your knowledge and experience to others in the group, including your business struggles.
- You are willing to learn from your peers and share with them as well.
- You believe in attracting abundance.

Benefits Of Masterminding

The benefits of masterminding are different for everyone, but may include:

- Life-long friendships
- Mentorships
- Referrals
- Cross-industry collaborations
- Business partnerships.
- Faster success.
- Finding your tribe or network
- Being supported by like-minded people.
- Setting limitless goals and dreams

Well-known entrepreneurs talk about their first experiences in a mastermind group and tell you how they leveraged the principles of masterminding to reap the benefits of creating *smartcuts* (not shortcuts) to growth and, ultimately, industry domination.

Every entrepreneur in a mastermind group will tell you it's the best money they have invested in themselves and their businesses. The opportunities to leverage their situation and find a community where they can grow to their highest level are limitless in a mastermind group.

Moving Forward

There are a few things you need to understand before joining a masterminding group:

- It's not a networking group.
- It's not a place where you bring referrals.
- It's not a place for negativity.
- You will have to enter some moments of vulnerability, which can be defined as emotional exposure, being honest with yourself and those around you.
- You must be prepared to make paradigm shifts.

If you want to get started today, look for like-minded people around you and others who yearn for growth. Those people will be great candidates for your mastermind group.

Masterminding is a life-changing experience; my success today is credited to the principles mentioned here.

A Gift For You

If you are tired of being stuck, and want the accountability of those who strive for excellence to become your best self in a growth mindset community, please apply to join our diverse group of game changers at Paradigm Shifters Academy.

https://www.jennyhansenlane.com/masterminds

About Jenny Hansen Lane

Jenny comes from a long line of entrepreneurs (thanks pioneers) and she's tested positive as a carrier for the radical entrepreneur superpower. As a mother to three young boys, she implements mindset growth in all that she does. She obsessed with sharing all that she knows as she paves the way and makes room for others. Her core values for living life are based on vulnerability. Which means she's comfortable opening up to other people on demand. Because she cares deeply, everyone she helps succeeds. She launched a podcast this year and it became #2 for Self-Help on New and Noteworthy. Because she puts abundance first, she empowers others to do so too. Her superpowers include active listening and vulnerability.

CHAPTER TWENTY-EIGHT

What Preschoolers Can Teach Us About Marketing

By Lynley Hipps

As a copywriter, I spend a lot of time thinking about audience. In fact, when I meet with a new or even potential client, we spend more time talking about their audience than their offer. Why? Because no matter how good your offer is, if you don't know what your audience needs and wants, they won't buy. End of story.

However, when I ask a new client about their target or ideal audience, I often get an answer like this: "My ideal customer is a woman, ages 35-45, married with children, has a college degree, and works outside the home."

Many of my clients can cite the demographics of their audience, a list of characteristics that you can get from Google Analytics, Facebook Insights, or other market analysis tools. Demographics usually include information like gender, location, age, device (desktop/mobile), age of children, education level, living status (homeowner/renter), etc.

But demographics only scratch the surface of who our audience really is. To authentically connect with them, we need to delve deeper into their psychographics - their interests, motivations, culture, and emotions.

It's the psychographics that help us best position our product or service so that we can best serve our customers.

This misunderstanding of their audience was really hindering my clients' success, so I began to formulate a framework that would help them peel back the psychographic layers of their audiences. I soon realized the core of these questions was actually quite foundational and simple (though not necessarily easy). We needed to focus on the basic, innate techniques of connection and authenticity, which came so easily to us as children but seem more complicated as adults.

In this chapter, we're going to hone in on the psychographics of our audience by focusing on three techniques that preschoolers have perfected - curiosity, empathy, and story.

Curiosity

Think for a moment about a young child in your life. Like every child, they probably went through a phase of asking never-ending questions – most often, "Why?"

- Why is the sky blue?
- Why do I have to take a bath?

- Why does it thunder when it rains?
- Why can't I eat peanut butter and jelly sandwiches for every meal?

And they don't stop with one *why* - they keep asking, usually to the point where the adults in the room don't actually know the answer, so we get flustered and finally use the old standbys, "Because that's just the way it is" or "Because I said so."

Curiosity is a natural impulse for these little beings who want so desperately to understand the world around them.

And yet, as we grow older, we lose that curiosity. We stop asking why. We just accept things as they are or we figure we can't change them, so why bother? But curiosity is one of the most powerful tools we have as marketers.

To tap into that curiosity, we're going to borrow a technique from both the manufacturing industry and the preschool set, appropriately named The 5 Whys Exercise.

The 5 Whys Exercise helps you get to the root cause of a problem by asking the question "why" over and over until you get to the crux of the problem – the real reason why your audience feels this way, struggles with this issue, or is resistant to this change.

Let's say the mom from our demographic profile above thinks her family eats too much fast food. We sell an information product that helps busy parents plan healthy, delicious meals that can be prepared quickly.

How do we catch her attention with our product? Let's get curious about her.

Why #1: Why does her family eat so much fast food?

Because their busy schedules don't leave her any time to cook healthy meals

Why #2: Why is eating so much fast food a problem?

Because most fast food is high in fat, calories, and sodium, and low in nutrition.

Why #3: Why is this a bad thing?

Because she wants her children to eat healthy foods.

Why #4: Why is eating healthy foods important?

Because she doesn't want her children to grow up with body image issues and struggle with their weight like she did.

Why #5: Why doesn't she want her kids to grow up with body image issues?

Because her own body image issues prevented her from trying out for the basketball team, pursuing her passion for acting, or backpacking around Europe after graduation; all events in her life that she looks back on with regret and disappointment.

Now we're onto something. Maybe her concern isn't only about nutrition. When we get to the root cause of that motivation, we understand that she sees healthy, nutritious meals as an important step towards making good choices and developing a positive body image so that her children don't struggle with weight and don't live with the regret she does.

In short, she wants to protect her children from experiencing the pain she felt at their age. Pretty powerful.

This is psychographic data. This is what we need to truly understand our audience's fears, dreams, needs, and pain. And if we can show her that we understand that concern that she holds deep down, we can really connect with her.

And to do that, we must demonstrate empathy.

Empathy

I recently had dinner with a friend and her little boy. He saw that I had a bandage on my ankle.

"Oh, no." he gasped. "You have a boo-boo! I so sowwy. Does it hurt?"

I assured him it didn't and that I was okay. Then he patted my leg and said, "Be more careful when you're pwaying, so you don't get hurt again!"

This child did what so many adults fail to – he noticed. He offered me empathy for my ankle injury. He'd had booboos before. He let me know that I wasn't alone, that he'd been there.

And that's what our audience is pining for – empathy. They want to know that we understand, that we get it, that we see them and the pain they're experiencing.

So, once we've gotten curious about our audience and asked our 5 Whys, our empathy for them will help us craft a marketing message and copy to help them be seen, heard, and understood.

Let's go back to our example of the mom with the fast-food-eating family. How can we show empathy in our copy to show her that we understand what she's experiencing?

We might catch her attention with a headline like,

- How to Have Healthy Kids On a Fast Food Schedule
- Dinner: Healthy or Fast? You Don't Have to Sacrifice!
- How to Skip the Drive-thru and Eat a Healthy Meal Fast!

Suddenly, that mom who resorted to the McDonald's drive-thru for dinner tonight has stopped scrolling. She sees our headline and thinks, "Yes! I do care about their health, but I'm not sure how to cook healthy meals with so little time!"

Do you think she's going to read your whole ad? Probably so. Will she click-through to your sales page? There's a good chance!

But what if we hadn't gotten curious about our audience's real motivations and fears?

What if we had stopped with the demographic information and assumed, "Oh, she must be worried that she's wasting too much money eating out, so let's focus on how she'll save money with our product."

Would that mother feel seen and heard? Would she feel like we really understood her? Would she have stopped scrolling to look at our ad? Probably not. And we might've just lost a sale.

The Power Of Story

Everyone loves a good story. Classic fairy tale, blockbuster animated movie, or tale invented on the fly, with a good story, you'll have the preschool set (and most adults!) rapt with attention. But why are stories so compelling?

Stories allow us to exercise the other two points mentioned in this chapter - curiosity and empathy. Curiosity comes naturally to us as babies, and it doesn't abate as we become adults. Let's face it, social media is the ultimate curiosity fix. Learning more about someone satisfies our need to peek behind the curtain, to see how they do things in their life, and why. When curiosity isn't satisfied, we even make up our own stories to fill the gap – to scratch that itch to know.

Few things are more powerful than community and connection; to know that we're not alone, that our struggles are validated by the fact that others have them, too. Stories break down walls, eliminate differences, and allow us to connect over a common experience.

- Moms of newborns bond over midnight feedings and constant worry.
- Runners training for marathons bond over training schedules and race fuel.
- The #MeToo movement empowered victims of sexual assault to tell their stories, sometimes after years of hiding that secret, and enabled many of them to begin the healing process.

Sharing stories – your own stories, stories of your customers, even other people's stories – empowers you to connect through the power of shared experience. And your stories empower your audience to feel validated, seen, and heard, the ultimate victory of empathy and curiosity.

Moving Forward

Curiosity, empathy, and stories are some of the most powerful tools we have, both as marketers and as humans. We must stay curious, and we must keep asking questions to understand and truly empathize with what our audience is experiencing.

Great copy doesn't just happen: It takes lots of research, trial and error, and iteration. But if you can reach your audience on that deeper level – get curious about their struggles and strengths, empathize with them, and then use stories to connect authentically – they will reward you with engagement, purchases, and loyalty.

A Gift For You

If you'd like to learn more about how to use these three techniques – curiosity, empathy, and story – to better connect with your audience, visit lynleyhipps.com/audience to download the free info-graphic, "The 15 Questions Your Audience NEEDS You to Ask."

About Lynley Hipps

Lynley Hipps is a copywriting expert, funnel builder, grammar nerd, and all-around lover of words. Her passion is helping her clients translate their world-changing offers into compelling, persuasive copy to which their audience immediately connects and responds. When she's not writing highly converting copy or building beautiful funnels, she can be found hanging with her husband, daughter, Holly the Wonder Corgi, and Oliver the Copy Cat, who occasionally shares his sage advice on Lynley's Instagram page at @lynleyhipps.

CHAPTER TWENTY-NINE

Lead Generation

By Robert Segelquist

If you're like many entrepreneurs and small business owners, you've built some sort of Internet real estate – a funnel, website, or landing page – and you're paying for traffic to get there, by either running ads yourself or paying someone else to do it for you. All this work to generate leads takes time and money.

Lead generation includes any interaction that a person has with your brand that results in a request for more information or purchase of your offering. Leads can come to you from online ads, a how-to or other videos, word-of-mouth, social media posts, podcast reviews, etc.

We are going to discuss three things every entrepreneur or marketer should do to cut down on the amount of time they actively pursue leads using *passive lead generation*.

In The Beginning

As many in the online space do, looking for a way out. I felt that this online thing had to be the way and I started consuming every piece of content I could lay my hands, eyes, or ears on.

Like so many of us in the beginning, I was relatively broke. Between different training videos and courses, and just looking at profiles on the web, I noticed that the successful folks tended to have as much of their web presence as possible written as an advertisement. I realized that they were using social media as a business tool and not as a time waster.

I began to keep track of the different trends that I was observing and jotted them down in a master list of things to do and keep track of. None of the following is anything that I can take credit for, I've just curated the practices of the pros and made one list out of it all.

Customer Experience

There are four common steps prospects (leads) must go through to become a customer – Awareness, Interest, Decision, and Action – regardless of the lead-generation model used.

Awareness

During the Awareness step, the prospect becomes aware of your company or offer. They show this awareness by clicking on an ad, commenting on a blog, opting into a mailing list, joining a private group, liking a post, sharing a blog, etc. There are many ways they may fall into the pool of leads for you to pursue.

As a result of their action, you must respond or connect with them to build rapport and trust. The sooner you make initial contact, the higher your chance of conversion will be.

The first few minutes of interaction are critical for conversion rates. If you collect their email or cell phone number upfront, you should contact them immediately by welcoming them to your company and expressing your pleasure at helping them. You want them to enter the next phase of the conversion, which involves further communication to increase their interest.

Interest

Automated follow-up systems are very helpful to generate interest once a lead has become aware of you. The fact that they gave you some personal contact information confirms that they want to hear more from you.

Build a drip campaign to stay in touch with your leads by email or short message service (SMS) over time to stay in the front of their eyes and mind and ahead of the thousands of ads they see every day. Provide information to help them learn more about your offering. Offer discounts or bonuses for immediate purchase. Help them decide to buy.

Decision

As you build rapport with your leads and authority by providing valuable information, the conversion will begin to occur. It begins with the decision to buy.

Action

Once a lead hits the buy button, they have converted from a lead to a customer. But your interaction is not done. Proper follow-up care is important. Send them a message to see if they are happy with their purchase, for example, and be prepared for returns and be clear on your return processes. Once they have had your product or used your service for some time, be sure to follow up with them to ensure they are still happy.

Lead Generation

Businesses have participated in lead generation forever. The first caveman to trade a shiny rock for a piece of meat had to find someone with whom he could make the trade. Today, the process is more sophisticated, but the underlying principle hasn't changed: How to convince someone your product or service is useful to them.

It takes five to seven interactions (touchpoints) to convert a lead into a prospect and then a customer. Thus, you must take advantage of every opportunity to interact with your leads and you must generate new leads constantly.

You can upsell and resell to customers you already have but it's nearly impossible for your business to keep growing if you don't have new customers willing to buy.

Passive Lead Generation

Most people actively pursue leads. Indeed, they may dedicate huge blocks of time toward creating offers and interacting with clients so much that they end up ignoring other aspects of their business or life that need their attention.

The goal should be for a business or marketer to create a method or methods of passive lead generation so their valuable time can be spent doing other things to improve their business and life rather than constantly be searching for leads.

Here are four suggestions to create passive lead generation for your business:

Calls To Action (CTAs)

Your website is probably a beautiful thing that you poured blood, sweat, and tears into, or paid several thousand dollars to create, but is it doing to generate leads?

If you don't have Calls to Action (CTAs) on every page of your site, you're missing out on opportunities to generate awareness and leads.

- Place a CTA in the heading of your entire site.
- Place one big and bold CTA above the fold and at the bottom of every two to three sections down the page.
- Place CTAs on all other pages several where appropriate, depending on the length of the content.

Social Media

Just like your website, your business social media accounts must have CTAs. Use posts to draw people to your website. Be sure your business accounts are linked to your personal accounts. Have accounts on any social media platform that is used by your audience and participate in them. Use your business photo on every profile, whether personal or not. Go to each profile and see if a visitor can answer these three questions:

- What business or market is it?
- What service or product can I purchase?
- How do I pay?

Become The Authority

Position yourself as the expert in your industry or market in places you frequent online. Write blogs, give away valuable information, do guest blogs, podcasts, and videos.

- Any time someone asks a question that is in your area(s) of expertise, answer it. Remember to be polite and provide enough information that they can solve the problem, as they may just be starting out and not have any idea what they are doing.
- Help some people for free – once – to become their go-to person when they pay. People remember someone who helps them without expecting anything in return and are more likely to trust

Customer Feedback

Foster leads through customer reviews and referrals. Encourage your customers to share your business with their friends. Provide an incentive if you wish.

- Share customer reviews and testimonials in social media posts, within ads, and/or funnels.
- Services like Upviral™ provide points for users who share your links on their social media platforms; you can apply the points they earn as a discount system or give them a freebie – PDF, course, etc. – for earning a specific number of points.
- Offer incentives to customers who share an offer link on one or more social media platforms.

The four things discussed here can all be implemented in an hour or two.

Moving Forward

More leads generate more business, period. The more lead generating activities you do, the more leads you will generate, and the more business you will do.

I've never had someone approach me in the real world or online and ask what they can pay me to do for them, but I've had countless opportunities because I made the first move to tell someone about a service or product I provide and how it can solve their problem. Many of these opportunities came through passive lead-generation methods like those I've discussed in this chapter.

A Gift For You

Get a checklist of what your social media profiles should and shouldn't include to drive passive lead generation at cowboycopywriter.com .

About Robert Segelquist

Eagle Scout | Bad Employee | Forward Thinker

My father set me up for failure by teaching me to be resourceful and independent. While that's made me a failure as an employee, it set me up for success as a business owner. I've gained a variety of job experiences across many fields and roles in life, allowing me to draw on the good and bad systems from different places and fine-tune them to make one smooth and efficient business plan.

I started my business as a cash flow system to get more experience running a business and so that I could build my credibility as a business consultant. I have a passion for systems, automation, and helping small business owners find the freedom they really want from having their own business.

CHAPTER THIRTY

Email Secrets

By Clint Whitney

On the surface, email seems straightforward. In reality, there are several steps to consider. This chapter will serve as an outline for any beginner to advanced marketers to narrow their focus.

I've taken what I've learned from some of the best marketers in the world and created a successful framework that has generated thousands of subscribers and made non-performing lists generate consistent sales. I have helped take businesses from $160,000 to $500,000 during four of their toughest months of the year.

You'll learn about the following:

- Why email is an asset.
- The mind of an email reader.
- Your attractive character.
- Secret questions of the best marketers.
- Writing headlines and email frequency.
- The Technical: A Mini-Guide.

In The Beginning

I used to be the guy that would run ads and not track anything and complain about the cost per click. Then, I became the guy that would run ads and track them but, like a knucklehead, still not collect any emails. This meant I was never able to follow up with interested people. In other words, I was losing sales!

Finally, I was enlightened by an email course I took from Ian Stanley. He shared his secret sauce that led him to have a freedom lifestyle by simply writing amazing emails. More importantly, he helped me understand what it takes to create effective emails within an ad campaign and just how many sales I was missing because I wasn't collecting email addresses.

This was really the moment that my eyes were opened when I realised that most people do not purchase right away. It didn't matter what the business was – restaurant, e-commerce store, agency, etc. – the money really was in the list.

Why Email Is An Asset

Expert marketers agree that email is still the most critical marketing method today. The money is in your email list. On average, you should make $ 1-a month per person on your list. Sometimes it's more, sometimes less, but it's an average. Therefore, 1,000 people on your list will bring in $1,000 per month.

To generate at least $1, most marketers offer high-ticket upsells after an initial opt-in. Don't be alarmed that only 20% of your list buys from you, while 80% usually sit on the sidelines. Getting traffic to your website is not about making a sale, it's about building your list. This becomes traffic you own; traffic you control. Remember, your website or Facebook page could go down tomorrow; your email list is always yours.

When you control your traffic, you control your income. When I realized this, it changed the entire focus and results of my business. It will always be more expensive to acquire a new customer and turn them into a buyer. However, it is easier to get a buyer to rebuy. Your email list is people who are already warm to you (they gave you their email, so they trust you to some degree) and many have bought from you; these people are easier to convert than new, cold prospects.

Finally, email can serve as a launch platform. Launching a new podcast, product, or service? A quick email to your list gives you immediate traffic that didn't cost you anything.

The Mind Of An Email Reader

Trust and authority are core to success, email builds both. Trust is built through the frequency of the emails. Authority is built by the value of the content you provide. Often people wonder, "What's in it for me?"

To avoid coming across as a needy entrepreneur, limit your free offers. A big discount that is unavailable to the public is generally well-perceived. Helpful tips and tricks are useful and sharing personal stories shows you trust them and makes them feel good. Remember, you are entering their personal space with email, so treat the opportunity with respect.

It is essential to describe a problem they are having and then provide the solution (your product or service). Help them imagine something they want, dream, or desire. Most people are looking for a reason to buy something. If done correctly, your customers will feel like you're reading their minds. Playing on fears can be highly successful, but practise extremely high integrity when working with fears.

With email, people are unknowingly looking for leadership mixed with entertainment. Think about the amount of content we consume. People are looking for leadership in solving their problems. They subscribed to your list because they found value in your initial offer. They are waiting for you to lead them there.

People will do anything for those who encourage their dreams, justify their failures, allay their fears, confirm their suspicions, and help them throw rocks at their enemies.[15]

People look for email they want to delete, not what we want to read. Be entertaining. Share a funny story and relate it to the problem, then share the solution. The story must align with your customers' desires. This builds a level of trust that turns them into a Super Fan; someone that loves you, buys your stuff, and defends you.

[15] Warren, B. (December 18, 2013). *The One Sentence Persuasion Course – 27 Words To Make The World Do Your Bidding.* Kindle Publishing. Retrieved from https://geremiecamara.wordpress.com/2017/01/01/one-sentence-persuasion-book-summary/ on October 25, 2019.

Your Attractive Character

Your attractive character is not a fake personality you create – it is you, only a better version of yourself. It's a person that people will look up to. A person that likely shares the same values, ethics, hobbies, or life struggles with which your r relates. customer Avatar relates. Be yourself and lead.

Secret Questions Of The Best Marketers

I've collected a common set of questions extremely successful marketers use to examine their Avatar. Discover your ideal customers' three biggest desires or goals by asking:

- Where do they want to go (what are their dreams)?
- What is keeping them awake at night?
- What angers, frustrates or makes them scared?
- What are the three biggest issues keeping them from reaching their three biggest desires?
- Do they have any limiting beliefs for themselves or their businesses?

Once you answer these questions, you are ready to write your first email to your list. There are many strategies; I will only describe the Soap Opera Sequence.

The Soap Opera Sequence

Love them or hate them, soap operas are amazing at hooking you in at the beginning and leaving you hanging at the end. This is how you should write your first five to seven emails. Start with the highest action point. End by relating the story to their troubles or dreams. For example, "Tomorrow I will reveal the exact secret that helped launch my first business and allowed me to be a stay at home dad." Share your epiphany (a-ha) moment, stay brief, and make sure to drive them to your offer in every email.

Email Frequency

I recommend that businesses email their list every day. I've found that you receive fewer complaints and have fewer people unsubscribe than when you email only once per month. It's a misconception that if you email less you are more effective.

The moment you stop emailing your list, they forget about you. Celebrate your un-subscribers! Yes. This means you are weeding buyers from non-buyers. You are building more super fans who share your views and become part of your tribe.

Writing Headlines

Your headline should create curiosity or say it like it is. Use no more than nine words in a headline. Use multiple approaches for each topic and track the open rates to learn how your readers react and where your sales come from. The headline should match your email message and drive them to your offer. Keep it simple and be honest so you build trust. Don't mislead them with a headline that has nothing to do with the email. That's spammy.

Here's a headline formula you could use with two examples:

"The ______est way to ________."

The simplest way to save money.

The easiest way to get a date.

The Technical – Mini-Guide

You need a website and a domain email to get started with email lists.

1. Use your URL for your email: businessname@gmail.com is not a professional email but Clint@elevateapreneur.com is.
2. Choose a domain with Googledomains.com
3. Get G-Suite service for your domain email; it will save you time.
4. Write at a third-grade level.
5. Invest in an autoresponder. GetResponse or Active Campaign are good options.

My biggest mistake was avoiding the autoresponder expense; I lost buyers by not being prepared. Now I have an over 60-day sequence allowing them to buy from me every single day.

Moving Forward

Remember, email lists and using them helps ensure controlled income, controlled traffic, and a successful business.

Email your list every day and use honest, simple headlines. Don't let the technical stuff stop you. Once set up, your automated systems will allow you to work fewer hours and generate passive income.

A Gift For You

For a step-by-step course on how to get your email system and strategies working to free up time while increasing your income go to www.elevateapreneur.com/book

Do it now before the Launch discount disappears!

About Clint Whitney

Clint Whitney is originally from South Dakota and has been a professional musician in the United States Air Force for almost 20 years. Additionally, Clint is celebrating almost 20 years of marriage to Sandra. They are blessed with two children. Touring over 30 countries and performing for millions of people, Clint took up marketing to help musicians become better online entrepreneurs.

He discovered online marketing was the secret way every business could get more customers. Having successfully proven concepts through helping other businesses and musicians succeed, he knew he could help the masses.

CHAPTER THIRTY-ONE

Escape Your 9-5 With One Simple Sales Funnel

By Blake Nubar

Not long ago, I was a salaried employee grinding away at a decent job, but I craved something more. More money to have more freedom to do what I wanted when I wanted. Thankfully, it was that job that led to the discovery that set me free: Online sales funnels.

Since then, I have gone on to generate over $11 million in sales, partnered with sharks from *Shark Tank*, worked with HGTV stars, and helped thousands achieve financial freedom using funnels.

I don't say that to posture and peacock. I say that because I want you to understand that anyone can do this. If you are willing to put in the work, dedicate the time, and scale some obstacles that may get in your way, you can have any type of business you want using these incredible sales machines.

In The Beginning

In 2016, I was working for a fitness company that created personal trainer education programs. We had just finished developing our flagship program and we couldn't wait to get it out for the world to see.

Excited, I handed the entire program over to the marketing department who was responsible for creating the strategy to generate website visitors (traffic) and make sales. No one at the company had ever heard of a sales funnel or knew what one was. The marketing department was still operating under the notion that websites will get people to take action.

They drove visitors to the site, but nothing happened. I couldn't sit and watch our amazing product die a miserable death. We put too much work into it to not give it a fair chance at succeeding in the marketplace.

One night as I was browsing Facebook, I was hit with an ad from this guy named, Russell Brunson, that said "Weird Marketing Experiment to Increase Traffic, Conversion, and Sales Online!"

The ad brought me to a funnel, of course. I thought it was a website; it took me to a 90-minute video in which Russell talked about all the ways you can sell your products and services using funnels.

The next day, I started doodling on a whiteboard at work. People asked me what I was doing. My response, "I know how we're going to sell our program. We're going to use a funnel."

After about ten minutes, I had my first version of a webinar funnel completely sketched out. But a big part was still missing. The sales message and offer were both absent.

I called up our partner, who was the face of the program we just created. I explained what we were doing, and he quickly recorded a webinar. The webinar we created was like a live webinar. It was pre-recorded but the date on it was in the future, so it would appear to be a live event when it was broadcast. This was an important concept to ensure high show-up rates. It had to seem live.

We had the sales message, we had the offer, and we had the funnel. We were ready to rock and roll.

When the ads were turned on, people not only clicked to the page, but they were opting in; it was at that moment I became committed to funnels forever.

On the broadcast day, people showed up! We had people sitting at their computers all over the world, watching as we gave our presentation. Then we presented the offer, and ... nothing happened ... five minutes, ten minutes, 20 minutes go by, and the webinar ends. Not a single person purchased.

I was devastated. I walked out of the building and sat down on the steps that led up to the front doors. Head in my hands, I was defeated. Then I had a thought.

I went straight to my computer and decided to try something. My finger hovered over the Refresh button, then I pressed it. A sale had come in. Someone paid us $797! This funnel stuff worked. I felt like I was on top of the world!

The next day, I walked into work and quit. I had no savings and no plan, but I knew I was onto something great. Funnels had the potential to provide the freedom I craved and, more importantly, I would wake up every day to do something I loved.

The Funnel Described

Some of you are reading this and have never launched a successful funnel. Some of you have. Regardless of where you're at with your business, one thing is for certain: Funnels are your fastest ticket to the life you want.

The world of funnels is complex and there is no one-size-fits-all solution. To decide which type of funnel to use depends on what you are trying to accomplish at each step in your business.

There are three main types of funnels:

- Front-End Funnels
- Core Funnels
- Back-End Funnels

Front-End Funnels (Acquisition Funnels)

Front-end funnels are used to create new customers.

After you have completely picked all the low hanging fruit in your market (collected customers from other areas in which you operate online) and it's so saturated you can no longer find leads, launching a front-end funnel to generate new leads makes sense.

Front-end funnels are designed to break-even, and possibly even turn a profit depending on your offer.

Funnel Strategies: Squeeze, Reverse Squeeze, Lead Magnet, Quiz, Bridge, Tripwire
Goal: Break-even/profit

Traffic Temp: Cold (creating customers)
Offer pricing: $1-$297

Core Funnels (Ascension Funnels)

Core funnels sell your core products/services. This is the most important type of funnel because it is the backbone of your entire value ladder.

In this funnel, you must prove that you can solve a core problem with a solution. These funnels are designed for warmer traffic (people with whom you have some type of relationship or affiliates/influencers who have a relationship with the people to whom you want to sell).

Funnel Strategies: Webinar, Product Launch, Tripwire, Sales/Video Sales Letter (VSL)

Goal: Prove your core solution and generate a profit

Traffic Temp: Warm (collecting customers)

Offer pricing: $297-$2,997

Back-End Funnels (Monetization Funnels)

Back-end funnels maximize profits for your business. They are used with hot traffic, people who know, like, and trust you. These are where the lion's share of your money will be made selling high-ticket products and services.

Funnel Strategies: Application (App)

Goal: Maximize Profits

Traffic Temp: Hot

Offer pricing: Over $2,997

Where to Start

Selecting the type of funnel you need depends on the type of audience you currently have and what you want.

I recommend you start with the core funnel. You need to prove this idea out by solving a problem for your core audience. Once you have your core funnel and infrastructure in place, move to your back-end funnel. Because you have hot customers from the core funnel, the next logical step is to offer higher value (sell them more stuff). This is where you are going to maximize profits.

When you can systematize at the back-end level, then you can think about moving to front-end funnels to keep fueling the fire and bring new, potential customers into your realm.

The best order to implement funnels is: Core –> Back –> Front

Moving Forward

Give funnels a try. They are rewarding and can generate results very quickly. Start with your mail list, if you have one, or run ads on social media to your ideal audience. I swear by them and, I suspect, you will, too.

A Gift For You

If you want to learn more about Internet marketing and how to launch a $1 million sales funnel, I invite you to my Facebook group where I'll walk you through what you need to be doing every day to find the online success you are looking for.

Freedom Fighters: Launch Your First $1M Sales Funnel

www.facebook.com/groups/blakenubar

About Blake Nubar

In just a few short years, Blake Nubar has generated over $10M in sales and helped thousands of entrepreneurs launch a successful funnel online.

Having worked with sharks from ABC's TV series "Shark Tank" along with HGTV stars, Blake is on a mission to help as many people as possible achieve financial freedom.

CHAPTER THIRTY-TWO

Challenge Funnels

By Austin Ford

There's this myth out there in the internet marketing world that says in order to build your list and to get people to buy from you, you have to give something away for FREE first.

This couldn't be further from the truth.

I know this flies in the face of what you've been taught. It even goes against everything marketing gurus have been preaching for years. But the cold fact is, FREE typically tends to attract FREELOADERS.

Think about your own list.

Do you...

- Spend gobs of money on Facebook or Instagram ads advertising FREE stuff?
- Do tons of Facebook Lives to attract prospects?
- Spend time shooting web or YouTube videos delivering amazing FREE content?
- Write blogs that constantly give away your expertise and advice?
- Drive prospects to your landing page where you give away a free lead magnet with MORE great content?

Look, I'm not saying this is a bad thing. In fact, it's fantastic. Up to a point. But all of this giving giving giving amounts to an inordinate and disproportionate amount of your time, money, energy, and resources. And the result? You've literally trained your prospects to EXPECT your expert advice for FREE. So when you actually ask for the sale, don't be surprised if they get pissed at you. Or go away.

Ask me how I know.

I used to give away the farm. Content. Videos. My time. My energy. My money. Free consulting sessions. And I couldn't understand why clients and prospects weren't flocking to me. Until I realized that there was no need for them to pay for my services because I was giving it to them for FREE. And my list became a bunch of tire kickers, folks I didn't want to serve. They were needy, didn't take responsibility for their lack of results, demanded constant attention, and sucked the life out of me because they expected *me* to solve all their problems. They were essentially people who don't pay attention.

A Better Way

What I discovered was that my audience wasn't the problem. I WAS THE PROBLEM. My head was stuck in FREE mode. And when stuff is always free, you DE-VALUE yourself. If I was going to attract PAYING customers, I needed to find a better way.

As a marketing agency owner, I noticed that a lot of entrepreneurs were killing it with Challenge Funnels. As I talked to some of these successful marketers, there was a common thread among them...

1. They LOVED their customers

2. They got RESULTS for their Challenge Funnel participants FAST

3. And they got PAID right from the start!

Challenge Funnels became the most profitable front-end funnel in their business. I had to know more.

I'm going to share with you how you can attract hot BUYERS to your business...no matter what your product or service...by using a Challenge Funnel. And this includes COLD traffic. But first, you might be asking...

What's A Challenge Funnel?

A Challenge Funnel is a process that takes your customer through a series of simple daily tasks over a period of time, anywhere from 7 to 30 days, so that they achieve a specific result. Once they complete the daily task, they move on to the next one. So that by the end of the Challenge, your customer experiences the big result you promised them. And the beauty is, people will PAY to take your Challenge! There's no need to butter them up with free lead magnets or a bunch of free 'discovery sessions.'

Here are some examples of successful Challenge Funnels:

"One Funnel Away Challenge" - 30 Days to Launching Your First (or Next) Funnel

"Traditional Cooking 28 Day Challenge"

"Video Gamechanger Challenge" - Get All Your Marketing Videos Done in 21 Days!

"The Dream 100 Challenge" - How To Find Your Ideal Customers

As you can see, these challenges cover a wide variety of niches. You can implement a Challenge Funnel for just about any niche or industry.

High Ticket Sales: The Beauty of Challenge Funnels

Because Challenge Funnels are SO dang effective in getting prospects and leads to take your low-priced offer ($37 - $297) on the FRONT END of your funnel... Challenges make it EASIER for you to sell higher ticket offers on the backend. And more of them. Here's why: You've already 'primed the pump' by showing your new customers you can get them the RESULT that they want. You've made it easy for them to achieve their goal by showing them HOW to get the results they desire. And you've kept them ON TRACK and ACCOUNTABLE so **they achieve their goal in RECORD TIME.** And by doing all this, **you've earned their trust** - the most valuable asset in keeping and growing your customer base.

You Instantly Establish Yourself as The Expert. They'll now follow you anywhere. And they'll buy more of what you have to offer, again and again. Your backend offers can include:

Memberships...Software...Training...Courses...Coaching...

Consulting...Live Events...Masterminds

There's no limit when it comes to adding value and transforming your customers' lives.

Why Are Challenge Funnels So Successful?

There are 3 big reasons Challenge Funnels work so well as a front-end offer.

Reason #1: Challenge Funnels Promise and Deliver RESULTS

Did you know that most entrepreneurs and business owners think AND believe that their customers buy from them because they offer an amazing product or service? Yes. That means a lot of their marketing and advertising is focused on selling the PRODUCT. But the reality is, customers could care less about your product or service. See, people don't buy STUFF. They buy the RESULT that your product or service promises to deliver. For example, people don't buy ASPIRIN. They buy the PAIN RELIEF that aspirin provides them. People take action based on just 2 Things in this world...

1. The Avoidance of Pain
2. The Pursuit of Pleasure

As humans, we are biologically hardwired to respond according to these two laws of nature. Think about ANY instance in your life – it can relate to your career, relationship, finances, health, purpose. No matter what, the basis for anything you do in life is predicated on pursuing pleasure or avoiding pain. And if you can solve one or both of these EMOTIONAL NEEDS for your customer, you've won them for life. So, when create your Challenge Funnel, and have an offer that your audience WANTS... You'll attract hordes of buyers because you'll give your customer a RESULT that either alleviates their pain, gives them pleasure, or both.

Reason #2: Challenge Funnels Deliver QUICK WINS

Everybody LOVES to win. People want to experience SUCCESS. And they want to experience it FAST. As you already know, there's nothing like the feeling of WINNING. **You've SUCCEEDED IN ACHIEVING YOUR DESIRED RESULT.** And that feels SOOO good! People WANT those Quick Wins. And Challenge Funnels give your audience quick wins every step along the way to their ULTIMATE GOAL... So that they feel and STAY excited, happy, and validated all the way to the end of the Challenge. It's like playing a computer game. Think Candy Crush or League of Legends. You get excited every time you hear a bell, score points, defeat an opponent, or make it to the next level. You constantly get REWARDED for your QUICK WINS...and it's addictive. That's why people keep playing. They can't get enough. The game FEEDS your biological and neurological need and craving for Quick Wins. That's why Video Gaming is a $43 Billion Dollar a year industry.

Challenge Funnels are based on these exact same scientific principles.

Reason #3: People LOVE a Challenge

Let's face it...people can't resist a good challenge. Especially when there's an enticing goal involved. People who truly WANT to get "from here to there" are willing to challenge themselves to get to their destination. Plus, Challenges are a FUN way to achieve your DESIRED RESULT. And this is key for 3 reasons:

- Your customers get to compete against themselves.
- Your customers get to prove that they CAN DO IT themselves.
- Your customers feel Proud that they achieved their goal

When they take a challenge, they WANT to SUCCEED. They WANT the pot of gold at the end of the rainbow. They WANT to silently pat themselves on the back and say, "I did it!" This is why TV shows like "Survivor" and "The Amazing Race" are two of the most popular reality shows ever. The contestants put themselves through hell for months to achieve a goal. Why? Because, as humans, we're WIRED for it. Each win along the way triggers the release of what's called "happy brain chemicals." They are Dopamine, Serotonin, Oxytocin, and Endorphins. Everyone has them. And every day, you do things in your life to trigger these mini 'highs' because that's the reward you get each time you achieve a goal or get a quick win. If you take a step back, look at it this way... The show *Survivor* is a "Survival Challenge Funnel." *The Amazing Race* is also a "Racing Challenge Funnel." You can see this pattern in ANY reality TV show where there's a goal involved.

- ✓ Do these steps, get this result.
- ✓ Do these steps, experience these quick wins.
- ✓ Do these steps, get the big prize.

And just like these wildly successful shows, your Challenge Funnel triggers the release of the same Happy Brain Chemicals in your audience. You help them feel GREAT about the Challenge, about themselves, with the quick wins they get along the way, and the results they achieve.

Challenge Funnels are unique in that they have these built-in, internal 'invisible drivers' that stirs a primal desire in your prospects... So that they want to experience every step of the Challenge. It's why they want to jump on board to take the challenge and buy from you. They can't wait to come along for the ride.

5 Keys to a Successful Challenge Funnel

Now that you know that Challenge Funnels are a great way to attract BUYERS right from the very start of your sales process, let's take a look at what makes for a GREAT Challenge and a great experience for your Challenger.

1. Know Your Audience

This is where it all starts. First, you have to ask yourself, "Who do I want to serve?" Once you know the answer, find out what their biggest PAIN point is. What keeps them up at night? What will scratch their itch?

2. Create the Perfect Offer

Now that you know their pain point, figure out how to solve their problem. Create an offer that helps them to eliminate their discomfort. What result can you promise them? Build your challenge around their core desire. Keep the Challenge affordable. Anywhere between $47 to $297. Some marketers offer their challenge for free to customers or members who've already purchased from them, and then charge non-members. Once you dial that in, now think about your BACKEND offer. What can you upsell them once they've completed the challenge? Make sure that it's in alignment with what you just delivered. If they just took your "Attract 10 New Leads In 7 Days" Challenge, a good upsell might be "How To Sell Those Leads Your High Ticket Offer" or a group coaching program that helps them scale their business.

3. Structure the Challenge For Wins

Figure out how many days you want your challenge to be. 7 days, 14 days, 30 days? There's no right or wrong. Just make sure that they experience the BIG RESULT you promised by the time the challenge ends. Keep your daily modules or tasks challenging. Don't make them too easy, and avoid making them too hard or impossible. The key is for your customers to experience WINS each day. This is the juice that keeps them excited for the next day's challenge. (Think happy brain chemicals).

4. Keep it Exciting and Be Supportive

Keep your energy and enthusiasm high. Not only are you the Expert, you're also their cheerleader. And keep your customers accountable. Help them to SEE their progress and share in the progress of others. This is easy to do with a private Facebook group.

When participants can see what others are doing and share in the successes and setbacks, you create a true community where your participants help and cheer on each other.

5. Your Message

Now it's time to get the word out and promote your challenge. This is where good copy and a marketing plan of action is vital to your success. First, come up with a compelling name for your challenge. Something that makes people go, "I want that!" Something that they can easily and readily identify with. Next, focus your efforts specifically on the places where your ideal customers hang out or congregate. Is it Facebook? Instagram? Forums? Joint Venture partners? What pond do your customers swim in? And if you already have a list, fantastic. Promote to your in-house list. Whatever you do, don't skimp on good copy and marketing.

A Gift For You

You can get started right now by taking advantage of my *Challenge Creation Bootcamp.* In as little as 14 days, you can be up and running and hear the cash register ringing with your very own customized Challenge Funnel.

The Bootcamp includes templates and an easy step-by-step strategy for building your Challenge Funnel without any experience whatsoever. No matter what your product or service.

Go to www.challengecreationbootcamp.com right now to secure your spot in the *Challenge Creation Bootcamp.*

About Austin Ford

Austin Ford is the world's leading expert on Online Challenges. He's the owner of the Funnel Build Marketing Agency and the creator of Challenge Creation Bootcamp.

He's analyzed and dissected the world's most profitable challenge funnels in a multitude of industries and infused all the winning patterns, structure, psychology, and persuasion into his proven system. Austin has built hundreds of funnels for a variety of multimillion-dollar companies and his training has helped hundreds of entrepreneurs and business owners massively boost their bottom line.

He loves his wife Jessica and owns a 200lb great dane named Andy.

If you would like to skip the learning process and want to work with Austin and his team personally, you can go to www.funnelbuild.com to book a Free Challenge Funnel Action Call.

CHAPTER THIRTY-THREE

Content Marketing – "Content is Not King"

By Becky Koyle

"Will you Marry Me?"

I imagine you've never been proposed to on a first meeting, but if you're anything like me, you have probably been bombarded by inexperienced marketers who dropped a call to action within moments of you accepting their friend request on Facebook or connection on LinkedIn. When this happens to me, I usually immediately block the person, which means their opportunity to reach out to me again is forever lost.

I realize it's a bit dramatic to compare customer acquisition to marriage. Obviously, it's far from the same, but the concept of building relationships of trust is the same. Whether you are talking about a romantic relationship, a friendship, or a business relationship, the likelihood of any transaction ever taking place without a level of trust established first is next to none.

If you are one of the marketers guilty of the unprofessional practice of spamming your links all over the place without providing value first, PLEASE. STOP. NOW. If you keep doing things this way, your business just might end up single and ready to mingle for eternity. Now, if living in mama's basement is working out for you, then don't change a thing! But if you are ready to stand out among the rest of the fish in the sea and get more admirers for your business who want to commit to you long term, then you might want to listen up. There is a better way.

There is ONE thing you can do to get people to "fall in love" with you and trust you so much that they will be lining up at your door and begging you to put that proverbial "ring" on their finger. They will also become committed and loyal to you and if you do it right, they will stick by your side for a long time to come. Without it, however, your business may never get a date, let alone a suitor that is willing to commit to a long term relationship with you.

Unless you've been living under a rock, (or been spending a little TOO much time in mom's basement!), then you've heard the term "Content is King."[16] Well, I'm going to have to disagree.

[16] Evans. H. (January 29, 2017). Content is King: Essay by Bill Gates. Retrieved from https://medium.com/@HeathEvans/content-is-king-essay-by-bill-gates-1996-df74552f80d9 on October 21, 2019.

Now before you go and report me to the internet marketing police as a fraud for spreading vicious lies, please hear me out. Of course, content is an important part of the game. But as far as being the king on the board that has the power to WIN the game, content alone is not enough.

If you are not creating and promoting your content in a way that gets your message in front of your target audience, then you are wasting all of your precious time making content that is never going to bring the desired results you want for your business. Therefore, the ultimate truth is that content is not king, but content MARKETING is king.

What is content marketing? It is a method that businesses use to build an audience for their message. The goal is to create and promote multiple forms of content to entice your ideal "match" of a potential customer to metaphorically "swipe right" because something you said or did in your content made them "attracted" enough to you to want to learn more. See what I did there? ;)

There are 3 main aspects to content marketing: planning, creation, and promotion. We'll talk about those in a bit. The goal of content marketing is to become visible everywhere that your target audience hangs out. The valuable content you deliver to your audience will get them to know, like and trust you. When they like what they hear from you, they will want to friend you, follow you, join your groups, subscribe to your list, and ultimately buy your offers, services and products.

1. Content Planning

In order to effectively attract your tribe, you need to make a plan to get the right content in front of the right audience. Not having a plan in place would be just about as effective as showing up to speed dating night with your mother. Seriously though, in order to have a successful content strategy, you need to make a plan, create a calendar, and post consistently every day. In making your content plan, be sure that you structure it in a way that you are providing 10 times as much value as you are making offers. A good content plan would be to post something valuable a few times a day on different platforms. 3-5 times a week, post something about your family or personal life so your audience has a peek into your life and who you are. After all that...THEN, you can extend an offer. By doing it this way, you'll become this magnetically attractive character that people are drawn to and before you know it, they'll be clicking and buying your offers right and left and you'll be known as the "ClickMagnet" you were always destined to be!

2. Content Creation

To have the most far-reaching effect, you will want to create several different forms of content that can be shared across multiple platforms. The most effective and easiest strategy is to take one piece of content and repurpose it into multiple forms of content. For example, create a video, and from that one video, you can repurpose it into a podcast, an article, a quote meme, a tweet, a pin, etc. Here are several examples of content you should be focused on creating. The "other" category is optional, and there are others I haven't listed here, but this is just to give you ideas:

1. Videos
2. Blogs / Articles / Stories
3. Case Studies
4. Webinars / Live Streaming videos
5. Pictures (Infographics, Memes, GIFs)
6. Chatbots

7. Other- Email campaigns, slideshares, podcasts, checklists, surveys, contests, social media posts, quizzes, interviews, product reviews, successes & failures, etc.

3. Content Promotion

Once you have some great content created, you will want to begin promoting it across various social media platforms. There are tons of different social media sites, but we're only going to focus on the top ones that you will want to use to share your content. Note that some platforms limit the number of characters you can use, so if you are repurposing content, be aware of those limits as you are creating your content.

1. Facebook & Facebook Messenger

2. YouTube

3. LinkedIn - Limited to 1300 characters

4. Instagram -Limited to 2200 characters

5. Twitter - Limited to 280 characters

6. Pinterest -Captions limited to 500 characters

7. Other - Reddit, Snapchat, Slideshare, Tumblr, Flickr, Medium, Soundcloud, Tik Tok, Outbrain, paid ads, and many more

Moving forward

Remember that your mentors, coaches and the people you look up to in marketing didn't start out where they are today. They were once in your same shoes, and only became experts and influencers by consuming and studying someone else's content and then teaching what they learned to others like you. No matter where you are in your journey, whether you're just starting out or whether you're well-established, there is someone ahead of you and someone behind you, learning.

If your goal is to level up, then your job is to learn as much as you can from the guy ahead of you, so that you can teach it to the guy behind you. That's all there is to it. That doesn't mean you go and copy everything they are doing and rip it off or duplicate it. But, the process will involve learning, applying, documenting your journey, and then showing and teaching others in your own way what you learned.

If you are wondering what to put in your content, consider this: Zig Ziglar once said, "You can have everything in life you want if you just help enough other people get what they want." In order to have the greatest impact, your content needs to be geared toward doing just that. Helping them get what they want. Think of what it's like to be in their shoes. You've been there. You know what it's like to be pitched to, and you know what it's like to receive true value. If people in your audience feel like you are selling them, even if it is subtle, they will be turned off.

However, if you are sincerely offering consistent value and people are able to apply your teachings and get results, they will not only rave about you to all their friends, but they will be happy to pay you for your services. Before you know it, you will be in the position to "pop the question" and ask for their hand in business.

A Gift For You

For a free brand strategy session , as well as a 12-month content planning calendar, book a call here: beckykoyle.com.

About Becky Koyle

Aside from her bowhunting skills, nunchuck skills and her affinity to Napoleon Dynamite, Becky Koyle is a piano playing, church-going, shower-singing, unapologetic foodie turned marketer. She has four kids, a husband, 2 dogs, 8 horses, and a boat. When she isn't practicing Rachmaninoff on the piano, concocting some new recipe in the kitchen, or catching some air on the wakeboard, she is probably creating content.

She has some mad skills in graphic design, web design, video editing, and especially writing. Whether it's webpage content, email copy, print content, or even your grandmother's eulogy, She is a wordsmith that can make you laugh, cry, sigh or more importantly...BUY. She has created content for some big players, including Joe Vitale, Ryan Stewman, Jeff J. Hunter, Nate Bailey and others. She has published hundreds of articles, and assisted many small businesses in web content, social media content, graphics, videos and more.

She has done SEO, SMM, SEM, PPC, and even help you with your CTA so you can get some good ROI and increase your LTV, even if you're in the CIA or FBI...now if that doesn't make you LOL or ROFL, then you need some lessons in marketing. She can help with that!

Fun Facts about Becky Koyle: ♦ She went to the same high school as Russell Brunson ♦ She was on Candid Camera once ♦ She was a competitive classical pianist ♦ She sang the national anthem at a Utah Jazz game ♦ She was a contestant on the Pillsbury Bakeoff ♦ She has juice fasted for 40 days and water fasted for 5 days ♦ She can walk on her hands ♦ She lived in England as a missionary for her church for 18 months ♦ She makes the world's best chocolate chip cookies ♦ She once delivered 2 baby goats by hand...literally!

CHAPTER THIRTY-FOUR

How To Acquire High-Ticket Clients

By Bryan Fuentes

Have you ever talked to a prospect that you thought was amazing but you couldn't enroll them at all or they wanted to wait? Maybe you heard something along these lines:

"I need to check with my wife or business partner first."

"I'm nowhere near being able to pay that amount."

"I have 60 days left with my current person, so we have to wait."

"I have a few other calls lined up. I will get back to you."

Not getting that sale is the worst feeling in the world.

Imagine if you could consistently pull in $20,000, $30,000, or even $50,000 a month by yourself using your expertise, with no overhead and no staff. How would that change your life?

Think about it. No more of being on the phone with someone and at the end of the conversation, you hear that dreaded phrase, "I don't have the money." No more struggling to get leads, mediocre months, headaches from unexpected bills, and no more financial struggles. Financial freedom can be yours.

This chapter will show you how to create pipelines of new leads and create systems that filter through those leads so you spend your time talking to the prospects who are actually ready and able, right now, to pay you the money you are truly worth.

The exact system described here has generated six-figure incomes for businesses working with dream clients and has resulted in a huge shift to many businesses, including mine.

Know Your Audience

The first thing you have to do is know your audience. In other words, know your Avatar or buyer persona. You have to zone in and target the people who need and want what you do. It's not possible to help the entire world. Your time and effort will be spread too thin, diminishing the value of your offering, and causing personal burnout quickly.

When you know your perfect audience, you can create an effective and strategic marketing plan that draws them in. You must understand your perfect clients' pain:

- What keeps them up at night?

- What are the top three things that frustrate them daily?
- What's the biggest problem the client has?

Once you understand their deepest needs and desires, it's your job to deliver the solution to their problems and provide the best service possible. And, don't be afraid to charge a premium price for your services.

Mindset

The value you place on your expertise is critical to the price you charge. This is your mindset. Your mindset is the foundation of your value. If your mindset is off-kilter, then everything will be. Your expectations – whether high or low – create self-fulfilling prophecies.

This means that what you *think* is going to happen *will end up happening* (for better or for worse). Thus, the power of positive thinking, mindset, and manifestation will transform your life for the better and it is key to success.

The Mindset Training section of my course goes more in-depth with this, however, here's one huge value nugget I want to share to help you with mindset: No one, and I mean *NO* one, is better than you at what you do. Not the Pope, the President, Bill Gates, no one can do what you can do. The only difference is they simply know something about mindset that you don't know: They believe they are great and that belief makes great things happen for them.

Your mindset is something you can change very easily.

The Client-On-Demand System

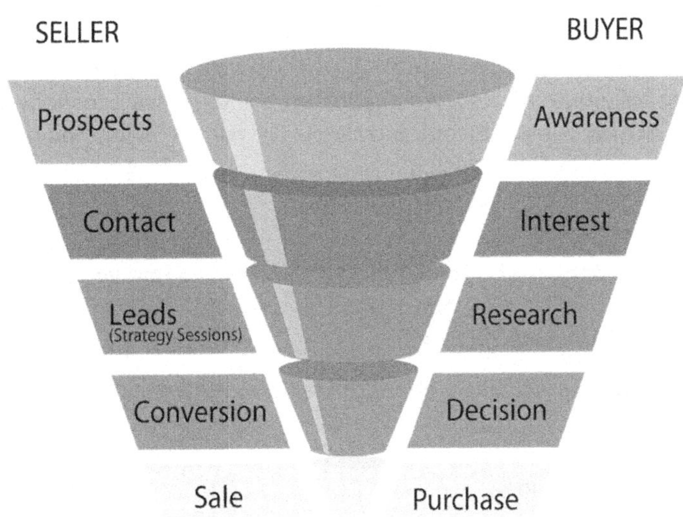

Imagine a funnel. At the top of the funnel are all the people who come into your marketing system. At this level, you must demonstrate that you're able to deliver value. You establish rapport, build trust, and show that you are the expert. It is here that the Client On Demand System starts filtering out those who don't have the money – or are not prepared – to pay for what you're offering.

The Client On Demand System cherry-picks the people who are perfect for you, puts you in contact with them, and will have you booking clients constantly. That is, it helps you move prospects further down the funnel. This is a game-changer. It's all about getting quality traffic coming to you day in and day out.

So how do you get quality traffic to come in? To set up your Client On Demand System, you have to use two techniques: the Bait and Hook System and Paid Traffic.

The Bait And Hook System

The Bait & Hook System attracts people to you. You provide massive value and then you hook them in. Instead of going out to contact clients, your clients come to you because you offer them something they want. Examples of "bait" to attract clients can be many things, including:

- Organic posts on Facebook and other social media platforms
- Webinars
- Free Training
- White papers & reports
- Video Training Series
- Free Trials
- Contests

So, instead of going through call after call and dealing with hang-ups, gatekeepers, and rude people, all you have to do is attract the right people (your Avatars) to you.

A good bait and hook system establishes your greatness; it builds the connection and rapport you want. Your prospects are getting huge value by learning something new and it makes them want to work with you.

This system gets you clients on demand and it's just as easy turning a light switch on and off. You can go on vacation or have time off and, when you're ready to go back to work, you turn the light switch back on and -- BOOM -- instant leads and clients are coming in left and right.

Paid Traffic

Paid traffic is composed of people who come to you through an ad that you pay for. You can run ads on any platform (including print, radio, and TV) but online paid traffic is already where you want them – online. Examples of paid ads include:

- Social media advertising (Facebook, Instagram, Twitter ads)
- Google Adwords
- Pay Per Click (PPC) ads
- Pay Per View (PPV) ads
- Banner ads
- Sponsored content

Facebook Ads is my personal favorite because it's dependable and scalable. Running paid traffic is like turning on the light switch. When it turns on, leads just flow in. and will soon turn into clients.

Most importantly, these are quality, qualified leads.

Clients on Demand System = Bait and Hook + Paid Traffic

Automated Systems

Your Bait and Hook and Paid Traffic Systems find the most qualified people; automation puts them on your calendar. Every morning you wake up to strategy session applications. These are the people who have raised their hand and say, "Yes, everything sounds good, I want to work with you."

You can be at the beach, a doctor's appointment, or on vacation – as long as you have your light switch on -- you will get strategy sessions booked.

Imagine this: You're having dinner with your spouse, you decide to check your emails and at the top of the page you see you have four new strategy sessions booked! This can be your everyday reality.

I have a client who's a Personal Transformation Coach. He has been in the industry for over 15 years and has a lot of knowledge and experience, yet struggled to find clients. He was only getting clients by referral or word-of-mouth.

I taught him this system and he landed a couple of strategy sessions and made $30,000 almost overnight. Now he is set to make over $300,000 a month. This is in stark comparison to before using my system when he was only making $10,000 a month. That is the power of having proper strategies and systems in place.

A Gift For You

If you're a Consultant, Coach, or Service Provider, then this is for you. My system teaches you how to double and triple your income and attract high-ticket clients so you can have the financial freedom you've been seeking.

If you want to learn more about my class, go to www.2dgmedia.com/training.

About Bryan Fuentes

Bryan Fuentes, founder of 2DG MEDIA, specializes in Hyper-Growth Marketing for struggling and established businesses seeking to maximize their revenue and grow to the next level.

From selling avocados as a kid door-to-door, to being almost homeless at 22 and working three jobs, to present day, Bryan has grown into managing marketing systems and media buying for multimillion-dollar businesses.

After seven years of trial and error, Bryan found a system to consistently pull in up to $50,000 a month in income and revenue from his expertise.

Bryan says, "If it wasn't for my family, I wouldn't be where I am today. Thank you for everything: Chep, Capitano, Paolita, Jinita and Don Teo."

CHAPTER THIRTY-FIVE

Influencer Marketing

By Latasha Mitchell

This chapter discusses how to position your business to attract influencers for lucrative joint ventures (JVs) that allow you to scale your business and reach.

Influencer marketing is a buzzword these days but it's far beyond connecting with some travel blogger for a shout out or paying a fashionista to post a story on Instagram wearing your latest creation. The reality is that Influencer Marketing has the highest return on investment (ROI) of any marketing system. It's a $10 billion industry that continues to grow exponentially, with 92% of survey respondents saying Influencer Marketing is highly effective.[17]

How do we find leading influencers who will give you and your business the time of day? Don't you need a massive following, an established presence, and a product ready to go?

No. Not at all. Influencer Marketing can be adopted by any business, whether you're just starting or have a two-comma income. I know because I started from zero and, in less than two months, was able to make more than most people do in a year.

In The Beginning

I learned how to leverage influencers out of sheer desperation. Recently separated, I was a single mom suffering from depression with $0.56 in my bank account and a repossessed car. When life hands you a big bag of rocks, you've got two options: Give up or dig in to find the diamonds.

I chose to dig in and go hard because my life, and my son's, depended on it. I knew that the fastest path to getting back on track was to connect with the right influencers. I went to work and within 50 days I made over $60,000. Needless to say, I was ecstatic, but I wanted to make sure it wasn't a fluke. I tested and tested, and my bank account kept growing. Then I taught a few clients how to do exactly what I'd done and they, too, had amazing success.

I've since created a system that works insanely well, no matter the niche or the market. Now, I want to teach you how to use it to tap into the incredible power of Influencer Marketing.

---

[17] n.a. (n.d.). *The State of Influencer Marketing 2019: Benchmark Report*. Retrieved from https://influencer-marketinghub.com/influencer-marketing-2019-benchmark-report/ on August 26, 2019.

Advantages Of Influencer Marketing

Why should you incorporate Influencer Marketing as part of your overall scaling strategy? Let me count the whys:

1. **Build instant credibility and exposure.**

When an influencer gives you their approval, your business becomes legitimate to everyone in that influencer's audience. That's the power of association!

2. **Promote your offer to thousands of eager buyers, even before you've created it.**

Verify that your offer will sell before you spend even a minute working on it. Influencers know what their audience needs and if you can offer the right solution, you'll be hearing that sweet notification sound cha-ching over and over again.

3. **Leverage specific social media sites and platforms to connect with the right influencers who will skyrocket your business (and we're not talking about Instagram).**

There are free websites full of valuable information that anyone can access to find the perfect JV partners, such as JVZoo, Clickbank, and Warrior Plus.

4. **Zero ad spend.**

Yes, you read that correctly: No money needed for ads of any kind. Imagine launching your offer successfully without giving Facebook or any other social media platform a single penny. What a difference that would make to your bottom line!

5. **Speed.**

Influencer Marketing is the superhero of the marketing world, catapulting you to new heights in record time. No other method scales as quickly.

Convinced now? I thought you would be. Let's dive into the wonderful world of Influencer Marketing and start putting its power to work for you!

Getting Started In Influence Marketing

First, position your social media profiles so anyone who visits them will know immediately what you do, who you are, and how you can help them.

Think of your profiles as billboards for you and your services or products. People are curious creatures and will likely check out your profile after you've provided some value in a post wanting to know, "Who is this genius and what other brilliant words of wisdom do they have?"

In all your profiles, include a professional headshot photo, a clear statement of what you do, who you help, and – most importantly – a clear Call to Action (CTA) such as *Join My FB Group* or *Click Here to Download the Only email Swipe File You'll Ever Need.* The CTA will build your email list while you demonstrate the mastery you've already shown.

Second, get visible! Attend as many events and networking opportunities as possible, being sure to document like mad on your social media. Can't make it in person? Take a shot of you doing a Zoom call with an influencer. Just get those photos of you with influencers out there so people see you with them. Your perceived influence will start to explode.

Third, provide real value to Facebook groups relevant to your niche. This is the most important and the key to getting quickly noticed as an expert.

Make long posts, filled with actionable tips, explanations, and clear instructions. Give away your best advice. Give advice for which people would normally pay top dollar. No one ever went broke by giving away great advice. Remember, you're positioning yourself as knowledgeable, the go-to guy or gal in your niche, brimming with incredible ideas and helpful tips. When people read your posts, you want them to think, "Wow, if they're giving this away for free, how sensationally life-changing is their paid stuff?"

Be generous and post often, especially in your chosen influencers' groups so they notice and take an interest in you. You want to influence each influencer so when it's time to connect with them, they already know, like, and trust you.

At this point, you need to step your image up a notch, so hire a professional videographer to shoot your origin story. You'll use this video on your website, sales page, and welcome page and will use edited clips for your Facebook profile and social media posts. You want to make a strong impression, showing you are professional and know what you're doing, so spend a bit of cash; it will pay handsome ROIs.

While you're at it, invest in professional photos and not just headshots. You'll use these for quote posts as well as all your marketing materials. Let your personality shine so you stand out from the crowd and make an impression that's not easily forgotten.

Fourth, employ cohesive branding across all your profiles and posts so potential clients and JV partners see you as a serious professional, not a hodgepodge of styles thrown together. Choose your color palette, your fonts, your voice and then keep them consistent with every piece of content you post. I recommend Canva.com; it's a great tool for branding (and free).

When you inject Influencer Marketing into every aspect of your business, you can scale quickly because you're leveraging the power of influencers over their audiences. No need to build up your own audience, create a ton of content that you hope gets noticed, or throw thousands of dollars on ads, praying that someone – anyone – says yes to your offer.

Moving Forward

When approaching an influencer, remember that they have an audience with a voracious appetite for fresh content. Their followers have challenges that keep them up at night. If presented with the right solution, those followers will gobble it up and they'll be looking for more.

If you post great value, are truly helpful, and are engaged in the community, the influencer will be grateful. Truly. Build that relationship and never feel intimidated because they have a name and a following. They need your help to keep their tribe entertained, engaged, and feeling good. Influencer Marketing works best when both parties value what the other brings to the table so it's a win/win/win for both of them and the audience.

Now's your time to shine. Can't wait to see you in the spotlight!

A Gift For You

Grab a copy of Latasha's ebook The Joint Venture Playbook here:

https://www.thejvplaybook.com

About Latasha Mitchell

Latasha Mitchell is an Influencer Marketing Strategist. She helps business owners, like you, harness the untapped power of influencers to scale their businesses faster and easier than they ever imagined, all without spending a dime on ads. Her Real25 system is revolutionizing influencer marketing, shifting the paradigm to a fresher, more effective method of making a quick impact. Working with many Two Comma Club winners and coaches, she is regarded as the authority in Influencer Marketing and is in high demand to show others how to grow their business without using conventional marketing strategies.

CHAPTER THIRTY-SIX

Business Growth and Marketing

By Tammy Donnell

"I'd love to be able to grow my business online!" I hear this daily from experts, entrepreneurs, business owners and e-commerce brands.

There has never been a greater opportunity than now to grow your business online. Forbes reports that e-Learning will hit $365 billion by the year 2025.[18] Selling your expertise is the wave of the future. You can join this massive online learning movement by leveraging your expertise and selling it. You can launch an e-commerce website or a funnel and 100X your product sales. Or you can grow your local or service based business with a fresh new Website, SEO, and professionally managed Social Media.

There are millions of people looking for a way to shortcut increasing their business income. Traditional society tells us to attend college, get a degree, and get a job. The problem is that we learn outdated information and spend thousands of dollars to get a degree to earn $50,000 per year (on average).

Today, people with experience and knowledge can start making more than ever before online with or without a college degree. The key is to get started; go ahead and launch your online business idea. Start selling the products you know people will purchase. Increase your sales by growing your business online for your local business or service business.

In The Beginning

Many years ago, I filed for divorce and found myself as a single mom. I knew I wanted to provide for my daughter and me and help other business owners. I have been a serial entrepreneur my entire life. I've started, grown and sold retail, e-comm and manufacturing businesses. I knew that in my next business, I wanted to serve other businesses. I knew how difficult it was to find reliable website developers. I knew that SEO and Social Media were things that business owners didn't want to have to spend hours managing. I learned by being a business owner just how difficult it is to do what you do best in your business and also be effective in online marketing. Now I help business owners grow their business online.

One of the most life-changing marketing events I've attended was Funnel Hacking Live, an annual event hosted by ClickFunnels. There I learned the most successful marketing techniques, the most

---

[18] McCue, TJ. (July 31, 2018). *E-Learning Climbing To 325 Billion By 2025 UF Canvas Absorb Schoology Moodle*. Retrieved from https://www.forbes.com/sites/tjmccue/2018/07/31/e-learning-climbing-to-325-billion-by-2025-uf-canvas-absorb-schoology-moodle/#5a8bbed13b39 on October 25, 2019.

up to date marketing strategies, cutting edge technology and all the systems to grow successful businesses online. The first year I attended, I added to my marketing knowledge; the second year I attended I spoke on stage in front of 5000 incredible entrepreneurs and business owners.

Now, I help businesses grow their business online with the most up to date technology and strategies in Websites, SEO, Social Media and Consulting. I've been in your shoes as a business owner and I get it.

Let Me Ask You a Few Questions

Are You Ready To Grow Your Business?

Are you spending all the hours you possibly can, working on your business yet not increasing your income?

How many years have you been stuck at the same level of income?

Does your income depend solely on how many hours you work? And there is no time left for Marketing?

Do you expect to double your income in the next year doing exactly what you're doing now?

Are you an expert?

Do you have an online business?

Do you have a local business?

Are you in a service industry?

Do you have a skill or knowledge that others wish they had?

Have you created a course that you can sell online?

Have you been successful in a business area for which others would gladly pay you?

Do you know the ins and outs of what you do so well that you could easily teach it to others?

Do you have a story to tell that will change lives?

Can you solve a problem for people?

Have you been through significant pain that you can help others get through?

If you answered yes to any one of the questions above, you are ready to launch and grow your online business helping countless other people learn what you know.

Here are just a few stats to help you understand just how valuable your skills, expertise, and knowledge are: Forbes reported in July 2018 that e-learning is the future of all education. "Market research firm Global Industry Analysts projected e-Learning would reach $107 Billion in 2015 and it did." As already mentioned, that is expected to more than triple by 2025.[19]

Five Steps To Launching And Growing a New Online Business

---

[19] McCue, TJ. (July 31, 2018). *E-Learning Climbing To $325 Billion By 2025 UF Canvas Absorb Schoology Moodle*. Retrieved on May 29, 2020 from https://www.forbes.com/sites/tjmccue/2018/07/31/e-learning-climbing-to-325-billion-by-2025-uf-canvas-absorb-schoology-moodle/#253e8bda3b39.

You have the business and I can help you grow your business. I help you determine if you need a Website or Funnel, or maybe an E-Commerce Shop, which Social Media accounts you need, your Marketing Strategy, SEO and can help you with business growth Consulting.

1. Need an idea for an Online Business?

There are many things you can do to start a new business online. The following is just one way you could launch a new business online. You could create a digital asset. The digital asset could be a course, a coaching program, a monthly membership, weekend Mastermind(s), a video course, a webinar, or a combination of these.

Courses should be five to ten modules long in which you share your expertise in a step-by-step system guiding your client from start to finish to help them create the same income you've created.

A coaching program may consist of weekly group calls that you host on an online meeting platform and share your expertise, answer questions, and give advice.

A monthly membership may be a private Facebook group for which you do weekly Facebook Lives, sharing and teaching.

A weekend Mastermind may be a weekend away at a select location with a small group of 12 to 24 people. You would spend the weekend teaching what you know; this concentrated format allows your clients to significantly shorten their learning time.

2. Discover Your Superpower.

What do you have to offer others that they would gladly pay you for? That is your superpower (or superpowers). You have spent years gaining skills and knowledge and now you can sell your expertise.

Think about the following:

What three things make you and your business stand out from your competition?

What specific skills have you developed to make you successful at what you do?

What are two or three success stories that were turning points in your life that relate to your superpowers?

Get very specific and detailed about your superpower(s). Clarify why someone would pay you money to teach them what you know.

Experience is valuable; it's gained only through our own experience and it has massive value. How many years did it take you to acquire the experience you have? How much time, money, and energy have you invested to gain this experience? People will pay to have you share your knowledge and experiences with them.

3. Identify Your Ideal Client.

Great marketing attracts the clients you do want and ignores the clients you don't want. To do that, you must know who your client is. Understand that you can't serve everyone. The more specific you become about who your ideal client is and is not, the more you will succeed.

The most common way to understand your client is to describe them. Some call this creating an Avatar:

Identify your ideal client's biggest pain points or problems. Narrow this down to the top three.

Identify their biggest desires. What would they gladly pay to accomplish a certain level of success?

What is their gender?

How old are they?

Where do they live and where do they buy online?

What are their values and beliefs?

What are their personal and professional goals?

Which relationships are the most important to them?

Be specific and take your time. As you work, you will start to see your Avatar in your mind and will start understanding the types of knowledge sharing and marketing you need to pursue.

4. **Create Your Offer.**

Take your time on this step. Your offer is critical.

Always remember that your perfect client has a problem or pain. Your focus has to be solving that problem or pain. People are very willing to invest a lot of money to solve their problems or pains. So, identify your potential customers' needs and fill those needs.

For your clients to trade their money for your solution, they have to feel like they are getting more than they are paying for. That is, the perceived value of your offering must be evident. People gravitate to what they perceive as something worth more than it costs.

Don't hold back on what you share. Give more than you think you should. The idea is to stack the value so high that your offer is completely irresistible.

Do your research: Look for competitors offering the same knowledge. Look at their offers and give more than your competitors.

Create urgency in your offer. Give potential clients a firm deadline and consider adding a bonus for those who sign up early. Stick to the deadline, and once it passes, your offer is closed until the next launch.

Consider starting with a beta launch. Initially, present your offer at a reduced price to a handful of people; mention that the beta launch will be the lowest price that will ever be offered. Launch with the plan of figuring out what works and what doesn't work. After – or even during – the beta launch, ask for videos and/or written reviews from your beta group. Tweak your offer to add more of what worked and remove whatever didn't work well.

Offer a 30-day money-back guarantee, or some type of guarantee, if a client is not completely satisfied. You always want happy clients. Some clients simply are not a fit and it's most beneficial for you and them to end the relationship if it's not working. Just try to have them go happy rather than regretting their investment.

5. **Build a Community.**

Finding your people online and sharing valuable knowledge with them is imperative. Trust is nurtured when we show up daily and give them what they want and need. Speak to your ideal client, talk about their pain points, problems, solutions, and ideas.

Create very specific content that you know your audience wants to see. Share information that will only attract them. You don't need massive numbers of clients; you just need the perfect clients. Your perfect clients will find you when you share your message. Once you build trust with your followers, they will gladly pay you to share your expertise with them. We connect with and purchase from those we trust.

Once you have the previous five steps ready to launch, I'd love to help you grow your online business.

Maybe you already have an existing business and need help growing and marketing to increase ROI.

Maybe you have a local business or a service based business and need a new marketing strategy.

Whatever you need to grow and increase sales, I can help!

Here's what I offer to help you grow your business:

- Website Design & Development
- Funnels
- E-Commerce
- SEO
- Social Media
- Consulting

I'm fully aware that Business owners have to wear many hats. I can help you by doing what I do best, so you have more time to do what you do best. Marketing and growing your business online is my superpower. Don't make the mistake of spending hours and hours creating your business, then shortcut your business online.

Your website is the face of your business online. You're competing for many eyeballs online and your competitors are growing and marketing. Don't allow your competitors to steal your customers with their stellar online presence. Make sure your website represents your business and your brand.

SEO is how your business gets found online with search engines. How you rank in searches is highly imperative to increase business growth. Ranking highest in search engine results is the difference in whether or not your business grows.

Social Media is where your business connects with your target audience. Social Media is almost a national pastime; it's where your target audience spends most of their free time. Managing Social Media is a full time job and requires entirely too much time for most successful business owners to be effective. Yet, Social Media is massively important to keep your brand and your business in front of your customers/clients.

Consulting is like coaching to win. I've been a business owner most of my life and understand what works and what doesn't. Sometimes a new perspective and a new approach can make a significant difference. We all get stuck sometimes in doing the same thing over and over, whether it's working or not. When you're serious about growing and increasing revenue, I can help because I've been there.

A Gift For You

Let Tammy help you grow your business online! Who better to help you grow and market your business than a successful business owner?

Reach out to Tammy on her website: GrowthManagmentAgency.com

About Tammy Donnell

Tammy Donell is an online Business Growth & Marketing expert. She helps entrepreneurs and business owners grow their business online.

She started her first business at age 15, paid cash for the sports car of her dreams at age 17, ran a successful business while attending college, graduated, and never worked one day in the field of her degree. She started another business at age 22, grew it to six-figures in a year, and sold it in the high six-figures. Tammy has repeated this process multiple times with businesses in many different niches and every business has been successful.

CHAPTER THIRY-SEVEN

Messenger Bots

By Larissa Banting

Messenger bots are the Facebook Messenger version of a chatbot, which are small pieces of software that use Artificial Intelligence (AI) to talk to you rather than you having to use a menu.

They're programmed to understand questions, provide answers, and execute tasks,[20] not unlike Alexa or Google Home. They are user-friendly and save time. Using Messenger bots should be an integral part of your marketing for lead generation, customer service, and sales.

What's all the buzz about Messenger bots? Aren't they just some fly-by-night app that will soon go the way of MySpace and Viber? They must be complicated, and you just don't have the bandwidth to learn yet another type of technology or the cash to throw at some bot developer.

Well, Messenger is huge. More people download Messenger than Instagram, Snapchat, and Twitter combined. Over 1.3 billion people use it per month with over 8 billion messages sent daily.[21] So you better think about using it and Messenger Bots

This is where it gets really interesting: Studies show that there are over six million advertisers on Facebook, yet only 300,000 active bots in Messenger. That means you can be an early adopter and beat your competition. Imagine if you'd jumped into Instagram or Facebook in their early days, where would your business be now?

More Messenger Bot and Chatbot Statistics

- Chatbots are expected to cut business costs by $8 billion by 2022.[22]
- Up to 90% open rates are normal with bots versus up to 30% for email.[23]

---

[20] Cooper, P. (May 9, 2019). *What Are Facebook Messenger Bots (a.k.a Facebook Chatbots)*. Retrieved on November 4, 2019 from https://blog.hootsuite.com/facebook-messenger-bots-guide/.

[21] Threlfall, D. (2019). 27 Facebook Messenger Statistics That Will Make You Think Twice About Marketing. Retrieved on November 4, 2019 from https://mobilemonkey.com/blog/facebook-messenger-statistics-facebook-messenger-marketing.

[22] n.a. (July 24, 2017). *Chatbot Conversations To Deliver $8 Billion In Cost Savings By 2022*. Retrieved on May 29, 2020 from Chatbots are expected to cut business costs by $8 billion by 2020 (Juniper Research).

[23] Stelzner, M. (March 23, 2018). *How To Get Started With Messenger Bots*. Retrieved on May 29, 2020 from https://www.socialmediaexaminer.com/how-to-get-started-with-messenger-bots-dana-tran/

- A combination of conversational marketing and chatbots can result in 182% more qualified leads.[24]
- Website visitors who chat to a business first are 82% more likely to convert to customers.[25]

In The Beginning

A couple of years ago, I started to hear about Messenger bots. My initial reaction was, "Ugh! More technical stuff I need to learn and won't understand!"

I resisted and largely ignored what little bits of bot information was knocking on my already over-loaded brain. That changed, however, when someone I respected presented a webinar to sell her bot course. And sold me she did.

Before I knew it, I had a bot up and running, without any drama or throwing computers out the window. It felt too easy. Rather than question it, I ran with it. Bots are now my jam and I'm on a mission to spread the word about how easy building bots is.

Why Do You Need A Messenger Bot?

Let me count the *whys*:

1. **You can easily program your bot to act as a customer service representative who never takes a coffee break, a day off, or a vacation.**

Statics show that a bot can save you upwards of 30% in customer service time and cost because your staff doesn't have to answer the same questions over and over again, thanks to automated responses. Customers don't have to wait for an email, a live chat, or a phone call and they get the info they need in mere seconds. A win/win for all!

2. **Get those seven to ten touchpoints a customer needs to say, "Yes!" faster.**

Consider social media for a moment. Perhaps 2% of your audience will see a Facebook post; maybe 22% of recipients will open that email you sent out. How can these new subscribers get to know, like, and trust you if they don't see your content?

A Messenger Bot has a 90% open rate. A drip sequence combining emails with social media posts will warm your audience in mere days, priming them to say, "Here, take my money!"

3. **Tag your subscribers to create a personalized experience.**

Gone are the days of one-size-fits-all marketing. The more you can narrow down your list and offer them information specific to their needs, the more success you'll enjoy. Bots give you the ability to instantly tag and segment according to various actions your subscribers take. Use more tags, make more money.

4. **Sell with your bot.**

You can use your bot for e-Commerce, so your customer never has to leave the application. This lowers the drop-off rates below the typical ad-to-webpage pipeline. Cart abandonment is handled

---

[24] Wood, R. (n.a.). *Supercharge Your Clients' Growth With Chatbots*. Retrieved on May 29, 2020 from https://offers.hubspot.com/thank-you/supercharge-your-clients-growth-with-chatbots?submissionGuid=5d4bf6a0-453c-4c73-a5f6-53fddeaf83b7.

[25] Yin, S. (n.a.). *How Live Chat Increases Conversion Rates*. Retrieved on May 29, 2020 from https://www.intercom.com/blog/why-live-chat/.

by bots that send a reminder message about those snazzy pair of sneakers they didn't finish purchasing. Your bot can even offer upsells, suggesting funky socks to pair with those sneakers.

5. **Book appointments with one touch.**

Connect a Messenger Bot to your booking system for a seamless experience. The makeup chain Sephora created a simple Messenger Bot to book free in-store makeovers that eliminated five steps from their old booking system. The result was an 11% increase in bookings. Considering the average makeover customer walks out with $50 in makeup, that's a beautiful boost to their bottom line.

Five Things You Need To Do For A Top Performing Messenger Bot

1. **Use the Menu.**

Set the menu up as a directory – complete with subcategories – to drive sales, offer instant customer service, and increase your social media followers. Include your phone number (one touch and they're instantly ringing you), links to your website, links to all your social media accounts, and a link to Google Maps for driving directions. Don't forget your online catalogue for seamless sales.

2. **Program Keywords.**

Make a list of all your frequently asked questions related to one another, such as: What are your store hours? When do you open? When do you close?

From these questions, create a list of appropriate keywords, in this case, including *time, hours, open, close, etc.* In your Messenger Bot, use the function *Message contains* in the Rule field to list the keywords and add an appropriate answer like, *We are open from 9 AM to 5 PM, Monday to Friday.*

You've just eliminated the need to individually answer all of those repetitive questions.

Bonus Tip: Include the Live Chat growth tool on your website or blog. Genius!

3. **Off-line use.**

Create a URL growth tool in the Messenger Bot with a welcome sequence that drips information over a few days. Connect to a QR code and print the code onto menus, receipts, signs, and business cards.

When customers scan the QR code with their phones, they automatically become a bot subscriber.

Bonus Tip: Create a giveaway with a QR code at your next conference booth with a PDF of your brochure, price list, catalogue, etc., as part of the subscriber welcome sequence. No need for printed materials or entering hundreds of handwritten entry forms.

4. **Birthday Giveaway.**

This is a great strategy for brick-and-mortar businesses.

Each month, run a Facebook Messenger ad targeting everyone within a 20-mile radius who has a birthday in the month, offering something enticing for free. When they click on the ad, they enter their birthdate (uploaded automatically to a Google sheet via your bot) and receive an instant gift certificate. Since no one celebrates alone, they'll bring along a friend or ten and if it's a free product, they're likely to do a bit of retail therapy while picking up their gift.

5. **Facebook Live.**

Program a Comment Growth Tool. Connect to an upcoming, scheduled Facebook Live post and viewers can get an instant download when prompted to post a comment. Dramatically increase webinar attendance by broadcasting the link minutes before you start.

Bots are powerful, yet incredibly simple to set up. One word of caution, however: Play by Facebook's rules, especially with Subscription messages, or you will run the risk of being shut down. The rules are easy to follow, so don't panic, just be aware.

Moving Forward

Messenger Bots can boost your profits and decrease you customer service costs while increasing client satisfaction. Bots offer a myriad of options for reaching your clients in unique ways, including audio, video, images, instant downloads, and interactive conversations. New functions roll out almost daily, making bots smarter, more intuitive, and better for both businesses and customers.

So, what are you waiting for? Get your bot in gear!

A Gift For You

Special offer! Get your own free Messenger bot, ready to personalize! Just go here to get started: https://m.me/larissabantingbiz?ref=Playbook

About Larissa Banting

Larissa Banting is a marketing strategist and copywriter who adores working with Messenger Bots and teaching others the ways of the bot via her courses on bot building and marketing.

She's been featured by IBM as an expert on using humor in bots along with appearances on various podcasts and video interviews. Larissa is an award-winning film producer, the author of the best-selling *Costa Rica – The Bradt Guide* and publicist for various Canadian film and television productions. She is also the owner of Weddings Costa Rica, a destination wedding planning firm she built from a laptop in a spare bedroom to a seven-figure business in only four years. Larissa is included on the A-List Top 30 Destination Wedding Planners in the World and a regular contributor to *Martha Stewart Weddings*. She calls the hills near San Jose, Costa Rica home along her husband, daughter, and pack of rescued street dogs.

CHAPTER THIRTY-EIGHT

How To Build A Passive Income Using Automation And Systems

By Spencer Meecham

Every entrepreneur dreams of making income with as little effort as possible. It's known as making passive income.

For your online business to be passive – that is, making money even when you aren't working – it must be *fully* automated . You must take the time to systemize every part of your business to achieve it.

That means automating everything from driving traffic to the initial sale, the sales transactions themselves, remarketing, and all your follow-up sales and upsells. This chapter will teach you how to set up all four of these important processes. When implemented correctly, an online business owner could disappear for months, or even years, and see little impact on their income.

Traffic

Traffic is the lifeblood of any online business. it represents the number of visitors you can get to click over to your funnel or website.

Traffic typically comes from two places online – search engines and social media platforms. You can either pay these platforms to get visitors to your offer or you can use free methods to organically get in front of an audience.

In this chapter, we will focus on free organic methods to passively generate traffic.

There is only one secret to getting organic traffic. That secret is to create lots of really good content. This is easy to understand, but it can be challenging to implement.

The problem with creating content is that it takes so much of your time! Especially if you want content that doesn't do more damage than good. Fortunately, systems can massively eliminate that barrier.

Content Creation System

Content creation will be slightly different for every business, but the principles remain the same. Much of what I'm about to discuss I learned years ago from an entrepreneur named Peng Joon and I'd like to give him credit for that.

With Peng Joon, I learned three principles we must discuss:

Principle #1: The only time your business needs you to create any content is when it's video or audio. Those are hard to fake.

Principle #2: Every piece of content should be utilized across every platform.

Principle #3: Any task that is repetitive should *not* be done by you, the business owner.

Principle #1

In my business, my biggest sources of traffic are YouTube, my blog, Pinterest, and a Facebook group.

YouTube obviously revolves around videos. A blog revolves around written content. Pinterest revolves around images. Finally, the Facebook group is a mix of all three.

I could hire someone to get in front of the camera and do my videos, but then that person becomes associated with my business instead of me.

On the other hand, I could hire someone to ghost-write my blog posts, with me just adding a few edits at the end, and no one is any wiser. In fact, it is likely that the article will be better if I am not the one who is in charge. The same goes for Pinterest, and can often be true in the Facebook group as well.

You are the face and voice of your business. Anything that doesn't require that face or voice should not be done by you.

Principle #2

I mentioned in the first principle that my sources of traffic are YouTube, my blog, and Pinterest. Many businesses run each of these exclusively.

However, I know that these three traffic sources are actually very similar. They are just relaying the same information in a different way. Some people like to search YouTube for answers to questions they have. Other people prefer to search Google and read about the answer to their question in blogs or posts. And finally, a certain demographic of people likes to use Pinterest to search visually for pictures that will lead them to answers to their questions.

So instead of me spending hours coming up with content ideas for YouTube, while my writer does the same for my blog, and my Pinterest manager does the same for my Pinterest page, we use the same content!

I create a YouTube video. That video gets handed to my writer. She doesn't transcribe the video, but instead recreates it in a logical way that makes sense on a blogging platform. And finally, my Pinterest manager makes a set of images that point to the video and to the blog post without having to create additional content to send traffic to.

Principle #3

Once you start pumping out content, it doesn't take long to realize how repetitive a lot of it really is. Once I film a YouTube video, everything that takes place after that is essentially the same every time. We edit out personal information, add intros and outros, write descriptions, add tags, add to playlists, etc.

If a task is repetitive then it can almost always be outsourced very inexpensively. The key is to come up with a system that you use on every single video, then you can simply make a checklist and a training video and then almost anyone can run your system.

I use Asana for all this because it is free and allows my freelancers and assistants to check off one task at a time. For YouTube, it looks something like this:

- Each step can be clicked to pull up a better description of the task, with some having links to video instructions.
- Every time I make a video, I upload it, then duplicate my template with a new video title, then a team member takes care of everything else.
- The last task in the YouTube section has my YouTube assistant create a new task in Asana for my writer who then takes over from there and starts turning the video into a blog post.
- As you may have guessed, the last task the writer does is assign the blog post and video to the Pinterest manager who starts with images.

Selling

For your sales process to truly be automated you need to have a funnel. Sending people straight to a website's homepage will result in far fewer leads and sales. Send the visitor to a specific landing page where you tell them what you want them to do.

I am not going to write much about sales funnels because this book has other chapters written by those far more experienced with funnels than me.

Suffice to say that you need all of your content to have a specific Call To Action (CTA). That CTA should capture an email address as soon as possible and then proceed to sell.

Email Automation

No matter how good your funnel or product, you will inevitably lose a majority of people once the selling begins. Sometimes this is simply because it is not a good fit for the potential customer. However, more often than most entrepreneurs realize, it is due to something else.

Sometimes visitors don't understand the product, sometimes they don't believe that the product or service can solve their problem, and sometimes it's just a technical bug.

We can use email automation to follow everyone that falls in any of those categories, then resolve the issue, and help them make a purchase.

I use Active Campaign as my autoresponder to make this all happen, but you can do it in most autoresponders.

Everything is run using a system of tags and lists. Most tools that take payments and collect email addresses can integrate directly with your email autoresponder and add people to lists when they do certain things.

When someone puts their email address into one of my forms, it adds them to a list in my autoresponder. In my autoresponder I have already created a ten-day email automation that attempts to resolve any concerns that they may have about the product. I use *Inside Peek* videos to help them understand the product better and I use testimonials, reviews, and case studies to help them trust that the product is legitimate.

If they decide to purchase in the very beginning through my funnel, or after reading an email, my sales funnel software (ClickFunnels) will add a "purchased" tag to their contact profile in the autoresponder. The autoresponder then removes them from the "prospect" list and stops selling them any product they have already purchased.

It looks something like this (visually complicated, but it takes about five minutes to set up).

- Whether a person purchases or not, they are added to the appropriate list.
- Everyone that did not purchase gets added to another email automation that sends out emails every couple of days that help build a relationship and build trust.
- Those who did purchase will receive emails that will offer additional products.
- This email automation is nearly six months long and I add one email to the end of it every week. My goal is to have at least two full years of automated emails to go out to every email address I capture.

Moving Forward

Systems help me to pump out large amounts of content that would otherwise be impossible. You can set up similar systems.

Each piece of content has a CTA that sends people to a funnel. The funnel captures their email address by offering something for free, and then attempts to sell them a product. Email automation continues to attempt to sell those that didn't purchase in the initial funnel. Another email automation takes all customers and leads and continues to build a relationship and sell additional products for six months (you can start with something shorter or longer, as required). This maximizes the value of each lead I (and you will) capture.

A Gift For You

If you want to learn more about how I use this system to exponentially grow my business, my income, and my impact go to buildapreneur.com webinar and I'll share the three secrets that makes it all possible.

About Spencer Meecham

Spencer has spent the last three years pursuing a passive income through his online business. He firmly believes the truly wealthy have lots of time, not money. He has automated large amounts of his business and now spends his time trying to teach others how to achieve similar results. He recently started traveling and vlogging with his wife and two children and putting his online systems to the true test.

CHAPTER THIRTY-NINE

Drop-Shipping on Amazon and eBay

By Waseem Rahman

Don't have capital?

Not sure if a certain product will sell?

Don't have room at home to store hundreds or thousands of products?

If you answered *yes* to any of these questions, drop-shipping could be for you. It's a great way to start your venture into the world of retail with a lot less overhead than traditional selling models require and – by doing so – you can reach seven-figure sales like I have.

People always ask:

- Where do I find suppliers who will drop-ship?
- How do I make money using this method?

These questions and others will be answered in this chapter.

What Is Drop-Shipping?

Drop-shipping is a non-traditional retail method in which you do not hold stock of any kind; no stock will ever be shipped to you, the retailer. Drop-shipping skips housing and managing an inventory by circumventing that step of the tradition sales model.

Instead of bringing in stock or inventory of the products you are selling, as a brick-and-mortar store must when selling to walk-in customers, you sell items virtually, online. You don't order the product until a buyer places an order with you; then, you buy the product from a retailer or wholesaler who agrees to ship the product to the customer rather than you. You simply manage the purchase and collect a tidy profit for doing so, in the end.

A lot of drop-shipping is done through third-party marketplaces such as Amazon, eBay, or Shopify. Officially, neither Amazon nor eBay allow drop-shipping, but it happens every day. It's critical you follow the marketplace's rules.

Successful Drop-Shipping Methods

There are several ways to implement a drop-shipping business and you can create your own hybrid systems but, from my experience and what I've seen my students accomplish, drop-shipping falls into one of the following categories:

Manual Drop-Shipping

Using this method involves listing and checking stock for products yourself or with the help of a Virtual Assistant (VA). This is the least expensive way to approach drop-shipping but is time-consuming and costs if you use a VA.

Automated Drop-Shipping

This method involves using software to list items, deal with suppliers, and follow up with customers, which is a simpler method of drop-shipping, but comes at a cost.

Hybrid Drop-Shipping

One of my favorites is a blend of online and traditional drop-shipping. In this method you list the product, deal with supplier, but have the product shipped to yourself, and then send it on to the customer.

International Drop-Shipping

This method involves listing products in countries other than your own.

Secret Method

It's taken me eight years to perfect and is not known to many till now, but I'm going to share my secret drop-shipping method with you here at a special discount (see *A Gift For You*, below).

Methods to Avoid:

Aliexpress

I've seen many in the past get burnt drop-shipping from China. There are too many moving parts you have to consider that could go wrong here, mainly shipping times and whether the retailer actually sends the products out.

Amazon to eBay

This, by far, has been one of the most popular and, quite frankly, the riskiest of all the ways you can drop-ship. The margins are extremely low, the competition is high, and you must track thousands of price fluctuations on both sides of the deal (purchasing and selling prices).

Drop-Shipping on Amazon And eBay

According to the rules of Amazon, to be a drop-shipper, you must be the seller of record, take responsibility for customer returns, and identify yourself as the seller of your products on all packing slips. This involves bending the system a bit and making sure your suppliers don't add any slips to the shipment by indicating it's a gift during the checkout process on Amazon.

eBay has similar rules but, when done properly and by ensuring the customer is well cared for and providing a good buying experience for them, eBay won't have any problem with you drop-shipping.

Drop-Shipping on Shopify

Shopify drop-shipping involves creating a store – either from scratch, or by purchasing a premade template – and then adding products, ensuring the title and descriptions are done, taking and posting pictures, and making sure there is an audience to purchase the product by using paid promotions, like Facebook ads, Google ads, or other platforms.

The products are usually sourced from China using AliExpress, Alibaba, DHGate, and other online commerce companies. This model has a few disadvantages such as long shipping times and communication issues with the suppliers.

The first step in using Shopify is completing a lot of research on what products will sell and then spending a lot of time and money testing to find winners.

Advantages of Amazon/eBay Drop-Shipping

- Easy to get started.

Simply find a supplier, choose an audience, and keep a tab on stock levels on your supplier's website.

- Little investment.

Imagine not spending thousands on stock and, even worse, on stock that doesn't move!

- Flexibility.

You can do this from anywhere in the world.

- Scalability.

You can keep adding new products, as often as you want, because the responsibility of fulfilling the orders is on the supplier which gives you time to focus on growing your business.

- FREE Traffic!

Amazon and eBay have millions of customers and have a massive market-share of all online purchases so, as long as your listings are optimized, you needn't worry about getting people to see your listings.

Disadvantages of Amazon/eBay Drop-Shipping

- Stock

You are relying heavily upon your supplier(s) to have stock available. This means you must ensure the item is in stock when you've made a sale. You can rely on software to check the suppliers' sites once or multiple times a day but what if they have a sudden surge in sales and you now can't fulfill that item or, worse, if they don't maintain their inventory records accurately? (Don't worry, there are ways around this.)

- Competition

Any business model with a low barrier to entry will always have more competitors on the same listing. However, if hybrid models are used, you can beat that competition both on price and delivery times or, better yet, be the only seller on a listing getting all the sales for yourself.

- Margins

If you do it the way everybody else does, the margins of drop-shipping are often discouragingly low but, if done differently, you can easily make a full-time living or even – one that I know everyone loves – a passive one.

How to Find Suppliers And Products to Sell

Like traditional retail stores, who maintain a physical stock of products, you can contact individual suppliers to inquire into whether or not they will ship their products to a third party (the consumer) and start selling their products with that agreement. However, here are some other ways to find good suppliers and products to work with:

- If you find a seller you like on eBay or Amazon, you can sell anything they have for sale. You may find specialty items by following Google Trends, Seasonal Holidays like Halloween, Christmas, etc.
- Software that lists items from specific sellers will allow you to sell everything they have on offer.
- There is software available that can show you how much an eBay seller has done in previous sales and what their best-selling products are (you can find out more through my offer below).
- Supplying niche products allows you to have a more targeted audience and then branch out into related products.
- Finding suppliers isn't hard but you need to have some patience. Use Google to find contact information to approach manufacturers and wholesalers directly or, if you want to build a unique relationship, you could visit them so they know you face-to-face.

Needs for Starting Drop-Shipping

1. A seller's account on Amazon or eBay.
2. Software to extract stock levels from suppliers' websites daily.
3. At least one supplier who will send products to your customers directly.
4. Initial capital to cover expenses for the first three to six months on eBay or Amazon because they cover themselves for any potential chargebacks if items aren't delivered to their customers.
5. A business attitude that takes this seriously and puts systems in place to ensure success.

Endgame – Scaling and Automation

No, I'm not talking about the Avengers here, but if done correctly you can create your own team of superheroes and automate this business with VAs and outsourced one-off projects to free up your time and truly create a passive income for yourself.

Scaling would be the next thing to do and you should create different phases of growth. For example, trading on both platforms at once and then adding more suppliers and products or markets. I've traded in Japan and been invited to trade in China, Australia, and other countries.

Working less on the administrative side of the business and focusing on growth can open a lot of opportunities to work exclusively with suppliers once you have shown healthy sales and a proven history on the biggest sales platforms on earth.

Moving Forward

Drop-shipping is a great way to start your online journey and if you treat drop-shipping on eBay and Amazon like a business rather than a hobby, you can truly accomplish fantastic sales going into six- and seven-figure incomes, especially if you think outside the box. I've used drop-shipping as a stepping-stone into many other online ventures while providing a full-time income, and you can do this as well.

A Gift For You

Only for readers of this book, a 75% discount on a coaching call with me is available at https://www.passivedropship.com

About Waseem Rahman

Waseem's entrepreneurial journey took off in the early 2000s in the UK when he paid for his University education in full by selling products that he purchased from a retailer and then started selling them on eBay for a tidy profit. He did this part-time for many years.

Later, in 2010, he realized that, with a little more effort, he could turn this into a full-time income rather than a side hustle.

With his first child on the way, the pressure was on as he gave himself one year to turn his idea into reality and, within nine months, he had already started doing 5-figure months, which then turned into six-figures, and he hasn't looked back since.

Waseem now has multiple income streams which all started from humble beginnings in his living room to become a seven-figure business year-on-year.

CHAPTER FORTY

How To Use Instagram For Business

By Kelly Sturtevant

When most people think about Instagram, they think of visually appealing images in a nine-grid pattern and influencers like the Kardashians who share their latest sponsored promotions on a constant basis and they think, "My business has no place on there!"

This is what stops many entrepreneurs from seeing the potential that Instagram has to offer.

In this chapter, we are going to discuss using Instagram for business; more specifically, how to use Instagram's features to enhance your reach, attract your target audience, and grow your brand.

Why Use Instagram?

As a personal user, I enjoy using Instagram for connecting with friends and family, sharing photos of our family, and getting the highlight reel from those I follow. But there is a whole different side to this platform when it comes to business.

As a Social Media Strategist, understanding the power behind all social media platforms is a huge part of my role. Each one is unique and attracts different age demographics for a business. Instagram is no exception. When used in the correct manner, Instagram has the power to help a brand grow to unbelievable new heights, attract a larger audience and create brand awareness in a creative manner.

There are many benefits for your brand by using Instagram. With over 1 billion users, Instagram is the fastest growing social media platform with millions of new accounts being added daily. Instagram users are far more engaged with brands on Instagram than any other platform, including Facebook, even though Facebook has more than double the users.[26] By using some of the features on Instagram, businesses have been able to generate more revenue through the use of stories, influencer marketing, and engagement with their followers.

Most businesses think that Instagram is not for them, but in actuality, all types of businesses can thrive on Instagram if they know how to best utilize the features of the platform.

---

[26] Walton, J. (June 24, 2019). *Twitter vs. Facebook vs. Instagram: What's The Difference?* Retrieved on May 30, 2020 from https://www.investopedia.com/articles/markets/100215/twitter-vs-facebook-vs-instagram-who-target-audience.asp.

Hashtags And How To Use Them

It's no secret that hashtags have become critical in exploring brands on Instagram and giving businesses the ability to listen to the social conversation going on with their audience. But I find most businesses use hashtags incorrectly and, therefore, don't reap the benefits they should.

Hashtags are meant as a way to search for content and topics that interest you the most. But many businesses end up posting hashtags that are either unremarkable, or too generic, instead of focusing on who they are trying to attract. Using hashtags should be done with the customer in mind; think about what they are searching for in order to reach them.

Hashtag Do's

- You get 30 hashtags. Use as many as you can to reach a wider audience.
- Choose hashtags that vary in size and topic.
- Use hashtags that relate to your business and what your audience is searching for.
- Use a good mix of hashtags that are searched in the 100k-900k range for the bulk of your list. Have a couple tags in the million range and a couple in the under 100k range.
- Have a rotation of different hashtag groups so you aren't using to the same ones all of the time.
- Have one or two branded hashtags so your audience can find your content easier.
- Engage with your hashtags! Use them as a way to start a conversation with your audience.

Hashtag Don'ts

- Don't use generic hashtags like #instagood or #red or #travel. These are over 100 million posts and your content will never be seen on them.
- Don't use hashtags that are part of a phrase or sentence like #donttrythisathome or #whatareyouwaitingfor These are never tags anyone searches for.
- Don't use the same hashtags over and over. This can cause you to be shadow banned.
- Don't hijack another brand's hashtag. If it is clear that tag is another business's brand, don't post all of your content to it. Not cool.
- Don't use tags that have no relation to your business or your audience. If it doesn't make sense to your brand, avoid it.

The key to hashtags is to know for what your ideal customer searches and to have your content show up for them. Once your content is connected to the right hashtags, engaging within it is where the magic really happens.

Engaging With Your Audience And What To Avoid

Instagram has the most engaged audience out of all social media platforms. Its engagement rate is 10-times higher than Facebook, 54-times higher than Pinterest and 84-times higher than Twitter, and out of the 25 million branded accounts on Instagram, 80% of users are following at least one of them.[27]

---

[27] Smith, K. (January 20, 2019). 50 Incredible Instagram Statistics. Retrieved on May 30, 2020 from https://www.brandwatch.com/blog/instagram-stats/.

Engaging with your followers and hashtags is the most important way to grow your brand. You should have time set aside at least once a day during which you (or someone on your team) engages with your followers and targeted hashtags. This means commenting on their posts, commenting on their stories and commenting on posts within your targeted hashtags.

In order to engage and create an open dialogue with your audience, you need to leave comments that are more than, "Nice post" or a series of emojis. Those kinds of comments reek of automation which shows a follower you are not genuine in your comments and likely not worth engaging with. Comments don't need to be long (four words or more) in order to be picked up by the algorithm.

People ask me constantly if they should be using bots to engage or follow other accounts. There are many companies out there whose sole purpose it is to automate the engagement process by using bots – whether for comments or creating a huge new list of accounts following you.

While it can be tempting to create immediate growth on your account, using these types of tools are never in your best interest. These tactics violate the Instagram terms of service; and you will get caught and Instagram will ultimately delete your account.

Growing a genuine following may take longer and may yield less followers overall, but focusing on genuine engagement first and foremost will bring you the right audience and attract the followers you need to grow sales.

How To Use Stories To Grow Your Business

When Instagram Stories came out in 2016, they immediately became one of the major strategy components to growing on the platform. Using stories can drastically increase your reach and engagement, thus growing your brand in the process.

What Are Stories?

- They are video or image-based posts that last for a 24-hour period before vanishing.
- They allow brands to share content that's set in real-time.

They are engagement explosions for your brand, giving you many options for engaging your audience.

What Makes A Good Story?

Get creative when it comes to Stories; because they are short-lived, a brand can have a lot of fun with them.

- Create polls or questions to ask your audience. Market research!
- Show behind-the-scenes action.
- Share your day.
- Collaborate with other brands/influencers and share content.
- Have an influencer do a Story takeover.
- Giveaways and contests.
- Tease new products.
- Highlight team members or customers.
- Thank supporters and shout them out.
- And, so much more!

Because Stories are only live for 24 hours, you can have a ton of fun just experimenting with them. Test out different methods and just enjoy connecting with your audience in a casual and unique way.

Using Instagram Reels for Business

During the 2020 pandemic, video content quickly became the leading method of how social media users got in front of their audiences due to the insurgence of TikTok.

Social media users began flocking to the platform due to its short video length, the virality of videos, and the ability to jump on trending sounds and topics without needing a production company to film.

Instagram saw how fast users were adapting to this new form of content, and in August 2020, they added Reels to their product suite.

What are Reels?

Reels are short (under 60 second) video content, filmed in portrait style. They are quick, educational, and a way for businesses to engage with users with video.

Reels can also be found in two places, under the Reels tab on a user's profile, and they can appear in the user's grid, making it easier for followers to engage and react to the content.

Hashtags can also be used with Reels, and the same recommendation of using 30 hashtags in your captions is strongly urged for increased virality.

What to post in Reels

Reels are a great way for brands to showcase their business with the unique use of video.

- Demo a product
- Share a quick hack
- Showcase your location
- Give value with short lessons or ah-ha moments you've encountered
- Jump on any trending topics or video styles
- Showcase team members/their favorite things etc
- Influencer video shares
- Testimonials

Video content will not be disappearing any time soon. It's important for businesses to pivot fast when new platforms and creative tools become available. Reels allows brand to showcase content in a unique way with video.

Moving Forward

If you are reading this and wondering if Instagram is the right platform for you, my advice would be to stop wondering and start doing. Create your account and begin. Set your profile and optimize it for your target audience. Pick a good image of you (personal brand) or a logo of the business (business brand). Create a plan for content and plan your first set of images around it. When crafting your posts, think about how you can create ways for your audience to engage with you.

Spend some time looking through your competitors on Instagram; look at what they are posting and who is following them. Search their hashtags to see if your target audience is engaging with them. Make notes of the content they are putting out and how you can post similar content or better content (keep in mind that your competition may not being using Instagram well, so this gives you a huge opening to crush your market)!

Instagram has the power to create brand awareness, an engaged following, and attract the audience you want when you utilize the key elements it has. Spending time learning the platform (or hiring someone to do it for you) can drastically increase your reach and revenue through a cohesive and consistent presence. Don't miss out on reaching new potential clients by failing to have a presence on Instagram.

A Gift For You

Need help creating content for social media?

My Social Media Content Machine can help: www.bluepagesocial.com/365

About Kelly Sturtevant

Kelly Sturtevant is a Social Media Strategist and Facebook Ads Manager who specializes in digital marketing strategies to help 6-and 7-figure entrepreneurs grow their online presence, generate leads, and attract ideal clients to their products and services. Kelly is a coffee lover by nature who enjoys reaching new weightlifting goals in the gym. When she is not busy helping her clients achieve massive social media success, she can be found in her kitchen decorating cakes, enjoying quality time with her family, or being ignored by her cat, Gizmo.

CHAPTER FORTY-ONE

Pinterest

By Tereza Toledo

When I got my first iPhone, I found an app with a catchy name, it looked like a virtual pin-board. It let me search, find, and save dreams, beautiful images, inspiring quotes, recipes, and articles, just like I used to do with magazine cut-outs in my teen years.

Pinterest, a search and discovery platform that launched in January 2010, allowed users to search visually for products, ideas, and solutions. The platform not only allows them to easily share their finds but also save them for future use.

I had no idea how powerful the platform was or that I would be so passionate about it seven years later.

In The Beginning

Entrepreneurial blood runs in my veins. A passionate multi-entrepreneur, I explored different business possibilities from comic book and hiking equipment stores to foodservice, until becoming a mom in 2007.

Having a child pushed me to explore even more diverse business possibilities because I had to find something that could be executed while caring for a child. Garage sales hunting combined with eBay selling was one of them; I also became a certified personal trainer.

In 2016, I was asked by a health and fitness company to learn how to use Pinterest to generate traffic and share content that could improve people's lives. This virtual pin-board board was becoming a visual search engine that was changing the way people searched and discovered.

Pinterest Basics

Upon signing up for Pinterest you are asked a few questions about your interests and hobbies. Then Pinterest starts showing you beautiful images (pins) related to your chosen content. You can just scroll down or search for anything you'd like to discover. From there you can click on each image to view the full content, purchase, download an app, view a recipe and more. It allows you to save that idea for later in organized boards and share it.

People use Pinterest to: shop , plan a trip, find party ideas, learn how to decorate a cake, do any Do-It-Yourself (DIY) you can think of, learn new skills, collect recipes, get advice, dream, discover, solve problems, envision what they want, and manifest their goals all in one place. It's the best way to create a vision board that is handy and fits in your pocket.

You may already be using Pinterest to generate traffic and leads for your business but, chances are, you are not taking full advantage of its potential.

You should be using Pinterest to create brand recognition, to warm-up your audience, to grow your email list, and to generate leads and sales.

Why Use Pinterest?

Pinterest is the perfect platform to share and market your blog or business content. People use the platform to discover, search, and find new products. Every pin is allowed a keyworded description, which helps people discover you, and a URL, which leads traffic to your company website.

You can use Pinterest to market your product or service without being too salesy, to showcase without being spammy, to inspire without being an extrovert. It's a place to market your value, where people are ready to buy or try new things.

300 million people use the platform monthly, 98% of them have tried something they found on Pinterest, 84% of them use Pinterest when they're trying to decide what to buy, and 77% have found a new brand or product on the platform.[28]

The reasons you should have a presence on Pinterest are clear.

For example, by organically sharing content on Pinterest, one of my clients, Alex, went from 1,000 website visitors a month to a high of 8,000 visitors in one day. No ad spend was used. Not only was she able to increase her email list, but she also influenced many lives with her inspiring content. Her ad revenue increased as well.

Five Steps To Getting Started on Pinterest

There are many things to be said about how to use and strategize with Pinterest, but do these five things to start on the right foot:

1. **Know Your Audience and Use What You Know.**

Make sure your profile is complete and is a reflection of your company's brand. The profile description is your elevator pitch in 160 characters. Use your logo or picture for the profile image and use the same image across all platforms.

Create boards and pin relevant content to them, either yours or from other accounts. Only pin content that is relevant to your audience and related to your brand and mission. Anything else, of personal interest or unrelated content, must be stored on secret boards.

Use keyword-relevant titles and descriptions for your boards. Put yourself in your ideal clients' shoes and research what they may be searching for, the exact words and terms to use for board names, descriptions, and text overlay in your pins.

2. **Start With A Strong Foundation.**

Add your business website to your profile and claim it by clicking on the "Claim Website" tab. Pinterest will then verify your site. Also apply for Rich Pins.

---

[28] n.a. (n.d.). *About Our Audience: Meet The People Who Use Pinterest*. Retrieved from https://business.pinterest.com/en/pinterest-stories on October 13, 2019.

Rich Pins are Pins that have extra information available to provide context for a Pin. For example, a Rich Pin for a product you sell may have a description of the product from your website and the price, along with a link to your website, etc.

To set up Rich Pins, you'll need to add a small code to your website. That is what allows the extra information on your website to appear on your Rich Pin in Instagram. It's a simple process and free feature that gives your content more authority within the platform. Rich Pins make it easy for people to see you, reach you, and share your content.

This may sound a bit techy but it's fairly easy, and Pinterest gives you step-by-step guides to do everything.

3. Share and Cross-Promote.

Be active on Pinterest. Share on your email newsletter and social media platforms. Encourage everyone to save and share your content. The more people share and interact with your content, the more people will see it. Don't be afraid to send them from one platform to another and ask them to share on all platforms.

4. Optimize Your Blog Posts or Website Content for Pinterest.

If it doesn't already exist, add a Pin-it button to your website so people can save and share your content. The Pinterest widget is easy to install and can make the difference between someone reading your content and forgetting about it or saving for later and sharing it right away.

85% of Pinterest users are on mobile. Check your website from your phone and see how it looks and if it needs to be tweaked. Update the images on your website; make them attractive and ready to be pinned. Vertical images, 2x3 with text overlay and your logo or website on the bottom are excellent. Square images are OK, but you'll find they don't perform as well. And just remember, add a Call To Action (CTA) asking your audience to Pin it.

After working on the platform for so long, I can now anticipate what people search for and can offer content with solutions to questions that will be asked next. The longer you work on the platform, the more you will understand your audiences' preferences.

5. Pin Your Content and Stay Consistent

Be creative. Repurpose your existing content or create new content. Add it to the platform by creating your pin directly on Pinterest, from your website (that widget will come in handy), or using a scheduler (like Hootesuite).

Pin others' content and don't be afraid to pin your competitor's pins. Always wear the shoes of your ideal audience: Pin what they are looking for; pin about their problems and about solutions to those problems; and, always serve them high-quality content with clear images.

Be consistent with the look of your posts and the frequency. Both of these keep your audience interested and looking forward to your next pin.

For content ideas, look up the most successful pieces of content on the platform and look at your competitors' pins; both will help you create relevant content for your audience. Allow yourself to be inspired and motivated by others and your audience, too.

Moving Forward

The steps I've presented here are the same steps I take when working with a new client. The next steps involve content strategy, social listening, split testing, and consistency in putting out great content.

With strong foundations and the right strategy in place, I've been able to take website views from 1,000 a month to 1,500 a day within a few months. Turn Pinterest into your first traffic source and establish brand awareness for your followers, bloggers, and other businesses.

A Gift For You

Give it a try, with the steps above and my play-by-play free extended guide (download here: http://www.terezatoledo.com/pinterest). In no time, you will have your account primed to generate leads and conversions!

About Tereza Toledo

Tereza Toledo is a mom to two kids and a cat, an international traveler, a garage weightlifting enthusiast, and a Pinterest Marketing Specialist.

CHAPTER FORTY-TWO

Solo Ads

By Wayne Crowe

Solo ads, as the name suggests, are single ads sent to a list of subscribers. The trick here, though, is that the subscribers are not already on your email list; they belong to another company's list.

For example, you have a list of subscribers (leads) and are looking for more leads. Another business has a lot of subscribers because it has been operating for a long time, is well branded, and is trusted by those on its list.

That established company agrees to send a single email from your lead-gathering page (offer) to their subscribers. Those subscribers, who trust the company sending the message, are exposed to your offering with an implied endorsement from the established company. This builds trust and leads to many of those contacted to join your list. Of course, you must pay the established company a fee for the solo ad, which is often based on the open rate of the message, but it is worth it because the number of leads you will gain from that single ad will be amazing.

Solo ads are one of the easiest ways to get traffic compared to other traffic sources. I have gained millions of subscribers, had over 10 million clicks (on emails), and helped customers and students make five- and six-figure incomes per month by either using solo ads or becoming a reputable solo ads vendor. I consider myself well versed in most traffic building methods and my real love is split testing, reading the data, and taking action to make the figures work in my favor.

In The Beginning

I had an e-Commerce business and was fairly successful working with large warehouses, many staff, lots of stock, and high overhead costs. The problem was, although I was an Internet marketer, I realized I had become an HR manager, looking after staff, rather than doing what I love. I decided to look at what was earning money for my company. I simply followed the money backward and discovered the most money was coming from email marketing. So, I decided to focus on that.

The Five Benefits Of Using Solo Ads

1. Solo ads are the easiest traffic method with which to start building your business.
2. Solo ads are predictable, once you find a source that works, you can normally scale as much as you want with predictable results and costs.
3. You can turn solo ads off and on, at will, and as your budget allows.
4. You can make sales almost instantly (but optimisation is key).

5. Whether you are new online or a seasoned marketer, you can make use of solo ads to build your email list and make sales.

Things To Know Before Using Solo Ads

The most important decision about running solo ads is simple: Find the right provider.

Not all solo ad providers are created equal.

Because they are successful and people can make a great living just selling solo ads, there are a lot of solo ad providers out there. The problem is that most solo ad sellers build their list by buying lists from other solo ad vendors. This is not the best way for a vendor to build a list because the same leads end up on hundreds of lists and get thousands of solo ads that conditions them to either deleting the messages without opening them, or worse, opening the ad (so you have to pay for it) and opting in but rarely, if ever, buying anything from you. Those leads become clicked-to-death as a subscriber!

Some vendors mix in bots, run just bots, or provide fake reviews for each other on marketplaces and Facebook to outright scam ad buyers. These vendors are usually the least expensive and attract a lot of new people because they are cheap. They also have no results to show customers because they are so poor at what they do and, thus, don't have a good reputation.

Look At Vendor Reputation

The first thing you look for is a seller with a good reputation. Most of the time people will tell you to look in testimonial groups but don't because they are controlled by vendors themselves. Instead, simply ask other business owners for their recommendations. Look at who the big guns are using because – more often than not – they track engagement and sales so you can be confident the vendors they are using produce good results.

Look at Vendor Audience Strength

The other thing you can look at is the vendor's audience (followers). Bad vendors simply do not have an audience; their sole selling point is price. When a vendor has an audience, it tells you that the seller provides value and results to their followers and, thus, the followers stick around and socialize with the vendor.

About two years ago, I set out to completely change solo ads for the better. I produced several guides and tools to help people get the best results from solo ad runs. In the process, I built a strong audience by focusing on how to get quality traffic. A good solo ad provider should be able to convert their own traffic better than any buyer and try and teach this to others. This is how I keep my audience involved with what I am doing so they know I want the best results for them.

The quickest way to check a vendor's audience is to check their Facebook profile, look for the value and results they give others. Note that solo ad vendors with a strong audience are not prevalent, so this will narrow the choices down from hundreds of sellers to a handful quickly and, in my experience, this is the *only* way to narrow down top-quality vendors.

Once you have found people you think you can work with, spend time getting to know them and what they do. Finding a good provider is one of the toughest parts of running solo ads; you must work with someone you trust because this relationship is the foundation of every solo ad you will run.

Watch Out For Self-Promoters

Be wary of vendors who are very good at marketing themselves. They spend most of their time marketing themselves and normally sell or re-sell other vendors' traffic, which does not provide the buyer with positive costs and results.

You are looking for a vendor who has a track record of using alternative traffic sources, like native ads, email drops, Adwords, and others. Use of these alternate sources ensures fresh traffic that is more likely to get the results you want because they aren't being bombarded with hundreds of emails.

Finding a solo ad vendor you want to work with is just the start of your journey. You still have to choose your offer, optimize your offer around the traffic source, and more, but with the help of your vendor, you can scale to be successful faster.

Testing

Many solo ad buyers have one sales funnel they either built themselves, copied, or were given by their upline, leader, or sponsor and have been told to run solo ads to it. Most of the time, this simply doesn't work.

You can't use a funnel that is untested and unoptimized for your audience and expect it to result in sales (even if your upline says so). There are times when an upline or sponsor has done their homework and it does work but always look for the data proving it before using a funnel.

You *must* split test, optimize, and track everything (and that subject is far too big for this chapter) to ensure funnel success.

Consider The Audience Source

A funnel that works for solo ads may not work with Facebook Ads and other traffic sources so, again, optimization, testing, and tracking are key; always let the data tell you what to do.

I see so many people just focus on opt-ins because they are easy to track and it's an easy leap to think, *if I get more-opt-ins I should get more sales, clicks on my emails, and more subscribers*, but remember opting in doesn't mean conversion. Follow the data to know what is really happening. I have seen many campaigns were the opt-in was super low, but the sales were high, and a profit was made with each campaign.

Moving Forward

Solo ads in their basic form are very simple: Find an emaillist provider, buy 500 clicks, have the list vendor send their email recipients to your sales page, and job done.

It is because they are so simple that most people start with solo ads and dismiss them as unsuccessful. But that's because they haven't taken the time to research vendors and, instead, based their vendor selection on who is the cheapest. I am hoping, with this quick guide, to open your eyes to the fact that – with the right foundation (vendor), the right offer (funnel or program), and the right attitude (a willingness to split test, optimise, and be data-led) – solo ads work over and over again.

Always keep your end goal in mind. Is it to make as much money back on your funnel as possible? Is it to just build a list as fast as possible? Or, is it to look at how much money you can make over time per subscriber? Once you know your goal, you should measure it with data.

Remember, your vendor is the most important part; find the right one and they will help you become a success.

A Gift For You

Be sure to find your Free List Building Training at http://trdmn.pro/list-building

About Wayne Crowe

Wayne Crowe started his online journey full-time 12 years ago. Since then he has been part of many niches, all revolving around traffic generation and, in the end, realised that the most powerful thing you can own is an email list.

Wayne has built lists in the millions and sold more email traffic than anyone else hosting solo ads; he as well as spent 6-figures per month on traffic building his lists.

In November 2017, Wayne decided to try and change solo ads for the better and three years on has made a positive impact on the industry and the people who buy solo ads, but he knows there is still work to do and people to educate on how to use them.

CHAPTER FORTY-THREE

Podcasting: Scale Your Influence and Create Authority

By Ruth O'Neill

How do entrepreneurs position themselves to gain authority, display credibility, and grow their businesses?

One way that is often overlooked by entrepreneurs is podcasting, This is particularly true in recent years because of the explosion of self-produced videos online, but podcasts are listened to by millions of people. Fifty percent of homes in the US listen to podcasts. That's 60 million homes, and more and more people are listening to podcasts regularly.[29]

First coined by Ben Hammersley in 2004, the term podcast is the combination of *iPod* and *broadcasting* and refers to audio broadcasts that users download to a mobile device or computer to listen to whenever they choose.[30] Podcasters usually deliver a series of broadcasts over time and users often subscribe to the podcaster's feed.

In The Beginning

For two years, I worked my tail off to learn everything about branding, graphic design, and web design. I spent hours honing my skills and taking courses, yet my business was not experiencing the growth I wanted or felt I deserved.

After a lot of frustration, I decided something had to change. On a whim, I started a podcast in which I talked about business and mindset to try and connect with more people.

Turns out that whim was the best business decision I ever made. I went from just another graphic and web designer to a sought-after podcast host. Millionaires reached out to me weekly to see if they could get a spot on my show. It reached the point that I had to close down my design calendar for two weeks because I was booked solid with just podcast interviews. Launching my show completely changed my business.

---

[29] Winn, R. (June 1, 2019). *2019 Podcast Stats & Facts*. Retrieved from https://www.podcast-insights.com/podcast-statistics/ on October 14, 2019.

[30] n.a. (n.d.). *Podcasting*. Retrieved from https://en.wikipedia.org/wiki/Podcast on October 14, 2019.

Getting Started

Before you start planning your podcast episodes or creating any podcast cover art, there are basic steps you must complete:

1. **Declare Your Intention.**

This is so important. Declare your intention to start your podcast and announce the mission behind your show. Having a mission will give you clarity and also help you as you structure your show.

For my podcast, *Operation BOLD*, my mission is to empower my audience to embrace the BOLD within them and to accept that who and where they are, is enough. Once they've embraced they are enough, they can implement the actionable advice my guests and I provide on the show.

2. **Hype Your Show**

After you declare your intention, start creating hype around your new show. Get your audience (even if it's just friends and family) invested in your new endeavor by asking questions and getting opinions about the name of your podcast, the tagline, as well as the cover art design. This feedback will help you grow but, more importantly, it intentionally draws audience participation into your new project which makes them feel invested and more excited about the launch.

Create a separate Facebook business page dedicated to your show once you find a name and upload your podcast cover art to make it all official. Treat this podcast like a real business.

3. **Set A Launch Date**

Put a launch date on the calendar and stick to it come hell or high water. Make sure to give yourself at least three weeks to plan, record, produce, and set up hosting for your show. The devil is in the details and if you position yourself and your business properly you gain instant authority and credibility.

Create Your Listener Journey

We all know that confused buyers don't buy, and the same thing goes for podcasts: Confused listeners don't listen.

Before you launch your show it's crucial to do some planning. As boring as strategizing can be, it will determine the success of your podcast. Again, the devil is in the details:

Determine Your Topic and Angle

Determine what your show is going to talk about (e.g., business, real estate investing, self-development, health issues, etc.).

Think about your favorite podcasts (or radio shows). Why do you like each of them? Why do you listen to them? How do they make you feel after you are finished listening to each episode? Now, pick your favorite three.

Draw out a Venn diagram with three large, overlapping circles. In each of the circles write one name of your top three podcasts. Next, write the qualities you admire and that resonate with you in each circle for each show.

Doing this reveals why you identify with those particular hosts and why you listen to their content. In the small overlapping area in the middle of your diagram is the space that encompasses each of the shows, write the qualities that fit into all three of the shows here. It is in the overlapping area that your unique show is born.

You now know what you will be talking about and how you want your audience to feel after listening to your show. This direction makes the rest of the strategizing so much easier. Keep it in mind while creating the outline of your podcast season and the intended listener experience will be assured. Also selecting the right guests will be easier.

Authority Hacking 101

Once you decide to be the authoritative version of you, a change will happen. Not only will you be more confident but others notice will notice your confidence and start seeing you as an expert.

One of the questions I get asked the most is, "How do I find the right guests to come on my show to expand my reach?"

It's called authority hacking. Essentially, you piggyback off of someone else's reputation and success in an ethical way. When you release a new episode featuring an industry leader, you are viewed as a peer with that individual and, thus, recognized as an authority.

First, look for niche or industry leaders who have accomplished things you are wanting to accomplish. Do research, or recon, as I like to call it, on them to determine if they would be a good fit for your show. Next, build a relationship with them, and, finally, ask them to be a guest on your podcast.

Tell them about your mission, the purpose of your podcast, and how it will benefit them and your listeners. Remember an expert's time is extremely valuable and honor it. Prepare ahead of time, be thoughtful with your questions, and engage in meaningful conversation with them. Build a strong relationship with them so they are more likely to pitch your podcast to their audience. This value exchange means you can ethically use them, their name, and success to promote your brand and generate more revenue through the power of association.

One of my hacks to get more ears listening to my show is to post show notes on my website, send a new episode message via my messenger bot on Facebook, post a photo of the guest with my branded podcast logo on social media, and share what we discuss in the episode. It's a great way to inform your listeners (and potential new listeners) about the new episode. The more people that I get to download the episode, the greater impact I am making, and that results in growth of my business. More episodes equal more revenue.

Create A Digital Asset Vault

This may be the coolest asset you can have for your podcast: Create an asset vault.

An asset vault is a repository of digital assets that your guests usually give away for free or very low prices. Mention the asset in the interview and let listeners know where they can find it after the show. This will allow you to collect listeners' emails and build your list while helping your guests build their following as well; it's a win-win.

My favorite software to use to build this membership is Clickfunnels. My favorite thing about podcasting is how intimate you can be with your audience. As busy entrepreneurs, we are always on the go and our free time is limited. When we speak to our audience it's an intimate experience.

Moving Forward

Podcasts are a great way to build a following for your business. Podcasts aren't time-sensitive like Facebook Lives which require your listener to watch as it happens. They can be listened to as your subscribers do other things (like driving, cleaning the house, exercising, etc.) unlike YouTube or other videos that require full attention and eyes and ears to absorb.

If you follow the tips in this chapter, podcasts will position you as an authority, gain you instant credibility, and build a following who will buy again and again. Do your research, create epic content, and interview great guests to have an exceptional show.

A Gift For You

Connect with Ruth online via Facebook, Instagram, and Twitter @ruthoneillhq and listen to her podcast, Operation BOLD, on iTunes, Spotify, iHeartRadio, Stitcher and more.

About Ruth O'Neill

Ruth O'Neill is the founder and CEO of The BOLD Project. Her mission is to empower women to embrace their life BOLDLY, step into their greatness, and lead a life of purpose on their terms. Ruth and her husband Matt have two children and love to travel.

CHAPTER FORTY-FOUR

Monetizing Your Podcast: Create Predictable Profits On Autopilot

By Evans Putman

Podcasting entrepreneurs, your podcast is not just an audio channel to amplify your message and position yourself as an expert, it is also a powerful marketing and sales funnel. With a little effort, planning, and guidance, you can turn your podcast into a virtual, automated, money-maker.

This strategy does not involve filling your podcast episodes with ads or sponsorships for other companies. It also does not involve hiring an expensive agency to get you results; my model is easy to implement, as-is, by yourself. You maintain your listeners' trust because you retain complete control over your marketing and sales messaging. You keep all the revenue you earn from your podcast.

In The Beginning

In 2018, my business partner and I were struggling to sell our digital courses. We were frustrated and running out of options.

While watching Russell Brunson give a presentation at *Funnel Hacking Live 2018* he said, "Podcast listeners will also become your best buyers. This is proven. People who listen to podcasts are worth more money to you."[31]

Immediately, I put pen to paper and began sketching out the framework of the podcast monetization model for one of our podcasts and that became the model I use to help other podcasting entrepreneurs transform their business.

Once I discovered this secret, our business transformed almost overnight. The simple switch from a publishing and positioning mindset to a monetization mindset unlocked the true potential of not only the podcast but also the business.

The podcast monetization funnel strategy I created quickly generated over $500,000 in revenue while building an email list over 17,000 comprised of podcast listeners who turned into our best customers, by a longshot.

---

[31] Brunson, R. (March 21, 2018. *Conversation Domination Presentation*. Funnel Hackers Live 2018. Orlando, FL. Transcript retrieved from https://marketingsecrets.com/conversation-domination-part-3-of-3/ on October 24, 2019.

Along with those results, the podcast's subscribers list grew, and we had a corresponding increase in affiliate and Joint Venture (JV) opportunities as well as bookings with top-tier guests like Grant Cardone, Robert Kiyosaki, Barbara Corcoran, Dean Graziosi, Hal Elrod, and others.

Five Benefits For Focusing On Podcast Monetization

Here are five reasons why you should start focusing on podcast monetization:

1. **Higher-Value Customers.**

Podcast listeners are excellent prospects for your high-ticket offers. For example, our podcast listeners were responsible for 80% of our total sales revenue. They were our biggest source of repeat buyers, hyperactive buyers, and had the highest dollar amount spend per transaction.

2. **Shorter Sales Cycle.**

A podcast quickly builds rapport and trust, establishes you as an expert, and gives credibility to your products and services. Your sales cycle will speed-up because cold traffic will quickly turn to warm traffic and then hot traffic.

3. **Higher Profit Margin.**

Using this model, you will no longer have to run Facebook Ads or other costly means of acquiring customers; the majority of the $500,000 revenue we generated was pure profit.

4. **Predictable, On-Demand Revenue.**

Your podcast listener email list quickly becomes a source of predictable, on-demand revenue. In our business, this list is our go-to source for a quick influx of cash.

5. **JV / Affiliate Relationships.**

Your podcast becomes an asset by building relationships with other entrepreneurs, expanding your circle of influence, getting you access to thousands of potential new listeners and creating JV/affiliate relationships to increase sales of your products and services.

Five Tips To Generate Predictable Podcast Profits

Here are five proven podcast monetization tips you can begin using immediately to start making more money from your podcast.

Focus On Listenership Growth

Increasing your sales revenue through your podcast relies on increasing your number of listeners so you can continue to build your marketing lists. To grow listenership quickly, become proactive with your growth strategy instead of reactive.

Do not rely on listeners finding you via a podcast app. Instead, find where your target audience hangs out online and get your podcast in front of them. Use content and social media marketing. Provide your guests with promotional assets to get into their circle of influence.

Seed Your Podcast Episodes

Start seeding your podcast episodes with value, credibility, and offers to generate more leads and sales in the future. For example, make sure you (or your guests) always focus on delivering value.

When you do this, your listeners come to expect nothing but value in everything you offer (including your products and services).

Read listener reviews and customer testimonials on air. Provide subtle hints of offers and higher-ticket programs. For example, use phrases like, "When people get to work more closely with me..." or "When people are enrolled in my more advanced programs..." to plant those seeds in the minds of your listeners.

Fill Your Funnel, Build Your Tribe

Start growing your email, Facebook Messenger, and Facebook Group lists. This is your tribe, the people who eagerly await your newest product or service and quickly become repeat customers and hyperactive buyers.

When people I work with don't have the resources (time or team) to create all three, I tell them to focus first on building the email list. From my experience, our podcast listener email list was like an ATM. We sent them an email and they put money in our pockets.

Do not go the predictable lead magnet route of providing a simple .pdf checklist or e-Book in exchange for your listener's email address. You must overdeliver. Consider creating a free Members Area (ours was called the Agent Success Toolbox) with multiple, high-value items and update this Members Area regularly.

Create Action-Takers

During your podcast episodes, start training your listeners to go and do things with Calls To Action (CTAs). Ask them to subscribe, leave a review, share on social media, or to go and implement a strategy shared in the episode and report back via email or voice message with their results. Also, when asking them to take action, make sure to use CTAs like, "Go now to iTunes and subscribe."

In the future, when you drop in a CTA for buying your new course, booking a call, or applying for your high-ticket coaching offer, your listeners will be more likely to take action because you subtly trained them to do so.

Launch Events and Evergreen Customer Identifier Funnel

Create launch events – multi-episode podcasts – to build pressure, generate excitement and pre-sell your products and services with special fast-action bonuses only offered to podcast listeners. Promote these episodes, not only on your podcast, but also to your podcast listener email, Facebook Messenger, and Facebook Group lists.

Also, use this as an opportunity to grow your lists. Let your audience know that to get special pricing and additional bonuses, they must sign up for your email list.

I also teach my clients to use, what I call, a Customer Identifier funnel. This funnel is attached to your email list Members Area funnel and its purpose is to immediately identify customers so you can put them in the correct follow-up sequences.

We use this type of funnel to let us know which customers are our most valuable, based on purchase frequency and transaction amount. In some cases, we reached out to them personally to raise them to higher-priced offers with fast-action bonuses. With a 78% opt-in rate on the frontend, this evergreen Customer Identifier Funnel became a game-changer for our business.

Moving Forward

Once again, from Russell Brunson, "Podcast listeners will also become your best buyers. This is proven. People who listen to podcasts are worth more money to you."

I truly believe you are only one podcast away from your next million-dollar business and if you follow the tips shared in this chapter, you will transform your business. My best piece of advice for you: Get started now.

A Gift For You

To help speed up your success, I put together a free training video giving you access to the podcast monetization strategy that only people who are enrolled in my more advanced programs usually have access to.

Go to www.evansputman.com/playbook right now to get started. Remember, you're just one podcast away!

About Evans Putman

Host of the Infinite Impact Radio podcast and creator of the Infinite Impact Method, Evans Putman shows high-level, purpose-driven entrepreneurs, coaches, podcasters, speakers and authors how to make more money with high-ticket strategies, create quantum leaps in their businesses, and disconnect revenue generation from time using a proven, four-step pathway based on his 20-plus years launching and growing online businesses. Step into your purpose, share your message, monetize your mission, and serve your tribe with the help of Evans and his Infinite Impact Method.

Website - www.EvansPutman.com

Facebook - www.facebook.com/EvansPutmanHQ @EvansPutmanHQ

Instagram - www.instagram.com/evansputman @evansputman

LinkedIn - www.linkedin.com/in/evansputman

CHAPTER FORTY-FIVE

YouTube: A Recipe For Success

By Lyndon Scott

With over one billion active monthly users, YouTube is the second most visited website on the planet, placing just ahead of Facebook.[32] Google.com sits in the number one spot, mainly due to its widely popular search engine, which is advantageous once you start publishing content on YouTube. I'll explain why later, but for now, let me tell you what led me to YouTube in the first place.

Typical Success Was Not Enough

I was always an entrepreneur at heart. I dabbled with various business ventures in my 20s but wasn't disciplined enough to make any of them work. I always ended up going back to my life as a corporate slave, trading my hours for money rather than fulfillment. On the surface, things were great. I was the envy of many.

I was earning six-figures and actively building my little property portfolio but I was miserable. Working every day to build someone else's empire was soul-destroying. Our time on this earth is short and I was desperate to create my own dream life including leaving a legacy for my kids.

I'd been playing with e-Commerce and online marketing for a while when, in 2018, I left my lucrative job as a sales manager for a billion-dollar property development firm. Just like that, I was unemployed.

People tell me it was a ballsy move, but I didn't see another option. Trading my time, my energy, and my happiness for a paycheck just didn't seem right. I couldn't continue that any longer.

At the time, I was really enjoying my e-Commerce business but, I wanted to broaden it into something a little more passive, more hands-off in the long-term,

I decided that affiliate marketing was right for me. I started pestering all the big names in the business, hoping they would give me the secret to their success.

As it turned out, there was no magical secret to quick affiliate marketing success. All I kept hearing was, "It takes time and a lot of hard work."

"Ridiculous!" I thought.

---

32 (n.d.).YouTube.com July 2019 Overview. Retrieved on July 19, 2019 from https://www.similarweb.com/website/youtube.com.

OK, so maybe it wasn't ridiculous. It was the truth, *kind of*. Creating the holy grail of online revenue, the almighty passive income, definitely required a heavy investment of time *and* hard work but being the determined (i.e., stubborn and impatient) entrepreneur that I am, I still figured there had to be some sort of shortcut to success.

It turned out that there *was* a shortcut, and I found it, but there was one problem: This shortcut was like a big, red, scary, pimple right on the tip of someone's nose. Everyone knows it's there, people even stare at it, but very few people are brave enough to talk about it or do anything with it.

Yep, it was YouTube.

Publishing content on YouTube had the most potential to catapult my business to the next level in the shortest time, but it meant getting in front of the camera. For some, this signals game over, but for me, it was this or corporate slavery. For me, it was a no-brainer.

What's So Great About YouTube?

Consumers are in love with video and they watch over five billion YouTube videos per day, with an average session time of 40 minutes.[33] With that retention rate, it's crazy not to be part of it. Over half of the people searching on YouTube are looking for How-To videos.[34] If you have the solution to their problem, they'll find you.

As a bonus, actively publishing good content on YouTube increases your chances of ranking organically in Google search results because Google gives priority to videos when returning search results.

Five Reasons To Use YouTube

1. **It's free to use and easy to start.**

All you need is a smartphone to record yourself and you're good to go. There is no reason that you can't start publishing today!

2. **It's easier to build trust.**

Trust is imperative for people to buy. And, trust is built when people see your face. You should still blog and email, but throwing a killer video into the mix will skyrocket your conversions.

3. **Only 10% of US businesses currently use YouTube.[35]**

That means the market isn't saturated; an estimated 40% of businesses use Facebook.[36]

4. **Multiple opportunities for passive monetization.**

---

[33] Smith, K. (2019, July 15th). *52 Fascinating and Incredible YouTube Statistics*. Retrieved on August 24, 2019 from https://www.brandwatch.com/blog/youtube-stats/.

[34] Chi, C. (n.d.). *51 YouTube Stats Every Marketer Should Know in 2019*. Retrieved on August 24, 2019 from https://blog.hubspot.com/marketing/youtube-stats.

[35] Ledgard, J. (n.d.). You Should Be On YouTube: Here's Why. Retrieved on August 24, 2019 from https://kick-offlabs.com/blog/you-should-be-on-youtube-heres-why/.

[36] Ledgard, J. (n.d.). You Should Be On YouTube: Here's Why. Retrieved from on August 24, 2019 https://kick-offlabs.com/blog/you-should-be-on-youtube-heres-why/.

You can use YouTube to sell your own or affiliate products, and you can also become a YouTube partner, which earns you revenue from ads that are placed on your videos.

5. **Videos are on YouTube forever.**

Once they are up and ranking, videos can pull in revenue for years without you doing a thing.

Setting up a channel on which to post your videos is the first step to getting started on YouTube and it's easy. There are many online tutorials (on YouTube and elsewhere) to help you do that. What I'm going to suggest here are ways to make your channel successful.

The Recipe For YouTube Channel Success

1. **Cook up some helpful content that people are searching for.**

As mentioned earlier, over 50% of people on YouTube want to learn something: skills, how-to-fix something, how to use an app, travel information, etc. So, How-To videos take the cake.

2. **Make sure there is demand for what you're serving.**

I use the YouTube research tool VidIQ to see what people are searching for. For example, *how to write a blog post* is searched by 2500 people every month.

3. **Create thumbnails that are a feast for the eyes.**

It's one thing to show up in the search menu, but people still need to choose what you're serving.

This is where professionally designed thumbnails can help. Research your topic and see what your competitors are doing. Create a captivating thumbnail with the right amount of words and imagery so it screams, "Click me!"

You can create thumbnails yourself on Canva or Photoshop, or you can get them done quite affordably on freelance websites such as Fiverr or UpWork.

4. **Make use of the utensils that YouTube gives you.**

These are all native YouTube features that are designed to help you create a better channel. I won't go into detail for each (YouTube them), but you should use this checklist of tools in your YouTube strategy.

- Channel Artwork
- Channel & Video Tags
- Video Watermarks
- Cards
- End Screens
- Video Description
- Pinned Comments

5. **Combine consistency with quality in equal measures and mix.**

The YouTube algorithm loves to see that you are consistently uploading content, but not at the risk of sacrificing quality.

The most important metric is *watch time*: The more captivating your videos, the longer viewers will watch, and the more YouTube will love you!

Remember how, as a YouTube Partner, you can get paid for other people's ads on your videos? This is why watch time is important.

6. Don't forget dessert.

Include a Call To Action in every video, but don't come across too salesy or you'll put people off.

If you focus on providing quality content that your viewers enjoy, they won't mind a subtle pitch every so often, but don't go overboard. In every video, ask them to subscribe and also offer them something more.

An example script might be:

> *Thanks for watching this and if you want to see more weekly videos with free tips, please hit the subscribe button and notification bell. And, if you're interested in learning more about blogging, I've left a link to my Beginner's Blogging Course in the description below.*

You could also include a question in your video that prompts viewers to leave a comment. Make sure you reply to every comment on your videos, whether you asked for it or not. Your viewers will appreciate the engagement and it builds trust, as well.

Moving Forward

This chapter only scratches the surface when it comes to leveraging YouTube for your business, but it's more than enough for you to get started. That's the main thing that holds people back, getting started.

I've had others tell me that adding YouTube to their content strategy stretches them too thin, but I disagree. If you've written a blog or a series of emails about a certain topic, you can use that as your script for a video and vice-versa. Re-purpose your content and publish it across multiple platforms.

My first recommendation for everyone is to GET STARTED. You don't have to be perfect; being *flawsome* is great! You don't need expensive equipment or lighting; if you're delivering consistent, valuable content you will have massive impact on your audience. It may take a little time, but once you start seeing results they will grow and your business will explode!

Moving forward, in addition to setting up your channel and starting to film and post regularly, your next step should be competitor research. Take a look at what the top YouTubers in your niche are doing and look for opportunities to improve your content. Knock them off the perch!

A Gift For You

You can grab a free copy of my in-depth YouTube Success Blueprint, plus a heap more information from onlinestartupschool.com.

About Lyndon Scott

Lyndon Scott is a full-time e-Commerce business owner, affiliate marketer, YouTube publisher, and self-proclaimed comedian.

Born and bred in the land down-under, he currently enjoys life as a full-time, unemployed online entrepreneur on the West Coast of Australia with his wife, two sons, and a disobedient dog.

Lyndon regularly publishes content about how to make money online across a variety of online platforms, including YouTube, of course!

CHAPTER FORTY-SIX

Subscription Boxes

By Jessica Principe

The traditional subscription box business model is a company to which consumers pay a subscription to receive a box of products within a specific niche, delivered at regular intervals (often monthly). Birchbox or BarkBox are well-known examples, but did you know that there are thousands of others?

The subscription industry is booming and continues to trend upward. This e-Commerce market has grown by 100% per year over the past five years, with revenues of more than $2.6 billion in 2016 up from $56 million in 2011.[37]

Starting a subscription box business has a low entry barrier, so almost anyone can start one. It is also a fun and lucrative business model that many choose as a way to earn income online. Whether it's a side hustle, extra money while also raising a family, or replacing a 9-to-5 job with a full-time business, a subscription box business is a great choice.

In The Beginning

I started my subscription business, All Girl Shave Club, in 2016. What started as a side gig, quickly exploded, allowing me to leave my full-time job, to work from home and to enjoy a flexible schedule while raising my two little boys.

I didn't have any experience in online business. I didn't have an audience to sell to (I wasn't a blogger or social media influencer) and there weren't a lot of resources available about starting a subscription box business. I had to learn a lot on my own. But I was able to reach six-figures in less than a year and experienced a lot of growth, opportunity, and excitement along the way. If I can do it, you can do it too.

Four Steps To Subscription Box Success

I've created a four-step system to help get you started. See the Gift mention at the end of this chapter for a free workbook that will guide you through each of the steps outlined here.

---

[37] Chen, T., Fenyo, K, Yang, S., & Zhang, J. (February 2018). Thinking Inside the Subscription Box: New Research on e-Commerce Consumers. Retrieved from https://www.mckinsey.com/industries/high-tech/our-insights/thinking-inside-the-subscription-box-new-research-on-ecommerce-consumers on August 30, 2019.

Step One: Ideation & Concept Development

You may already have an idea for a subscription. If you don't, I've created an activity in the workbook that will help you come up with your idea and develop your concept. Once you have your idea, ask yourself two important qualifying questions:

- Does this idea fit within a niche market?
- Does this idea serve a passionate audience?

During concept development, you can be creative about the type of experience you want to provide to your customers. Is there a specific movement behind your box? Is your subscription box about the replenishment of consumer goods or food? Is it more about discovering new products and brands? Maybe it will be a guided experience that is themed monthly. There are so many different directions you can take your idea. Identify what you want it to look like. The three biggest questions to answer for this step are:

- Who will the box serve?
- What problem will the box solve?
- What is my unique selling proposition?

Step Two: Prelaunch

This is the most important step; don't skimp on this one.

Running a strong prelaunch is the most important thing you can do to set yourself up for success at launch. I have seen people rush to launch their product or subscription box and all they hear are crickets. It flops. And they're scrambling, wondering why no one bought from them. This is because they didn't execute a strong (or any) prelaunch.

During prelaunch you test product-market fit by building an email list of interested buyers and nurturing them throughout your prelaunch to create an exceptional customer experience, raving fans, and instant buyers at launch time. I credit running a strong prelaunch for All Girl Shave Club as the number one reason I was able to acquire over 100 subscribers at launch, to consistently gain hundreds of new subscribers month-over-month and to hit six figures in less than a year.

Start by building a very simple, single landing page with the sole purpose of collecting email addresses. Your landing page should include compelling information about what you'll be offering as well as pictures and/or a video showcasing a mockup box. Visitors need to be able to see what they can expect to receive in a box, so create a sample box and show them.

The goal of prelaunch is to collect as many targeted email leads as possible. I like to use landing page platforms that have a built-in social share feature to encourage visitors to share the page and earn rewards. This will grow your email list organically.

You can plan on 5-10% of your list to convert to buying customers. Thus, if your goal is to launch with 100 subscribers, then you'll need 1,000-2,000 leads on your list. Some of my students' favorite ways to drive traffic to their landing pages include running collaborative giveaways, guest appearing on podcasts, and influencer marketing.

Once you start collecting email leads, it's important to nurture them. Email them consistently, I recommend once a week. Send them sneak peeks, behind the scenes images and stories, ask them for their feedback via surveys and share valuable content that will keep them engaged with you and excited for your launch.

The information they share with you is a gold mine of ideas for building your business. Their feedback will give you the exact information you need to shape your marketing message and to hone in on their demographics so that you can easily find more customers just like them when you launch. And, it gives you the exact information you need to create a customer experience that will exceed their expectations. Customer feedback is powerful. The most important result of a strong prelaunch is having a built-in audience of eager fans who are ready to buy when you go live.

During prelaunch, you'll also tackle Steps Three and Four.

Step Three: Sourcing Products

One of the top questions I get asked is, "Where do I get the products for my subscription box?"

Most often, products are purchased wholesale directly from brands at approximately 50% off retail. As you increase your customer base and are buying larger quantities of product you can negotiate lower wholesale rates, or cost-sharing, in exchange for marketing efforts or other perks that you can offer your vendors.

In my prelaunch course, I teach my students to create a Brand Kit to send to vendors when approaching them about featuring their products in an upcoming box. A Brand Kit is a short PDF document that introduces your company, shares demographics about your customers, and provides information to show why partnering with you would be a good opportunity for their brand/products.

Some easy ways to find brands and products to feature in your subscription box include searching on Etsy for inspiration and contacting vendors there to see if they offer wholesale or bulk pricing, searching hashtags for specific products on Instagram, contacting brands directly through their website (sales or marketing teams), or using wholesale sites like Faire, RangeMe, and Wholesale Central.

Step Four: Know Your Margins

It's important to make sure you have a firm grasp on your margins. Make sure you are considering all the expenses that go into building one box (such as the box itself, packing material, products, shipping, stickers, etc.).

The best way to track your margins is to create a simple spreadsheet listing all your single unit costs and then subtracting them from the total cost that your customer will be paying for their box. You should aim for a 35% profit margin or higher to be sustainable.

Moving Forward

I believe that starting a subscription box is doable for anyone who has the dream to do so. Launching a subscription box can help you bring in extra income for your family, provide an opportunity for you to build a community of like-minded people, or even quit your full-time job and work from home. It's possible, and I'm living proof.

A Gift For You

For a more detailed description of the four steps to launching a subscription box, download my free workbook and **Dream to Launch** checklist at workbook.JessicaPrincipe.com

About

Jessica Principe

Jessica Principe is the Founder and CEO of All Girl Shave Club. A self-taught product and e-Commerce entrepreneur, she embodies the quote, "She believed she could, so she did."

Armed with a passion for business, a creative idea, and Google she self-funded and launched All Girl Shave Club, a women's shaving subscription service and online boutique.

She is a relatable and engaging speaker, author and mentor, whose greatest passion is teaching others who want to get started in the subscription box and e-Commerce industry. She teaches through free resources on her blog (www.JessicaPrincipe.com) as well as through her online courses.

She lives in southern NH with her husband TJ and their two boys.

CHAPTER FORTY-SEVEN

A Six-Step Framework For Creating Live Events

By Justin Stephens

Live Events Change Lives.

Live events take people on a journey. The attendees are immersed in the content and understand it at a deeper level. Attendees are surrounded – either physically or metaphorically by other like-minded individuals who want to experience the event as it happens. There is no way to re-create the experience that someone will have at a live event.

Hosting a live event gives you a platform to influence your audience and clients. It gives you a way to show appreciation for and recognition of your clients. You can invite them to come and speak from the stage, present them with an award, or have them host a discussion or breakout session.

Live events are a great way to bring your ideal clients together. Your tribe wants to get together; to be with others who are striving towards a common goal. They want that community. This is one of the great benefits of live events, they create an atmosphere that facilitates relationships and networking.

The relationships built at events are not limited to the people attending the event. When you host an event, you also get to strengthen relationships with vendors and suppliers and sponsors. You get to create new relationships that could blossom into strategic partners and life-long friends.

At your event, you create and demonstrate the culture of your business for your clients and prospects. It is a great way for you to show your audience exactly what it means to be a part of your community.

There is also no better way than an event to raise your clients from one level in your business to the next level. Events create so much energy and excitement, that your clients naturally want to ascend through your offerings. They want to get to that next level, whether it is an additional product or service, or maybe a coaching program. Events are the best place to sell because you get to immerse your clients in an experience and show them how you will serve them at a higher level.

Most people don't try and create an event because they don't know where to start and feel like it is too difficult. In this chapter, we are going to look at the framework for creating profitable and life-changing events.

Framework For Planning A Live Event

1. **The Avatar**

Determine your audience by creating an Avatar of your ideal attendee. You will build everything for your event based on your Avatar. There are many free resources to help you build an Avatar, which involves describing your ideal customer's demographics, job, family, attitude, needs, frustrations, experience, etc.

The most important thing to determine in this stage is the number one pain point for your ideal attendee. What is the biggest issue that they are trying to overcome in their business or life right now that you are going to help them with?

2. **The Offer**

Based on your Avatar, identify what you are going to offer during your event. What product, service, program, or result are you going to offer them so you can help them at a higher level. We look at the offer as the destination to which you are taking all your attendees during the event. The offer needs to be based on the issues that your prospects are facing; the products and services should solve those pain points.

3. **The Journey Within Your Event**

Once you have determined the offer that you are going to make at your event, you need to imagine the journey that your participants will take. Create a theme or story that can be used throughout the sessions. Build the journey based on their current situation, their current fears and struggles, and what they are trying to overcome. This journey determines the design of your event, the topics presented at the event, and even who you ask to speak.

Your entire event should be designed to make saying yes to attending easy. You need to make sure that you are pricing your offer correctly based on the audience and the result that it will get for your audience.

4. **The Journey To Your Event**

Now that you know the journey you will take them on during your event, it is time to get the right people to go to your event. This is an important part of putting on an event. If you fill the room with the wrong people, you will have very few sales in the end. You need to be sure you are identifying and targeting the right people.

Use your Avatar to determine how these people look for solutions and be sure to contact them there. Remember that the relationship you have with your audience will influence how you market your event. If you are putting on an event for current clients – people who already know, like, and trust you – you can send them straight to an event page. If you are trying to drive a cold audience to your event, it is much better to build the relationship first, then introduce the idea of the event after you have established some trust and rapport. Use lead magnets or short videos (even live ones!) to familiarize them with who you are and what you do before driving them to your event.

5. **Closing The Event**

How you close at your event matters. You owe it to your audience to offer a way to work with them at a higher level. You need to end on a positive, energizing, exciting note that encourages them to take your offer right away before they leave the event. They must see the value in your offer and want to take advantage of it right away.

6. **Re-purposing the Content**

Once the event has happened, don't think that it is all over! The end is only the beginning. At every single event, you create tons of documents, marketing materials, and resources that you can use in the future. Having a plan and strategy in place before your event on how you are going to use the resources after the event will let you focus on creating all of the resources as you plan, so you can maximize the investment without redoing documentation or materials.

Moving Forward

There are many ways that you can create a profitable and life-changing event. This framework has been used to create multiple events that have sold out and been wildly profitable.

If your mission is to go out and make an impact on the world, then you need to look at how you can use live events to push that mission forward faster. Events are a powerful tools that have been used for many years, and live events are evolving to include technology that allows our need for human interaction and engagement found at traditional live events to be addressed.

The most successful businesses out there use events to connect with their tribe and drive results. Events are used by all sorts of companies to create a compelling experience to wow their participants and create life-long fans. It's time for you to plan your event for your tribe.

A Gift For You

If you want to know more about running a live event, go to www.justindcstephens.com

About Justin Stephens

Just started his sales career at 13, when he went through the Sandler Training system. From then on, he was in love with helping people decide what they needed to do to improve their lives.

After nine years running the Sandler franchise in Boise, he sold his stake in the company to go out and start his own business in November 2018. The path on this new adventure was paved by the life-changing power of live events.

That is why he now focuses on helping business owners learn how to put on their own profitable and life-changing events. His mission is to connect the everyone in the world with the right live event to change their life!

CHAPTER FORTY-EIGHT

Ad Scaling Secrets

By Dan Ryder

These days, it seems like there's always a new advertising guru offering you their blueprint to millions in sales from running ads on networks like Facebook and YouTube. It's because buying media (i.e., running ads) has never been as competitive as it is now. Although this drives up the costs of advertising, it's not what will prevent you from scaling profitably. I'm going to give you the key to scaling your ads missed by 99.9% of your competitors and 99.9% of all the ad guru courses!

This chapter is *not* about writing more persuasive copy or designing killer videos for your ad creative. It is definitely *not* about converting more sales through your website or funnel. However, the secrets I'm going to share with you *will* help you get exponentially more sales than you could do otherwise.

In The Beginning

After a ten-year career in healthcare, and a long-time love of marketing, I made the jump into being an internet entrepreneur in 2014. During the last three years, I've become especially good at getting paid traffic to offers. After managing millions of dollars of ad spend across a variety of ad accounts with multiple six-figure monthly ad budgets for clients through my advertising agency , I've learned a lot about how to position ad campaigns for mega-success when scaling.

Advertisement Scaling

There are two main problems that stop most advertisers from scaling. The first is that the Cost-Per-Acquisition (CP) for a sale ends up being too high. It's hard to sell something for $10 if it costs you $20, right? Pretty obvious. The second problem arises when the advertiser can't figure out exactly from which ads the sales are coming.

Imagine that you've got a few ads running to your offer and it looks like they're all producing sales. Excited, you decide to spend more and eagerly anticipate cashing in big. Suddenly, the sky starts to fall! The same ads that were kicking butt earlier are now tanking! Your sales trickle down, your CPA goes through the roof, and – to stop the onslaught – you shut all the ads down and wonder, "How the heck did that happen?"

The Secret About Ad Platform Statistics

I have experienced the exact scenario described above running ads for my own offers as well as my clients; scratching my head in disbelief when I had to start over. I know how frustrating and heartbreaking it can be to pull the plug immediately after you start winning. I know too well that devastating feeling of failing and losing money on ad campaigns I thought were going to be winners.

The good news is that after overseeing millions of dollars' worth of ads running both my own offers and offers for my clients, I finally figured out the key scaling factor I was missing. Happily it has nothing to do with ad quality, which means if you are struggling to scale ads that were initially bringing in sales, your ad quality isn't at fault!

The truth is – even with advances in artificial intelligence algorithms used by the major ad networks – their conversion tracking can be wildly inaccurate. In other words, the measurements you are looking at to judge ad success are not correct!

This probably sounds dumbfounding but even with Facebook's all powerful pixel and YouTube/Google having their own *Eye of Sauron* (geeky Lord Of The Rings reference) watching every person online, , from my experience, their ad campaign conversion tracking can be off by 10%, or more, at any given time. . That means, they may report a higher or lower conversion rate than the actual numbers.

To complicate things, when you have multiple campaigns running, many times the wrong ads are given credit for a conversion. The ad network tells you a campaign converting like wildfire when, in reality, it's a complete dud.

Imagine reviewing your results from several ads that have been running a few days to see seven conversions in one campaign when the number was actually ten and, in another campaign, you see several conversions being reported but those buyers actually came from another campaign altogether!

Each day, that is the reality of your ad account reports. From my experience, using that inaccurate data to make scaling decisions has the potential to compound losses on top of each other because you're at risk of misappropriating your ad budget.

Think of your ad budget and imagine you spent 10% more on campaigns that should've been cut, while simultaneously not spending 20% more on campaigns that were bringing you a great return. In this hypothetical scenario one thing is clear, you cannot make scaling decisions with a 30% error rate![38] You cannot sustain this level of wasted ad spend on failed ad campaigns as competition becomes more and more fierce

Don't get me wrong. Facebook, Google, and other ad networks aren't trying to mislead you. They actually want you to have accurate results so you spend more money with them. The truth is it's not their fault, either.

Ad Network Tracking Methods

Here's how most of us think conversions occur and get tracked:

[38] Personal anecdote from experience managing a million+ in advertising dollars

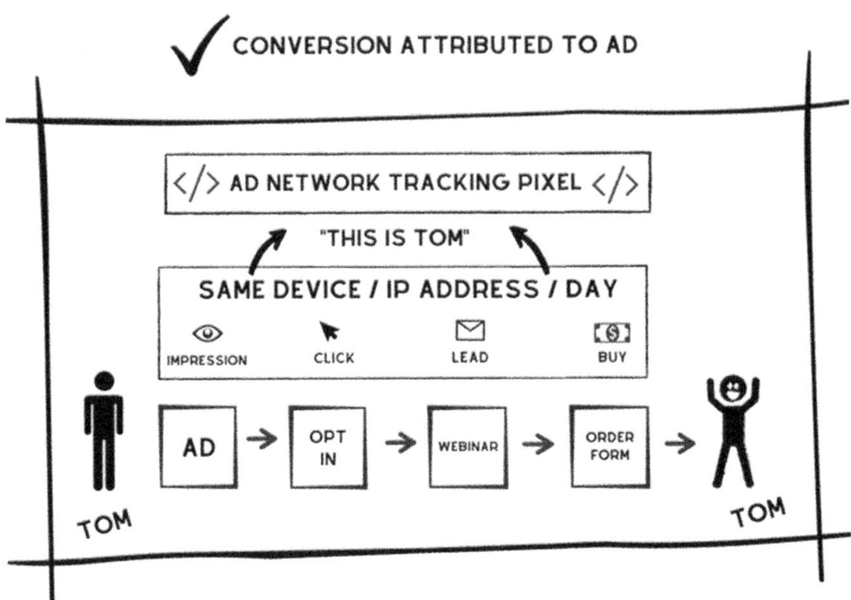

But, here is what may actually happen:

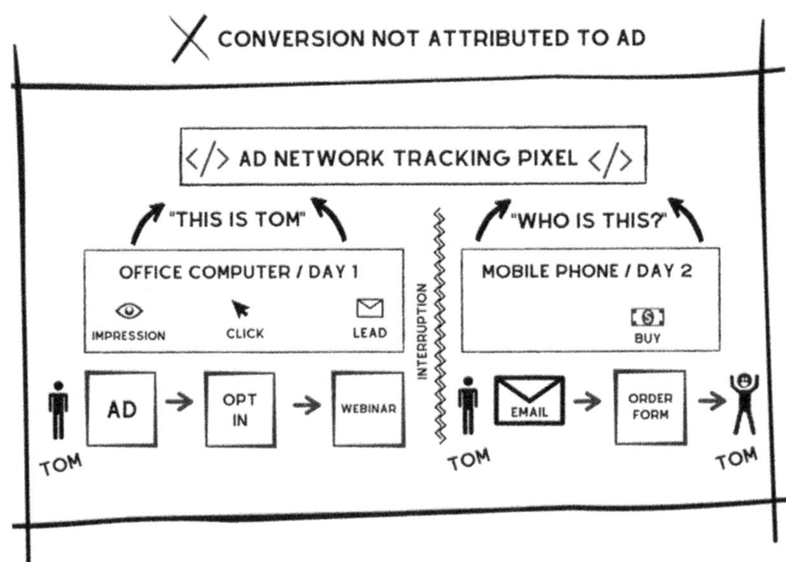

The unpredictable nature of peoples buying habits makes tracking much more difficult than it may seem.

You need some very in-depth and complicated tracking to catch people days after the first click and after multiple device/IP changes. You may say, well track them by their email address, but what if people subscribe with one email and then, a day later, come back and buy with a different email address?

Unfortunately, the ad networks' tracking capabilities fail with that and similar scenarios. They simply don't have all the data points to track the very complicated digital behaviors we all make every day online.

Even a simple example (see above images), like someone subscribing to watch a webinar, but then buying the next day (even with the same email address) can be too tricky for ad networks to track.

In addition to variable buyer behaviour and technical difficulties, user data privacy demands, that includes both regulatory constraints like the General Data Protection Regulation (GDPR) out of the European Union and other digital and personal privacy laws, make tracking difficult. And, popular web browsers waging an all-out pixel/cookie war continues to block the ability of ad networks to track conversions.

So, how do we fix this? What is the secret key to scaling ads profitably?

What To Do: True Lossless Tracking

The battle of advertising online to your target market rages on and the stakes have been raised. You need to come equipped or your business will die (dramatic but true). But, when you have true lossless tracking it's like carrying a bazooka to a gun fight.

Hopefully, by now, you have already heard the term Lifetime Customer Value (LTV). It's a calculation of all your revenue divided by your total number of customers to date, revealing the average value of a single customer to your business. For example, if your business had a total of five customers who spent $10, $25, $100, $50, and $5 respectively, the LTV of a customer to your business would be $38.

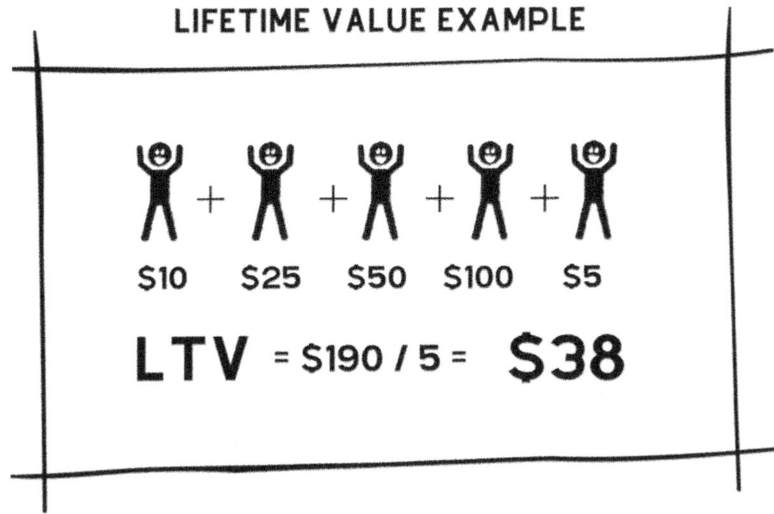

As I mentioned, you need to connect all the dots to have accurate reports. Flawless LTV tracking of your customers (through inclusion of LTV) allows you to know their true value to your business.

Your LTV is powerful because it allows you to raise your CPA threshold to acquire a customer that might result in a loss on Day 1 but put you in profit on Day 7 and beyond. This offers you the opportunity to scale harder and faster by outbidding and, therefore, outgunning your competitors (who aren't willing to spend as much as you) in the ad networks.

As awesome as that is, imagine you had the ability to track and attribute LTV down to the ad level. This would mean that you could find the origin of any customer down to the very ad they clicked, even if the sale occurs months or years after the first click. It also would allow you to see the true long-term ROI on every ad you run which means you can confidently spend as much as possible on your winning ads (regardless of what the ad network reports say). Pretty awesome, right?

Setting Up True Lossless Tracking

Setting up tree lossless tracking is simple: Connect the dots.

You need a tracking system with multiple touch points that allows you to track your leads and customers beyond their IP, cookies, or email addresses. A system that plugs into your ad account to uniquely profile your acquired contacts with ad level tags as they enter your business. A system that is also plugged into your checkout system and payment processor to make sure that no sale slips past without being tracked.

Here's a visual concept:

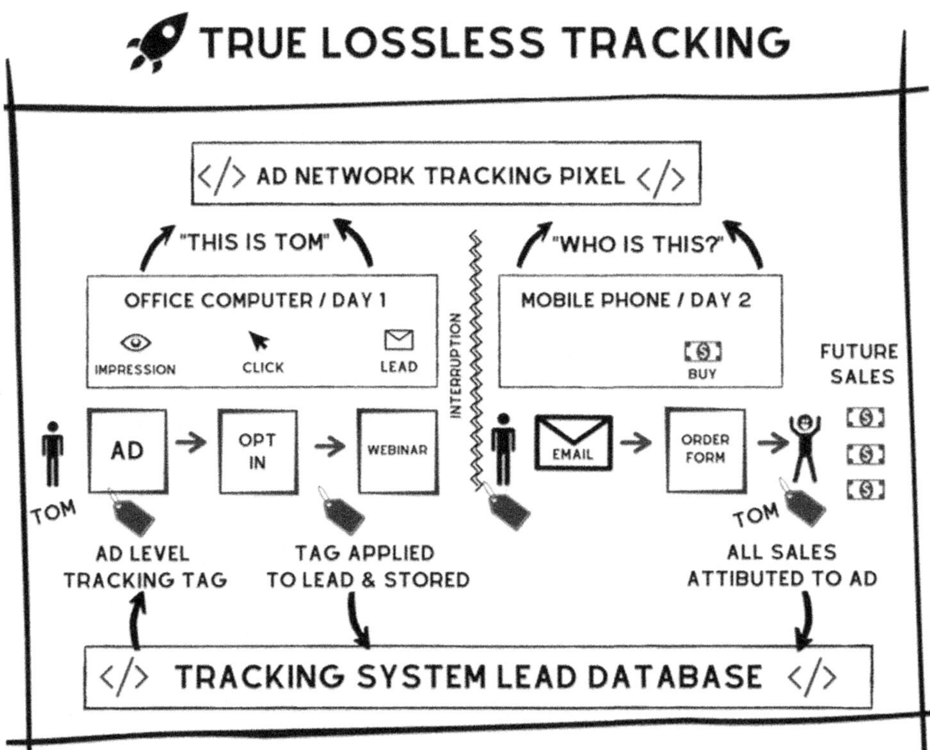

This set-up allows you to connect your ads to any sale, anytime, anywhere. It allows you to calculate the actual cash flow of your business effortlessly, which allows you to know beyond a shadow of a doubt your true LTV numbers without having to guess or assume. The result is true lossless tracking. It's the secret to scaling your ads for maximum profitability and obliterating your competition.

The BEST PART is that is not as complicated as you might think. In fact, it is push-button simple to implement.

Moving Forward

Following LTV using true lossless tracking is the answer to inaccurate ad network reports. It's the only way to get an accurate understanding of which ads are working and which are not and, thus, is the greatest way to scale your advertising to get great returns. When you're ready to get more out of your advertising (or save a ton of money), use true lossless tracking to make decisions easier.

A Gift For You

I'll make it easy for you. Get my fast and easy true tracking set-up guide (plus bonus ad scaling hacks) by visiting https://book.danryder.me/chapterbonus

Apply to see if you qualify to work directly with Dan's agency.

Visit: MediaMarketerPro.com

Facebook: www.facebook.com/DanRyderPublicPage/

LinkedIn: www.linkedin.com/in/danjryder

About Dan Ryder

Dan Ryder is a seasoned digital marketer and coach, currently making his mark on the internet as founder of Media Marketer Pro.

Dan specializes in developing results-driven advertising strategies for businesses that focus on business growth instead of "vanity metrics" that don't add to the bottom line. His clients have seen a 4X customer growth while achieving over a 350% increase in actual revenue.

Dan would be remiss not to recognize the loving support from his wife Eva without whose sacrifice and encouragement the transition away from a 10-year career in healthcare to pursue a passion for marketing wouldn't have been possible. They live in North Carolina with their kids, AJ and Gabby. They have two fur babies, a dog, Blue, and cat, Aidan.

CHAPTER FORTY-NINE

Modern Multi-Level Marketing Tactics

By Coulton Woods

"Network Marketing is the big wave of the future. It's taking the place of franchising, which now requires too much capital for the average person."
~Jim Rhon

Network or Multi-Level Marketing (MLM) is s a system for selling goods or services through a network of distributors.[39] In general, a company hires distributors to both sell their product(s) and to hire other distributors to sell the product(s). Distributors make money for both sales and hiring new distributors. Despite the promise of making as much money as you want for a small investment, many find making money through MLMs difficult because the costs associated with selling the product(s) often eclipse any profit that distributors make.

Like many people, I thought that Network Marketing was a total scam. I've learned some things over the past few years that have changed my opinion about it. I've discovered the model that the top earners are secretly using to make it big. The majority of top MLMers are telling those who follow them to do something different than they are doing themselves.

I am going to reveal why what leaders are teaching is completely wrong and show you what they are actually doing and how you can do the same thing.

In The Beginning

The first time I joined an MLM was through a colleague. He told me about a business he'd bought into and how I could do the same. I got really excited about the opportunity since I was looking for an easy way to get into business.

---

[39] Ward, Susan. 2019 May 19. *Multi-Level Marketing (MLM Meaning): Multilevel Marketing is a Huge Business*. Retrieved on August 22, 2019 from https://www.thebalancesmb.com/multilevel-marketing-mlm-2947187

I remember having a hard time sleeping at night because I couldn't stop my brain from thinking through all the ways I could be successful with it. I kept thinking of all the people I could sign up or sell the product to. I was going to make millions. Or, at least, that's what I thought.

I was so excited and convinced of success that I signed up with money I didn't have.

I remember the day like it was yesterday: I didn't know how I was going to get the money together to join the MLM. After running through all of my options, I realized the only way it was going to happen fast enough was if my dad would loan me the money.

I grew up in a home in which asking for money to pay for something that wasn't a necessity wasn't tolerated. That phone call scared me to death. I thought for sure my dad was going to teach me a lesson by refusing to give me the money and insisting on telling me why he thought it was a bad idea. You can imagine my surprise when he said yes.

I honestly think now that he wanted to teach me a different lesson than I expected. The lesson about buying into an MLM plan and learning the hard way that it wouldn't work for me. I didn't make anything on that first MLM venture, but I didn't learn my lesson either. And, thank goodness I didn't because I wouldn't be where I am today if I had given up after my first failure.

But, let's get back to joining my first MLM.

I had my money to buy in and I was super excited and got to work. I did exactly what my upline taught me. I reached out to those I knew and tried selling my friends and family what I thought they could use. I spent a ton of time communicating and trying to sell them my products, but it never seemed to make sense for them, so they didn't buy. I think I signed up three people in my downline and didn't sell a single product and I was out of friends and family to talk to. The only other advice I got from my upline was to talk to strangers about the opportunity. *Awkward.*

Training Is Key

Finding an MLM plan that focuses on training those who join so they too can be successful is key. If the MLM doesn't focus on helping you be successful, stay far away from it.

I wish I had looked into that before I joined my first MLM program, but I learned it eventually and now I'm in an MLM venture that not only cares about the product they sell but also about the people who are under them. The best part about it is we are trained on how to use a *Sales Funnel* and are also expected to help others use sales funnels.

Sales Funnels

A sales funnel is the golden goose of websites and leads your prospects through the exact sales process you want them to follow, instead of traditional websites that can be linked into anywhere and everywhere on the site but, it seems, the page you want them to see.

How MLM Leaders Use Sales Funnels

Websites provide a lot of content to the world and those in MLM are taking advantage of that by directing prospects to a web page where we offer them access to more content that is valuable to them in exchange for their email address.

Once we have their email, the next page they see offers them a Self-Liquidating Offer (SLO).

An SLO is a free offer that leads to a paid offer that generates enough sales to recuperate the cost of the entire promotional campaign. In other words, we drive ads to an attractive free offer (product or information or another enticement), collect prospects' emails, then sell them a fairly inexpensive product at a high margin to cover the costs of the whole promotion (including the free offer that initially drew the prospects in).

It is also possible to skip the free offer and send them straight to a fairly inexpensive product; the most profitable one I currently use sells for $57.

Think of the power of this: If we can spend $100 on ads and make $100 back on those ads, we can continue to run the ads over and over again without losing any money. Essentially, we are getting leads for free.

We tell the leads to how to join our team if they want to and that's where the money is! You can consistently get leads for free and be pitching people into MLM every day.

How it works:

You're probably seeing how this can work for you, too. It's simple, but it does take work to do. Once you create one piece of successful content it goes to work for you 24/7 and can be seen by thousands of people at the same time. It's kind of like recording yourself while pitching to one friend and then having that recording pitch people you don't even know all day, every day.

Moving Forward

If you like what you've learned in this chapter – applying sales funnels to MLM systems – and want to use it and teach it to your downline (or use funnels to recruit), go for it!

Be ready to work hard but, in return, you'll get a system of income that will support the life you want to lead.

A Gift For You

To learn more, go to *ModernMLMTactics.com/AirFryerExclusive* and get access to a special bonus I put together for buyers of *The Entrepreneurs' Playbook.*

Here's what you're gonna get:

- The audio version of this chapter (extended cut)... ($37 Value)
- FREE SLO (Self-Liquidating Offer) Sales Funnel... ($297 Value)
- FREE Examples of other SLO Products... ($197 Value)
- FREE videos on different ways you can produce high-quality content... ($97 Value)
- FREE video course on how you can do this too... ($97 Value)

Total Value: $725

Exclusive Price: $37*

* I wanted to make it completely free, but I couldn't stop adding extra bonuses, so I decided to only charge you for the audio version of this chapter and give you the rest for FREE!

About Coulton Woods

Coulton's goal in life is to help people get past their own roadblocks and just get started!

He used to think he was not good enough to do great things. He just about flunked out of high school and never dreamed of being able to become much more than just another guy.

It wasn't until he realized that other people, who were less educated than him, had done some amazing things that he started to believe he could too.

Coulton's first entrepreneur adventure was repairing and reselling phones and tablets on eBay; he was shocked when sale notifications started rolling in. Over the next couple of years, he fixed hundreds of phones and tablets.

His business was so successful, he opened a brick-and-mortar location and had a team of employees working with him.

Now, Coulton works with Stephen Larsen (stephenjlarsen.com) and has transitioned to an online sales business model where he makes way more money in a month than he ever did with his brick-and-mortar. And, he doesn't have to fix a single phone....

CHAPTER FIFTY

Facebook Engagement

By Kevin Steven Quinn

If you read the Preface to this book, you know that this book evolved out of a series of Facebook Live events I ran regularly on Fridays while I was cooking dinner in my air fryer. It was the engagement that those Live events generated that made things happen and building a following, an engaged following, turned into a digital marketing book covering many niches on how to do business online.

In The Beginning

Let's go back a few years to the eight-year-old version of me. The Kevin selling sweet corn out of the back of a farmer's truck to people driving by. I learned then how to sell. How to connect. How to get people to purchase two dozen ears of corn instead of the single dozen they stopped to buy. It's all about engaging with them. Conversations. Being creative. This was my foundational launch into connecting and selling.

At twelve years old, I started my first paper route. Part of having a paper route includes having to sell subscriptions to people on your paper route who were not already subscribers.

I was not afraid of hearing the word no. I've never been afraid to hear no. It's not, "No." It's, "Not now." I'd eventually get them to subscribe using persistence and hunger.

I used to trade a newspaper with the milkman every morning. For a prospective customer, I'd drop off the chocolate milk I just traded and a free newspaper that morning. I'd check back with them that night to see if they wanted to try a free subscription. This worked often.

I've carried this attitude with me for years. Fearless; totally not worried about being told no. And, that parlayed its way into today's digital space for me.

The Facebook Algorithm

Since 2009, Facebook has used an algorithm to provide a new sorting order during that year that, rather than displaying news items in reverse chronological order as it had been to that point, sorted newsfeed items based on each post's popularity.[40] Now, everything anyone does on Facebook is tracked in a so that Facebook personalize ads and delivery of content.

---

[40] Cooper, P. (January 27, 2020). *How the Facebook Algorithm Works in 2020 and How To Make It Work For You*. Retrieved on July 31, 2020 from https://blog.hootsuite.com/facebook-algorithm/

The algorithm monitors scores of things, chewing through data and delivering your content out to the audience that follows you. Whether that's content from your personal Facebook page or in a Facebook group, you can manipulate the system and trend higher in the newsfeeds.

I've been doing this for years, manipulating the Facebook algorithm. Lots of people tell me I am always at the top of their newsfeed. I'm the first name they see when they log into Facebook or when they log into specific Facebook groups. This is intentional.

Take the Click Funnels Facebook group, for example: 250,000 members and I trend number one in the Facebook algorithm for engagement in that group. Something I've worked hard to establish.

Reaching Out To And Connecting With Influencers

Did you know that connecting with or engaging with influencers and having them engage with you publicly on Facebook improves your credibility with the Facebook algorithm?

Engagement with influencers has a massive ripple effect on your audience because that influencer's audience sees your post or your video. This leads to massive engagement for you.

I've had Gary Vaynerchuk respond to a post in Gary's Facebook group. That engagement with a massive influencer created the ripple effect for that was huge. Gary's followers were notified that he responded on my post in his group and they all wanted to see that. From there, because he interacted with me, I gain credibility and some of his audience started following me. I've been seen and this creates social proof for me. The Facebook algorithm recognizes my credibiity as well and rewards me. My social proof with Gary's audience, and with Facebook itself, grew.

How To Trend Number One In Facebook Newsfeeds

Looking to increase your Facebook engagement in groups or on your personal page? Here are some tips to heat up that algorithm in your favor.

- Post controversial topics. These babies get hot quickly. I know from experience.
- Post questions and ask for responses/feedback
- Post interactive games, offer rewards
- Have great posts from friends or fans? Share it.
- Photos/images with quotes. Verify the quotes, though.
- Request likes during Lives, "Hit the like/heart button below if you agree/disagree."
- Ask for advice,"Hey ClickFunnels, how do I ...?"
- Post at high traffic times on both Facebook and Instagram.
- Be funny! Humor works amazingly well.
- Post on the weekends when people aren't at work and will see your posts.
- Go Live often.
- Publish every day.
- Teach. Provide value. Help people in groups.
- People follow you for reasons: Feed into why they followed you

- Be concise. Most people are using Facebook mobile. Reading pages of content from a phone screen doesn't happen.
- Provide quality posts and use videos.
- Respond to people's questions/comments.In other words, ENGAGE!
- Check your group Facebook Insights: zee where your fans are from, post during their high traffic time zones.
- Turn your personal Facebook page into a sales funnel. As you engage, people will want to know more about you: Drive them somewhere.
- Use Facebook Stories. Facebook Stories run at the top of everyone's feed and are seen first.
- Include Calls to Action, they help drive engagement.
- Get social media verified. That blue checkmark is everything.
- Be NICE. I know, controversy builds engagement, but sometimes controversy can hurt your brand.

Moving Forward

Buy an air fryer? Seriously. OK, maybe not seriously. But, find a way to create something unique to you that you do publicly on your Facebook page. Go Live and talk regularly about whatever amazing tool or subject you know, this will build a following of people who know, like, and trust you. They engage with you and your content. Their engagement introduces you to their Facebook audience.

When I started publishing on Facebook with Lives and engaging in groups, I had about 1,800 Facebook friends. Within six months, I had 5,000 Facebook friends and thousands of followers. That's the power of publishing and engaging on social media.

Mix up your posts. Motivational. Educational. Make the pitch (talk about what you do). Entertain. Create video and content around that model of motivating, educating, making a pitch, and entertaining. Balance your posts to keep it fresh and engaging.

There's a fine art to dominating the Facebook algorithm. It requires you to be diligent, publish often, and create engagement. Connect with your audience. You can totally do this, step outside your comfort zone and grab that opportunity to build your audience.

It's so easy, even I could do it. You've totally got this.

A Gift For You

Get my free mini-course on the power of connecting. Heck, those connections brought together 70 authors for this book. The 5 people closest to you and the ripple effect on how those connections can change your business, are included in this course. www.kevinstevenquinn.com

About Kevin Steven Quinn

Kevin spent 25 years in the corporate space running sales for large corporations in the technology sector. He managed up to 75 people on his sales teams and taught them the sales techniques that he learned as an 8-year-old selling corn out of the back of a farmer's truck. Sales is 100% about connecting with your audience and Kevin mastered that.

- 25 Years VP of Sales Management
- Launched Multiple Tech Startups in software and SaaS sector
- Has pitched over 100 investment groups
- Kevin and his teams have closed over $2 billion in sales revenue over his career
- Connector of people
- Marine Corps Veteran
- Author & Business Coach
- Brand influencer
- Hemp Farm & CBD owner

Connect with Kevin here: www.kevinstevenquinn.com

CHAPTER FIFTY-ONE

Facebook Ads

By Jessica Walman

Facebook advertising – if done correctly – can scale businesses from nothing to over seven-figures in revenues. It is one of the leading paid advertising platforms.[41]

My digital marketing agency currently uses Facebook advertising for our six- and seven-figure clients to broadcast their message to the world, sell their programs and/or services, and increase their revenues. We've had clients spend $9,000 and make $170,000 in a matter of weeks and other clients who've gained over 30,000 leads for less than $2 while continuously selling monthly memberships daily.

Getting Started

My love for marketing and Facebook ads started when I was pregnant with my first child in 2009. I decided I wanted to be home more with my son, so I had to start my own business.

I indulged in learning everything I could about marketing while still in my job at the time: online research, tutorials, videos, and more. I taught myself Google paid ads, SEO, affiliate marketing, and build-out Wordpress sites from scratch.

It was in January 2015 that I started dabbling in Facebook advertising to sell an affiliate product. In June 2015, I finished a business coaching program and – because she knew I had experience – the coach asked if I would run her Facebook advertising. I agreed, made her over $25,000 in just a few weeks, and – from that success – continued getting clients. I quit my full-time job and focused on my agency.

Why Facebook Ads?

Facebook advertising can be powerful; it provides a massive traffic stream to your paid offers. If you have a converting offer (which you can test organically or with paid ads) then Facebook ads can take pretty much anyone from a nobody to a go-to expert in their niche *fast*. Here's why:

1. **Target Audience**

Most of your ideal clients are already using Facebook, which means you're able to target your exact audience. Facebook is known for its extremely tight targeting so you're able to put the right offer

[41] Cherry, Baylor. January 22, 2019. Paid Social Media: Which Platform Should You Choose? Retrieved on August 12, 2019 from https://www.bluleadz.com/blog/paid-social-media-which-platform-should-you-use-1

and message in front of the right audience at the right time. The trust of that audience makes you an expert in your niche.

2. **Brand Awareness**

Facebook ads will amplify the reach of your content to all the world. This allows you to create an audience that knows your content and is interested in it. From there, you can retarget and promote to them directly. This is huge! You can increase your following from just a few to thousands. That larger following makes you an expert in your niche.

3. **Lead Generation**

Facebook ads allow you to quickly build an email list of subscribers interested in your content so that you can email market to them and sell your offers. With the right budget and strategy, you can have a list of thousands in a matter of weeks. Paid advertising platforms can change unexpectedly at any time, so having your email list is vital to the health and longevity of your business. Facebook makes this easy to do.

4. **Consumption**

With all the noise on the Internet, Facebook allows you to use retargeting to ensure the content you publish gets in front of your ideal clients, allowing them to consume the content and engage with it regularly. This, in turn, increases your expertise and credibility. Facebook makes it easy for your fans to consume your content. The more people consume your content – as long as it's good content – the stronger your influence and credibility become.

5. **Revenue**

At the end of the day, the most important piece of your business is profitability. You can't continue to change or impact the world or even run a business if you don't make a profit. Facebook has one of the highest returns on investments (ROI) out there. It's shocking how quickly you can get a ROI with a single paid Facebook ad. That financial success allows you to continue to impact lives and grow your business to the next level.

The 5C Grow And Scale Method

If you're ready to be not only a success in business but also a recognized expert, then I can help. I have a strategy I call *The 5C Grow & Scale Method* that I use with every client. This method has helped some of our clients enroll thousands of students into their programs, obtain hundreds of thousands of subscribers to their mail lists and multiply their investments, sometime 20-times.

It may sound simple, but please trust me when I say, most people aren't doing all of these and/or they aren't doing them correctly or consistently, and each needs to be done, done correctly, and done consistently for success.

Phase One1: Connect

In this phase, you build an audience through brand awareness campaigns. These campaigns promote relevant content without a Call to Action (CTA) to a cold audience. This is pure content only, no pitching of any kind. This starts building trust and credibility, gets your brand in front of people interested in what you have to say, and creates an audience to start retargeting. Use blog posts, podcasts, Facebook Lives, pre-recorded videos, long-form posts, and/or other publishing in this phase.

Phase Two: Convert

In this phase, you'll be generating high-quality leads by converting those interested in your offering into subscribers. Building an email list is incredibly important to the longevity of your business: in exchange for an email address, you give people useful, relevant, or interesting content. This, in turn, improves your trustworthiness and expert status with them. Plus, the subscriber list allows you to market via email as well as on Facebook, increasing advertising reach without increasing costs and, thus, increasing profitability.

Phase Three: Consume

This is the phase where content in Facebook Ads is critical. The goal is to make it insanely easy for your new subscribers to consume and engage with your content via Facebook ads. Converting interested individuals into new email subscribers is easy, turning them into loyal customers who buy is where most people fail.

With the open rates on emails increasingly dropping, converting subscribers to customers using direct email offers is becoming more challenging even though they are wanting what you're offering. In this phase, you must use relevant content, similar to what you published in the *Connect* phase, but use it in paid advertising. The content can be a bit longer because the goal is to develop deeper trust with your new prospects.

Phase Four: Close

Now that you've turned your new subscribers into loyal followers, it's time to make the sale. You've showcased your expertise, gained their trust, and are making an impact in their lives. Now's the time to create a bigger impact by selling your offering to them. This is done using calculated retargeting strategies to get your offer in front of your extremely warm audience. These types of ads can have a small budget but reap a massive ROI. That's why missing this phase could cost you tens of thousands in revenue and profit.

This is also the phase in which you'll send followers to your sales vehicle: a webinar, a challenge, a book, a video series, etc. The sales vehicle must provide massive value to make followers want to buy.

Phase Five: Continuity

This is the phase most people forget. They think they've won since they obtained a new subscriber and pitched their offer. The problem is, some of those new leads won't purchase. It always happens since only a small percentage will purchase up-front (within the first 30 days), the rest will need more nurturing to build up trust.

In this phase you create a continuity nurture campaign that you'll replenish daily and/or weekly with new relevant content sent to your warm leads, excluding purchasers, to continue to increase your trustworthiness and expert status. This phase is key to creating momentum in a business, key to turning subscribers in January to buyers in April. Plus, this is a pretty low-cost campaign with a pretty big reward.

The 5C Grow & Scale Method can be customized and changed based on your offer, funnel, niche, and initial results. Start by following the basic process, as above, and you'll be in the best shape possible to produce profit-generating Facebook ad campaigns.

I know this because Facebook ads have improved both my and my clients' businesses. I remember starting my first Facebook ad campaign for my agency. It was a simple PDF downloadable lead magnet with a tripwire on the thank you page. I then retargeted those new leads to an ad to book a call with my agency. Within the first week of starting this funnel, it was profitable and booking me client calls. I went straight to a beach vacation the day after I put the ad campaign live. That same funnel ran for over 2.5 years building up my agency clientele. Before that campaign, it was long days of organic posting and networking with dozens of people at a time in hopes of booking a couple of calls a week.

Moving Forward

Your next step is to get started! Until you get started, you won't know if it works. Start small, but make sure you cover all the phases to increase effectiveness and return.

Testing your funnel organically is a safe bet before putting ad spend behind it. However, if you're fired up to get started now, start with a minimum $20–a-day budget, focus on Phases One to Phase Three first, then once you've built up a small warm audience you can move to Phase Four and start pitching your offer.

Give, give, give, and then – don't ask for anything – offer an opportunity to serve them and change their lives.

Keeping that mindset of serving versus selling in your marketing is how to increase your sales and make an impact in the world.

A Gift For You

To grab the step-by-step checklist used inside the JW Agency, the breakdown of a profitable & converting ad, headline formula's, and target audiences used for high-end clients, download Jessica's free conversion kit now: www.jessicawalman.com/adkit

About Jessica Walman

Jessica Walman is a leading digital marketing strategist helping entrepreneurs share their message, impact lives, and 10x their revenue by selling their offerings to the world. Her agency runs thousands of dollars a day in ad spend helping clients launch multi-6- and 7-figure programs. Jessica has been featured in Huffpost, YFS Magazine, and Evercoach and alongside her agency is educating others how to run profitable Facebook ad campaigns.

CHAPTER FIFTY-TWO

Facebook Group Profits

By Chantelle Page Turner

I think we can all admit that, when it comes to selling our products or services, we all envy the cult-like following held by brands like Apple. Whether you're a die-hard Apple fan who lines up at midnight for the latest product launch or the anti-Apple person rolling your eyes, you have to admit that Apple has built a tribe of red-hot buyers who are constantly waiting for the next new thing for which they can shell out their hard-earned cash.

Having that tribe and die-hard following sounds great, but how do you build that for yourself? Especially if you don't have millions of dollars to spend on advertising?

The truth is, there are many great ways to build a following and turn that following into a tribe of buyers, but I will show you what I believe is the fastest and most effective way to build a tribe in today's crowded Internet space.

I am going to teach you how to quickly grow a highly targeted and engaged tribe through Facebook Groups. Once you have your own Group, you can leverage it to increase your authority and turn cold traffic into red-hot buyers!

In The Beginning

I actually stumbled upon this strategy almost by accident.

I founded my brand, Stronger Mommy, with the mission to empower special needs parents like me and help them get the resources, services, support and community they need. As a mom of a special needs child, a sense of community was one of the biggest areas I felt was lacking. There were plenty of Facebook Support Groups for special needs at the time, but I noticed that in most of them the same few people posted all the time and I really didn't feel I resonated with the way the Group was run.

In setting out to create my own Group for my Stronger Mommies (that's what we have come to call ourselves), I discovered that I had set up my Group and attracted my audience differently from other Facebook Groups. In no time at all, I was getting hundreds of requests a week from people wanting to join my Group.

And these were not just any people, they were my ideal Avatar! That perfect customer that I dreamed would one day become a member of my tribe and buy my products was coming to me! Even better still, because the Group quickly grew and over 90% of my members were active and engaged, Facebook began to actually send more members to me for free. So instead of having to spend a bunch of money on ads, trying to find people to join my Group or buy my products, those perfect people were finding me.

I went from having a list of zero and not even really knowing any other parents who had kids with special needs, to having people look at me as the expert in the field. As the Group grew and remained engaged, I received an invitation to join a private, invite-only group run by Facebook called the *Facebook Power Admins*. It wasn't long after that I had other entrepreneur friends begging me to teach them my Facebook Group methods and they too started to very quickly see the same results I had been getting within my own Group.

Benefits Of Facebook Groups

There are a lot of reasons why you should have your own highly engaged Facebook Group to grow an active and hungry tribe, but here are my top five.

1. **Instant Recognition**

As the Group administrator, you instantly elevate your expert status within your niche.

2. **Inexpensive Growth**

You can cultivate your perfect Avatar, warm them up, and turn them into buyers. All without creating a ton of content, writing a bunch of emails that never get opened, or wasting money on ads.

3. **Increased Sales**

Your social proof will skyrocket which, in turn, will generate more sales.

4. **Market Research**

You can easily do a ton of free market research. This means that you can test your offer on your tribe to make sure it's what they want, before wasting time, energy, and money to create it.

5. **Celebrity Status**

You elevate to celebrity status within your community and develop your own cult-like following. As the Group administrator and brand creator, you cultivate those die-hard fans so that competition is a thing of the past.

Starting With Facebook Groups

Now that you're excited to grow your own tribe through Facebook Groups, how do you make sure to set yourself up for success rather than ending up many Groups on Facebook that are full of crickets, with only the same few people posting all the time?

Simply follow these five tips to start your Group off on the right foot:

1. **Guard The Entrance**

Make the Group closed, which requires member approval by the administrator (you), and leverage your three entrance questions.

Facebook allows you ask pending Group members up to three questions. The questions you ask can make or break your Group,.

Your first question should determine whether you will allow a member to join the Group. Building your cult-like tribe of buyers requires that only your ideal Avatar be permitted to join the Group. For example, with my special needs parenting Group, I ask, "Are you currently parenting a child with special needs?"

If the answer is anything but, "Yes,", I do not allow them into the Group. You must be very firm on this. Remember, you're the boss.

Your second question should be a statement in which you tell them that, once inside the Group, they should introduce themselves. This allows you to welcome new members and very quickly help them feel a sense of belonging. This also increases engagement because you have given new members permission to participate.

Finally, the third question should be designed to get them on your email list. As great as Facebook Groups are, you want control of the asset you're building, so get them on your list. This can be done by asking for their email or giving them a link to a lead magnet/opt-in that you have created. If you ask for their email, make sure you tell them that you'll be sending them something and actually deliver on your word. This is your chance to make a good first impression so make it a great one.

2. **Set The Tone With A Welcome Video**

Create a welcome video and mark it as an announcement so it's always at the top of the Group postings.

TIP:, Pre-record the video, post it on your Facebook Business Page and then share it to the Group. This allows you to run ads to your Group members later on.

3. **Protect Your Group And Save Time**

Set *Admin Post Approval*, which means you must read every post and approve it before the Group will see it This might seem like it would cause you a lot of extra work and time, but it's actually the opposite.

By having to approve posts before adding them to the Group, you ensure that only the right content is added. This saves the Group from rule breakers, combats negativity, and allows you to increase your authority.

TIP: After approving the post, immediately comment on it. Your comment will have the administrator badge and the person who posted will feel important to you, which will make them more likely to engage with your Group in the future (comment, post, buy).

4. **Encourage Engagement**

One day a week make a self-share post. These posts allow your Group members to talk about themselves (which everyone loves to do). For my Stronger Mommies Group, it's called *Positive Monday*, and I invite members to share something great that happened for them within the past week.

TIP: Include a hashtag so it's easily searchable. For example, #positivemonday.

5. **Be Seen And Give Value**

Go Live once a week and give value. This will very quickly make you an authority on your topic and warm-up your tribe.

TIP: Always provide a Call to Action at the end of your Live event, even if you are not selling anything, as this will start to train your tribe to do what you tell them.

Over time, I developed a course called The CULTure Method and by using some of its simple but highly effective strategies one of my clients, Jamie Atkinson, got started in a brand new niche and quickly built his Group to over 250 members in just a few days. In less than 2 weeks, he sold 11 of them into his $997 course as well as a few upsells. Jamie went from an audience of 0 to selling $12,409, all with zero ad spend., by following this simple structure and leveraging his newly created Facebook Group!

Moving Forward

Most people put off starting a Facebook Group, or have failed with their Groups in the past, because they have been too focused on how they can constantly come up with engaging content to keep the members active, instead of actually leveraging a strategy that grows a highly engaged tribe on its own. By following my methods, setting their Groups up the right way, and leveraging the tools I teach, my clients are able to quickly grow highly engaged Groups of potential buyers. All with having no list, minimal content creation, and spending less than 15 minutes a day on it.

To me, nothing is better in business than having an amazing brand CULTure and tribe of engaged followers who know, like, and trust you!

A Gift For You

If you want more help growing your own tribe of engaged followers, head over to www.chantelleturner.com/book

About Chantelle Page Turner

Chantelle Turner began her online entrepreneur journey shortly after having her daughter. She was looking for a way to help cover the medical bills related to her daughter's stroke, and discovered network marketing.

While she did quite well early on using the traditional methods, she quickly hit a plateau and began looking for ways to leverage the Internet and automation. During this time, she was also working hard to get her daughter the medical services and support she needed. As she found ways to help her own daughter, she realized many other parents who had kids with special needs were not getting the support they needed either.

With her Internet and marketing skills, she founded her company Stronger Mommy to help other special needs parents like herself. Chantelle's Clients who adopt Chantelle's strategies, have seen massive growth both in their following and sales.

CHAPTER FIFTY-THREE

The VIP Visibility Formula: Show Up, Be Seen, and Get Paid

By Yael Bendahan

What is visibility in business? Visibility is equivalent to people knowing who you are and what you do, and it is critical to business success.

You can have all the knowledge and experience in the world. You can be the biggest expert your industry has ever seen. But, if you're not visible, no one will know any of that about you. And --- more notably – no one will pay you.

Using the power of visibility, I went from a stay-at-home-mom to meeting, working with, and befriending six- and seven-figure business owners and bringing my income from zero to a six-figure run rate in under two years.

In The Beginning

In June 2016, when I was a mom of four boys aged six and under, my husband and I realized that we could no longer subsist on one income. I needed to get a job.

There was just one problem. Due to moving countries as a teenager, I didn't finish high school or complete a degree. As far as employment was concerned, the most I could hope for was a secretarial job that would only cover the cost of childcare needed so I could work.

I knew there had to be a better way and, within just a few months, I realized that the best way was to stay at home with my children and bring in an income by building skills I could sell online. I'll never forget the day I sat in my mom's kitchen and told her, "Mom, I might even be able to earn $1,000 a month!"

I started off as a virtual assistant and, as I improved my skills, moved from blog management to social media to Facebook Ads and then to building sales funnels. My income increased with each change and I ultimately became a digital marketing strategist and coach.

But how did I go from being invisible to being contacted daily for my services?

Becoming Visible

Not only did I improve my skills, but I also improved my visibility over time, and I credit that with my success. With enough determination, anyone can grow their presence and authority in an ethically- and value-based way. I want to help you get visible so that you can get paid to have an impact.

Why Does Visibility Matter?

The more value you deliver to people, the more visible you become.

The more visible you become, the more authority you build.

The more authority you build, the more you'll be in demand.

The more you're in demand, the more you can charge.

The more you can charge, the more your life can change.

It can be hard to accept the idea that earning lots of money as a good thing and not a greedy thing, but money only amplifies what's already there. If you're a good person and strive to do good, you'll be able to do even more good with more wealth.

More Reasons to Get Visible

1. **To display your expertise.**

People want to hire experts and will pay more for their services.

2. **To display your personality and qualities.**

If you are professional, likable, and helpful, you will resonate with prospects and customers, and they'll hire or buy from you. And, if you don't resonate with them, they're not your ideal client anyway.

3. **To acquire new clients more easily.**

   Rather than depending on referrals, your visibility draws people to you. Providing value attracts people to you. The referrals tend to come naturally from customers in any case, but you're establishing a virtual business card that prospects can evaluate and start to trust.

The VIP Visibility Formula

Here is my VIP Visibility Formula that I used myself and help others use.

Mindset

The first step is to figure out *who* you are and what you're going to do. This may involve a fair bit of writing, journaling, and self-evaluation, but it is important.

What is your *why*? What do you stand for? What do you stand against? What are your core values? Whenever you create content, you'll do it through this filter so you need to identify it for yourself first before you show it to others. Everything you create will be aligned with this filter and your ideal clients will identify with it as well.

Create an elevator pitch now and get to know it intimately. Practice saying it to yourself and others (family & friends) to get it down to an informative, easy to follow minute that gives the essence of you and your business.

Elevator Pitch

I am a _______ and I help _______ do ________.

Understand your blocks. What might stop you from going all-in? What are you afraid of? Make a list of your fears and think about each one logically. Once you know and understand these fears, turn them into affirmations.

Positive Affirmations

Instead of saying, "I'm worried people will realize that I don't know what I'm doing," turn it into "I am extremely knowledgeable in _________ and I know more than a lot of people. I'm always learning and increasing my knowledge and I can help the people who are a few steps behind me."

Action Step Write out your elevator pitch and practice it on family and friends. For each of the fears you have identified, write a positive affirmation and read them often until you remember them all the time.

Find Your People

You must be clear on who you serve. I want you to be clear about who you're serving so that you know where they are.

People can get so overwhelmed by trying to be visible on every single platform that they end up nowhere. The important thing is to show up where your ideal client/customer is. If they're business owners, LinkedIn and Facebook will be your primary platforms. If they're moms, Pinterest, Facebook and/or Instagram. If they're millennials, Instagram or Snapchat. And, this is just in 2019! Things are always changing and so it's important to keep a finger on the pulse of where your people are hanging out.

Action Step: Decide on the primary and secondary platforms your ideal clients are using. Just two for now. You can work on the others later.

Content

Now that you know where to be, it's time to build your content strategy.

Video is currently the most successful content. Not only do people watch videos over reading text, but a single video can also be re-purposed many times. It can be a YouTube video, a podcast episode, numerous shorter clips, a blog post, quote graphics, and more.

However, if you feel strongly that your talents lie elsewhere, you can focus your content strategy on the written word (blogging) or your voice (podcasting). The important thing is that your passion and expertise shine through so pick the visibility strategies that feel best and most natural to you.

Plan content that establishes you as an expert and a thought leader. This can be a mix of actual teaching and inspirational content. Content without an objective is just noise, so be sure that your content is purposeful, delivers value, and always has a clear Call to Action.

Action Step: Decide on your primary content creation method (video, audio, or written) and plan out four core pieces of content for the next four weeks (my VIP Content Formula is a great resource for this).

Connection

Creating connections is the best thing you can do for your business. Relationships with other business owners and industry influencers will be the difference between propelling yourself to the next level and staying obscure.

Not only do you learn a lot through knowledge sharing, but the more people know you personally, the more people there are to refer you.

Action Step: Reach out to five new people in your industry or a connected industry this week. It can be people you've noticed in a Facebook Group or an influencer you've resonated with. Comment on their social posts, send them a message, or reply to their emails if you're on their list. Trust me, people notice these things!

Moving Forward

Now you're all fired up and ready to get visible your business will make huge shifts forward.

I strongly recommend you start with mindset. If you don't believe in what you're saying, all the visibility in the world won't help. Make the time for and schedule a couple of coffee chats each week. The connections you make will increase your momentum as you grow and you'll get some incredible friends along the way.

Now, go get visible!

A Gift For You

Be sure to grab Yael's Facebook Famous Framework to start getting your name and face out there on Facebook ... and everywhere else!

yaelbendahan.com/facebookfamous

About Yael Bendahan

Yael Bendahan is an internationally known digital marketing and visibility strategist for impact-driven business owners and entrepreneurs who want to increase their income by harnessing the power of social media, content, paid ads, and sales funnels.

She grew her own business from zero to six-figures within 18 months and has generated between three and five-times ROI for her clients' marketing campaigns. She has also masterminded and worked directly with six- and seven-figure business owners to create customized marketing strategies that have helped catapult their visibility and income with her signature formulas for authentic, ethical, and intentional content and marketing funnels.

Yael has been featured in publications and websites like *Funnel Magazine* and *Influencive*. She has also been a guest on podcasts like *Social Media Secrets*, *Work-At-Home Heroes*, and *Purpose Driven Marketing*. A New York expat, she lives in Israel with her husband and four sons.

CHAPTER FIFTY-FOUR

Publishing: Get Your Audience to Love You and Buy

By Kris Russo

My uncle was an excellent baker whose Italian pastry bakery, *Potito's Bakery,* had been a fixture in South Philadelphia since 1985. He was 45 and in remission for six months before his Leukemia came back in 2004.

He needed a bone marrow transplant to live. Because none of the five million registered donors in the Red Cross National Marrow Donor Program matched, my family organized a marrow drive. Businesses in the neighborhood got involved and handed out flyers to customers telling them Carmen Potito needed a bone marrow match.

Just three days before the drive, *South Philly Review* a local paper, reported, "More than 100 people already have signed up"[42] for the drive.

On the day of the drive, over four hundred people showed up! The number of donors quadrupled because that news article was published. That is the power of publishing!

Sometimes I think about how, today, with social media, one thousand people might have shown up, or more, and maybe my uncle would have found a bone marrow match and lived.

Customer Relationships

Many people who responded to the drive knew my uncle and how much he cared about his customers.

Your business will die if you don't connect and build meaningful relationships with customers to keep profits coming in.

Zig Ziglar says it well, "You can have everything in life you want, if you will just help other people get what they want."[43] In other words, serve your customers what *they* want to get what *you* want.

Another Zig quote that rings true is, "People don't care how much you know until they know how much you care." In other words, share *why you do what you do*.

That's when your audience falls in love with you.

---

[42] (2004, August 12). *Sweet Show of Success*. South Philly Review. Retrieved from https://southphillyreview.com/2004/08/12/sweet-show-of-support/ on August 6, 2019.
[43] Zig Ziglar Quotes. (n.d.). Retrieved on August 6, 2019 from https://www.brainyquote.com/quotes/zig_ziglar_381984.

If we show more people how much we care, we can help more people get what they want. And, in the process, get what we want, too.

Publishing And Relationships

A lot of marketers obsess over their email open rates. They read about a new, clever subject line that can lift their open rate by a half-percent and rush to use it.

But I know people who get 100% open rates and don't need "tricks"; they're not even marketers. Facebook, Messenger, email, SMS, LinkedIn, and Instagram, on every platform these folks get 100% opens!

Who are they?

My wife, my mom, my sister, my friends, and many more; I open all their messages and they open all of mine. People open messages from people with whom they have a strong relationship and publishing builds these relationships. So instead of looking for subject lines that get opened slightly more often, and often temporarily, it's smarter to build your customer relationships.

In a 2018 email marketing benchmark report, MailChimp reveals that, out of 43 industries, the hobby industry got the highest open rate, 27.35%, as well as the highest click rates, 4.78%.[44]. The non-profit industry was fifth overall with a 24.11% open rate.[45]

A similar email marketing benchmark report by GetResponse revealed that out of 18 industries the non-profit industry earned the second-highest open rate with 33.86%, as well as the third-best unsubscribe rate. [46]

The bottom line: People give most of their attention and money to where their heart is.

How to Never Need to Chase Money

In March 2017, my little blog site caught the attention of a Microsoft MVP and his IT Director, and this led to my first 6-figure senior IT engineering position.

Less than a year and a half later, I reapplied a similar strategy in my business using Facebook Live broadcasts (it's still publishing even though it's not writing). After my third Facebook Live, people privately messaged me. Why? Because they connected with my content.

Publishing instantly connects people with the heart behind the business.

Benefits Of Publishing

- Attention – Publishing gets what you have to offer out there; it also allows you to find out what your customers want (ask them).
- Relationships – Consistent publishing allows customers to get to know you and trust you – and you to know them – so you can sell more easily and give them what they want.

---

[44] Meaning the recipient was interested enough to click the link in the email

[45] (n.d.). *Email Marketing Benchmarks.* Retrieved on August 6, 2019 from https://mailchimp.com/resources/email-marketing-benchmarks.

[46] Leszczynski, M. (n.a.). *Email Marketing Benchmarks*. Retrieved on August 6, 2019 from https://www.getresponse.com/resources/reports/email-marketing-benchmarks#average-results-by-industry

- Organic customers – Organic customers can be more valuable than paid leads.
- Increased profits – Once people trust you, they will buy more and/or you can charge more. Offer a premium product or service they will pay for because they trust you.
- Happy customers – When they hear from you, your customers get to see that you don't just think of them as an order number.

Almost Illiterate But He Publishes Anyway

I failed English class in high school and scored 460 on my Reading SATs. I was assigned to a remedial writing course in college. But, I'm still publishing every day!

The trick is to keep it simple and be consistent (once a week is the perfect start). I'm going to share a few of my favorite shortcuts.

Shortcut #1: Stories

First, you'll need stories. You may have tons of them, but here's how to start nailing down some ideas. Draw three columns on a piece of paper (or in a spreadsheet like Excel). In the first column, write down the current year. In the second column, write where you're at now, professionally and/or personally, not physically. In the third column, add a comment about how you feel or a lesson you've learned. Then simply start working in reverse chronological order and record significant events in your life, both personal and business.

Here's how I would start mine:

Date	**Event**	**Comment/Feeling**
2019	Professional Development Coach for IT Professionals	Back in IT! But now I'm coaching IT Professionals in leadership & communication skills.
June 2018	Direct Response Copywriter, B1B Story Writer, & Consultant	My first attempt at writing sales copy was brutally criticized (and I'm thankful for that!)
August 2017	Rushed to ER the day before my daughter's 1st birthday	Scariest day ever!
July 2017	Began Sr. SCCM Engineer role with IBX	This was a dream job
July 2017	Finished a 5-year run as an IT engineer	This is the first job I ever left on my own. Weird feeling!
August 2016	First child born	I realized I didn't want to work 55-hour weeks anymore.

You're simply walking down memory lane, remembering the events and people along the way. Remember, you never know which story will be the perfect story to turn customers into diehards and non-customers into fans.

Shortcut #2: Momentum

The second shortcut is to get momentum.

Start with blogging if you like to write, podcasting if you like to talk, or do video if you like to be in front of a camera. Remember, whatever is simplest for you, do that. Keep doing it on a schedule, to build a habit and get comfortable with publishing. When you have momentum, you're more likely to succeed.

Shortcut #3: Be Honest

The third shortcut is to be real.

If you keep it real, then publishing it is super simple. Your story is already done for you because you've already lived it. Share the ups and the downs. Don't brag about the ups and don't dwell on the downs. When you share the ups, explain how you got there (i.e., explain how you earned it). When you share the downs, talk about what you did wrong and how you fixed it.

Moving Forward

The most important thing to publish is your origin story. This is the story that usually appears on your Home or About Us website page; it starts your relationship with customers. It's the background that customers look for to determine if they can trust you or not. And, it can turn customers into raving fans.

A Gift For You

Email Kris Russo to grab your FREE *Origin Story Template And Checklist* at kris@intentionalwealth.net

Mention this book and I'll do something special for you.

Facebook Messenger: m.me/itskrisrusso

Ph: 484-451-8655

About Kris Russo

A friend asked Kris, "Why would I hire you over a financial advisor from a big company like Fidelity?"

Kris knew he was different, but just saying, "I'm different," wasn't enough. Kris couldn't compete with juggernauts who were already household names.

But he realized something: he's walked a mile in his friend's shoes! Fidelity hasn't. Not Vanguard. And not Morgan Stanley either. None of the "big boys" had done that.

As soon as he started sharing his story, people listened because it was familiar; it was their story. Suddenly they wanted his financial expertise! When Kris noticed other businesses struggling to connect with their clients' core values, he knew they needed a story, too.

As much as Kris loves helping people manage their money, he found a calling to help business owners and entrepreneurs write their origin story. Why? Because he's been there!

CHAPTER FIFTY-FIVE

The Future of TV is Connected

By Angie Norris

The 20th Century was a time of huge advancements in technology. Many people thought the greatest invention was the television: It brought captivating entertainment to billions of people and became a driving force in consumer behavior.

Others believe the computer was the most influential invention because it revolutionized every area of our daily life with high-speed calculations, massive databases and retrieval systems, and automation.

Late in the Century, the Internet revolutionized communication and, like TV, had a significant impact on consumer behavior that is still being felt and changing at an astounding rate.

Initially, each of these technologies was at arm's length from the average consumer but soon, almost every household adopted first a TV, then a computer, and finally the Internet. Each has become an integral part of everyday life in many countries.

These three technologies are becoming integrated and, recently, the power of the Internet was married to TV to create a convenient, seamless way to watch our favorite shows. Connected TV (CTV) was born.

Connected TV (CTV)

CTV is a television that is connected directly to the Internet or is a device connected to the TV and the Internet (for example, Roku, Amazon Fire TV, Apple TV, Google Chromecast, Android TV, various gaming stations) that allows streaming of audio and video content.

Via CTV, as long as your Internet is not disrupted, you don't need the entire video or audio recording to download before playing it.

Viewers watch their high-definition CTVs in the comfort of their home, mimicking the traditional TV experience, but with the added benefits that streaming and on-demand TV provide.

Think about your favorite networks (Netflix, HBO, Prime Video, Disney, Hallmark, ESPN, etc.). All have leveraged the power of CTV by creating branded streaming apps.

When I say app, I'm referring to a software application designed to stream video content on devices like Roku, Amazon Fire TV, Apple TV, and others.

When you use your smartphone, every option on your phone is rolled up into an app. TV streaming devices work like your phone, they have apps on them like Disney channel, Hulu, and Hallmark, etc.

As a business owner and marketer, you should consider having your own CTV channel. CTV channels provide a new way to market your products or services to potential buyers. CTV channels are positioned to be the next big digital marketing trend. Your branded channel could be up there with Netflix, HBO, and other prominent CTV channels.

Why Does CTV Matter To You?

Marketing your brand digitally used to be easier but digital marketing methods have changed over the last few years. Messages are getting lost in a sea of messages and ads are now directly aimed at individual consumers. Getting your product or service in front of your target audience is more challenging. Having a branded streaming TV app is the newest way to set yourself apart from your competition and be seen by millions of potential buyers.

Imagine your TV channel app on Roku, Amazon Fire TV, Apple TV, and the other major streaming TV platforms. What messages would you want to get in front of people? What ads would you showcase to drive viewers to your products or services? How would it feel to have your business's brand on TV?

The Top Five Benefits of a CTV Channel

In addition to the prestige of having your own TV channel, there are several other benefits, including:

1. Reaching millions of people around the world.
2. Tapping into a multi-billion-dollar market.
3. Adding new income streams to your business.
4. Elevating your authority to stand out from the crowd.
5. Riding the cutting edge of technology and leveraging this new digital avenue.

How To Get Started

How do you develop your TV channel app on Roku, Amazon Fire TV, Apple TV, Android TV, Google Chromecast, and other streaming TV platforms? Here are five things to consider:

1. **Concept**

Determine what you want your TV channel to be. Think about the title of your channel as well as branding and color schemes.

2. **Collaborate**

Partner with a TV channel developer to either learn how to build TV channels yourself or ask them to build your TV channel for you. Partnering will ensure your channel strategy and technical needs are addressed.

3. **Content**

The most important component of a TV channel is its content. Your videos are imperative to the essence and success of your channel. It doesn't matter if you are a start-up or a well-established business, videos will be the lifeblood of your channel. Whether they are professionally produced or are do-it-yourself jobs, the important factor is that you are getting your message out.

4. **Channel**

The magic happens when your TV channel is developed into a fully monetized TV channel app across all of the major streaming TV platforms.

5. **Convert**

Once your TV channel app is up and running, you can harness the power of TV to get your message in front of millions of people around the world, while tapping into a billion-dollar market.

Moving Forward

Many business owners who want to elevate their brands have the misconception that having a TV channel is only for big brands with big budgets, but nothing could be further from the truth.

If you're a business owner who wants to reach millions of people around the world, having a fully branded TV channel as a streaming TV app is exactly what you need.

As more and more consumers cut the cord to cable and embrace this new way to watch television, businesses that are already present because they were early adopters of CTV will flourish and become the leaders of this new mode of digital marketing.

To get started, check out xtremefunnels.tv and find out information about how to develop your TV channel for Roku, Amazon Fire TV, and Apple TV with our team of experts.

A Gift For You

Be sure to access your free TV channel MasterClass at www.xtremefunnels.tv/masterclass

About Angie Norris

Angie Norris, Founder of XtremeFunnels.io, is an advanced online marketer focused on helping brands go from presence to profit using the power of online sales funnels and streaming TV.

Angie has worked in marketing for over 20 years, primarily in Information Technology working for Fortune 500 companies including Hewlett-Packard Enterprise Services and Computer Sciences Corporation. Since starting her own online business in 2019, Angie has become a speaker, coach, author, top affiliate for several software companies, the first Certified Groove Ambassador and an award-winning marketer.

Angie has a passion for helping brands leverage and harness the power of online sales funnels and cutting-edge tools and technologies. Check out angienorris.com to find out more about Angie Norris.

CHAPTER FIFTY-SIX

The Art Of The Interview

By Shannon Houchin

With the continued popularity of blogs, taped and live video, podcasts, and CTV the reasons for a business to conduct interviews are strong and growing. An interview with a subject expert, a recognized leader, or an engaging product or service user can build trust amongst your audience and result in more brand recognition, niche leadership, and sales for your company.

In this chapter, we'll review the interview process, including preparation for and conduction of the interview, whether it is for a blog, video, or audio format.

In The Beginning

It's 7 am on a Tuesday and my cell phone rings. It's the CEO of Pier 1 Imports. My stomach immediately tightens with dread. I consider not taking the call.

I wrote a breaking story on the company recently, and the CEO wasn't calling me to say thank you.

I answered and, sure enough, he was angry. "Who did you talk to? Who gave you the details for the goddamn story?"

Someone was going to get fired and the CEO wanted me to name names. Fortunately, I had performed over a dozen interviews for the story and couldn't recall a specific one that provided the details he was upset about. I was able to calm him down, make him feel heard and understood, and uncover his true concern: He wanted a follow-up story from his point of view.

That call confirmed what I already knew: I was good at getting people to talk about off-limit topics and I was an adept listener who could convince people to provide far more detail than they initially planned.

It's more than asking tough, invasive questions on sensitive topics; it's about the skill with which you handle the interview process and the interviewee.

Doing An Interview

It is no longer necessary to have expensive cameras and/or audio recorders to conduct interviews that people will watch. Set yourself up in a somewhat quiet, well-lit spot with your cell phone recording (voice only or video) and you're set to carry out an interview.

Do it live, if you like, or tape it and edit it afterward, the choice is yours. As long as the topic is pertinent and of interest to your followers and customers, you're sure to have people who will watch, listen, or read what you and your interviewee have to offer.

When you supply information that your prospects and customers want, you are creating value for and building trust with them. This helps create rapport and brand recognition, which in turn, results in sales.

20 Tips To Great Interviews

Here are a few hacks for conducting amazing interviews and creating compelling content that can make you an authority in the digital market:

1. Consider Your Audience First.

Determine who you want to consume your interview. Knowing this will help you select the interview topic, the questions to ask, and who to interview. The best interviews are those that dig into passions of or problems for the audience. Think about your audience throughout the interview process to ensure the interview will be useful to them.

2. Know Your Equipment!

Do all your technology learning before getting the interviewee on camera. Your audience doesn't want to spend any time watching or listening to you fumble around for settings, volume, or setting the stage. Don't lose authority or interest with your audience by not knowing your technology.

3. Select Good Interviewees.

Do your homework to determine who will give you a good interview. Don't select people who won't interview well. If the interviewee only offers one-word answers to your questions or lacks passion or conviction about the topic, your audience will lose interest quickly.

4. Do Your Homework.

This is true for the interview topic and the person you are interviewing, as well. Select three to five friends, colleague,s and/or partners of the person you are going to interview, and chat with them to learn more about the topic and the person. Having all this background information will make the interview richer, deeper, and far more compelling.

5. Write a Great Introduction for the Interviewee.

A good introduction will impress your interviewee and will also get your audience pumped-up about the topic and the interview.

6. Establish Rapport.

Use techniques to make your interviewee feel comfortable before and during the interview. For example, mirror their tone of voice and inflection, as well as their body language. Warm the interviewee up before you begin the official interview with a couple of easy questions, and perhaps share a personal story with them to establish an understanding of respect and openness.

7. Create A Mood.

Smile at your interviewee. Let them see your smile. If you're on the phone, let them hear the smile in your voice. This will flip a switch in their brain and elevate their mood as they mirror yours. Pleasantness increases rapport and motivates the interviewee to answer your questions.

8. Use Upward Inflections.

An upward inflection during speech puts people at ease while, at the same time, signals to them that a question needs to be answered. Avoid downward inflections on words unless you want the conversation to wrap up.

9. Have a Goal.

Determine a goal for the interview. What do you want the audience to know when the interview is over?

Prepare a list of possible questions that reflect your goal but be flexible as well. For example, if interesting topics come up during the interview, don't be afraid to go down an exploratory path. Try to avoid questions that have been answered many times before. Your interview should deliver fresh perspectives and content.

10. Use Open-Ended Questions.

Ask questions that can't be answered with a simple yes or no. For example, ask why questions or start with, "Tell me about...."

Open-ended questions usually require more reflection by the interviewee and will produce richer, deeper answers. Allow time for the interviewee to respond without interruption or interjection.

11. Prompt More Talk.

If you feel the interviewee has more to say but isn't, prompt them to continue. You can always prod with, " Tell me more" or, repeat the last three words the interviewee just said to encourage them to keep talking. Try picking three strong words from their answer and creating a question that will prompt them to keep talking to clarify their point.

12. Use Pattern Interrupt Questions.

Pattern interrupts questions are designed to interrupt the pattern of thinking and train of thought so a new idea or thought shifts the interviewee away from where they are going. Ultimately, a pattern interrupt question affects the flow of a conversation. These questions motivate thought from the interviewee and will lead to meaningful insights.

13. Let Silence Be.

Don't be afraid of silence in your interview. Silence can often compel an interviewee to answer a question or allow you to dig a little deeper. People tend to fill in silent gaps and will provide far more information in moments of silence than if you keep talking to fill the void.

14. Tell Stories.

Stories evoke emotion. Try to approach the interviewee from a storytelling point of view. Lead-ins such as, "Tell me what that was like..." or, "How did you feel when..." often get stories going. Audiences respond better to stories and emotion than factual unembellished short answers.

15. Show enthusiasm and passion.

Your attitude will be infectious! Ask follow-up questions that demonstrate your passion and interest.

16. Create Intimacy.

Talk to the person as if the interview is one-on-one, not in front of an audience. Try not to look at your questions during the interview; ask questions as they come to you, as you would with a friend. People want to be heard and understood, so don't be afraid to repeat something the interviewee has said to confirm your understanding so it is clear to all (the interviewee, you, and the audience).

17. Ask About Feelings.

People will respond in more depth if you ask about their emotions around a topic rather than a simple sequence of events.

18. **Practice Active Listening.**

Don't think about what you want to say next when your interviewee is speaking. Absorb what they are saying before asking more. If you want to delve into a particular point more, simply make a note and circle back to it. Stay in the interviewee's moment and show them you are listening. This builds trust and encourages the interviewee to open up even more.

19. **Let Them Pitch.**

Be sure to provide an opportunity for the interviewee to pitch their products/services or social media platforms at the end of the interview. Very often interviewees do interviews for free and allowing them to market themselves or their product/service is not only fair to them, but it may also be useful or interesting to your audience.

20. **The Final Word.**

In all interactions, the last impression is the strongest and is what your audience will remember the most, so make it count. Ask the interviewee if they have anything to add, or what they're strongest takeaway from their own story might be, or what's the best advice they would give to your audience. Let the interviewee have the final word.

Moving Forward

Interviewing others is a great way to gain authority, trust, and popularity amongst your followers and non-followers, too. Written, audio, or video, be sure to tape the interview so you can refer to it later, for excerpts, question and topic development for future interviews, and re-purpose the content.

The 20 hacks listed above will help you feel more comfortable conducting interviews so you can provide wanted information to your followers. During the process, you will likely learn some valuable information yourself and may even make a few friends along the way. Stay relaxed and listen carefully. Three, Two, One, Action!

A Gift For You

For more tactical practices on gaining the BEST interview possible, visit www.interviewlikeamaster.com

Find me at www.shannonhouchin.com and book in for an upcoming class where I teach you the tools of the trade for making all of your online interviews engaging and powerful.

About Shannon Houchin

Shannon Houchin is a multi-published author and award-winning journalist. She lives in Texas and divides her time between digital marketing and the marathon circuit.

CHAPTER FIFTY-SEVEN

Nine-To-Five Freedom: The Switch From Employee To Entrepreneur

By Bryan Rhodes

"A ship in the harbor is safe,
but that is not what ships are built for."

~ John A. Shedd

If safe and easy are what you're looking for, entrepreneurship is not going to be right for you. Rewarding, yes. Profitable, sometimes. But anyone who tells you that taking the path of the entrepreneur is easy is deceiving you.

There are ways to make the journey less tedious, products and services to eliminate some of the headaches, but there's nothing that will remove all of the risks and tedium of creating a business. Don't be intimidated, though. If everyone could just pay $47 and have a successful business created for them, everyone would do it.

This chapter (and book) is for people who want to free themselves from the nine-to-five hamster wheel. For the people who struggle each day with employment challenges that make their climb in life hard. I've decided to make it my life's goal to live for myself and help others do the same. After all, the top is a lonely place to be; I figure I might as well bring along a few people.

Every entrepreneur will have stories to tell you. People do business with people, not businesses. Not every story, however, will resonate with every person. Businesses aren't built to provide products and services for everyone. Keep this principle in mind as you go through your journey, and take this away if nothing else: You cannot please everyone.

In The Beginning

My story sounds similar to a lot of other stories; it's filled with struggle and frustration, fear and failure. If I said I succeeded more than I failed, I'd be a liar. I've failed a lot. And, from my failures, I've learned the lessons I needed to succeed.

Where my story might be slightly different from other entrepreneurs, however, is where and how my life began and what it's done to me. I wasn't born into a situation that would permit me to pursue my destiny. In all likelihood, had I stayed where I was born, I probably would be dead today.

I endured childhood sexual abuse at a very young age. I lived on and off the streets. My life's earliest memories are like flashes from a horror film. Eventually, I was adopted into a good home and my destiny was changed forever.

However, and perhaps because of my early experiences, I suffer from several mental disorders including bipolar disorder, autism, and attention deficit disorder. These emotional and behavioral disorders make even writing this chapter extremely difficult because, as I write, my mind is being pulled in 20 directions.

I'm not looking for pity; I don't need or want it. I'm grateful for my challenges because they've formed me into the person I am today. I tell you only to show you that if someone with my challenges can be an entrepreneur then anyone can.

Starting As An Entrepreneur

The first step in being an entrepreneur is to identify the people you most want to serve and tailor your products and services to their wants and needs. If you don't know whom you want to serve, the best place to start is by looking in the mirror.

If you're reading this book, it's likely because you want to escape the chains of the nine-to-five lifestyle. I refer to nine-to-five and shift-work jobs as Golden Handcuffs because you receive financial incentives in trade for your time. The handcuffs come in because you can't leave the job because you need the money from it to live.

Once you accept the job offer, you've started on a road that's difficult to leave. The illusion of safety provided by a traditional job is just that, though, an illusion. An employer can be empathetic, even kind, but the moment economic conditions become unfavorable your continued employment is in peril.

Don't get me wrong. I took a ride down that road myself; I'm still exerting time and effort toward a course correction. I grew tired of someone else deciding what my time was worth. It's difficult to put a value on time because it's the only asset we have of which we can never make more.

Before you can free yourself from the Golden Handcuffs and become an entrepreneur, there's one thing you *must* do. If you fail to do this, your chances of making it will be nil. You can learn everything there is to know about building a business, marketing, and creating products and services, but neglect this one concept and you'll be doomed to failure.

I once read something by Dean Graziosi, and I'm paraphrasing, but essentially it said if someone handed you a machine that printed hundred-dollar bills you'd ultimately go broke if you hadn't spent the time and energy mastering this one fundamental principle.

Mindset

You must adopt the mindset of an entrepreneur.

Mindset is the one thing you mustn't get wrong; you can't go into business with the mindset of an employee. You aren't going into business to work for yourself; you're doing it so that you can bring change into the world. As an employee you are limited in making changes by the scope of your role within a company or organization, having your own organization means the only limitations you have are those you place on yourself.

Changing your mindset from employee to entrepreneur begins, always, with the conscious acceptance that this is the path you want to take. Accept now that there will be challenges and trials you haven't encountered before but commit to overcoming them at all costs.

Money

You must also change how you think about money. Don't see money as a means to a desired end (or as the desired end); your abilities, talents, gifts, knowledge, and experience are the means to the desired end. The value you provide and the change you create in the world will yield monetary gain, but money is nothing more than a way to keep score. Yes, we live in a material world where cash is king, but money goes where value flows.

Paradigms

The way you perceive the world, the thoughts you have, the dialogue playing in your head, and your beliefs, all determine your reality. In the personal development space, these are called paradigms. Paradigms are like software installed on a computer. The paradigm will run continuously because ultimately the brain is obedient; it doesn't decide what is good or bad. Unless you consciously change your paradigm, it will continue to run as it always has.

You, as your brain's host, can change the paradigm because you can tell it what is good and bad. Thus, if you tell the paradigm it is wrong for you, it will have to change.

Paradigm change begins by taking control of what you allow into your consciousness. If you surround yourself with negativity (people, news, etc.) over time the paradigm you develop is negative. Systematically replace the sources of negativity in your life (avoid negative people, take a sabbatical from reading or watching the news, etc.) with positive ones (only spend time with positive people and read positive writings) and your paradigm will change. The better job you do of eliminating sources of negativity and replacing them with sources of positivity, the less you continue to feed the negative paradigm; you essentially "starve" them of what they need to keep operating and create a new, more positive paradigm instead. You're responsible for your own mental space and what it projects into the world.

Sacrifices

Be prepared to make sacrifices. You'll have to give up things you enjoy to free up time and energy for your entrepreneurial journey. This will be hard; I won't try to fool you. But the time and enjoyment given up is an investment. Imagine your life once you have what you want and you're the person you want to be. You'll look back and thank yourself for having the courage to make the sacrifices necessary to live the life you truly deserve.

Don't Gamble

Lastly, don't treat your business like a slot machine or an ATM. A business is a vehicle for change and some strategies and principles must be applied if you ever hope to successfully build a business that achieves what you truly desire. Respect your business and the people you serve. Trust and respect yourself and your abilities. The greatest asset or obstacle to your success is you!

About Bryan Rhodes

Bryan Rhodes is an Internet entrepreneur, business mentor, and coach. His passions center on helping new businesses grow and emerging entrepreneurs to develop the strategies they need to succeed, particularly those with mental and emotional health issues.

Bryan specializes in business development, having graduated with High Honors in a Master of Business Administration (MBA).

Also educated in Information Technology (IT), Bryan has specialized knowledge in incorporating IT services into businesses strategically for maximum efficiency. With a total of ten years of Internet Marketing and business experience, Bryan is aware of the challenges the modern entrepreneur faces. He prides himself on his ability to help others understand complex business and IT principles.

Bryan's business provides coaching and consulting to new or aspiring business owners, as well as several Done-for-You services. Bryan is a competent copywriter, web page designer, and product creator. His specialized training in human resource management allows him to source and hire highly qualified talent, an essential skill for any aspiring business owner.

Bryan currently lives in Northern California with his family and enjoys playing golf, road trips, and watching documentaries in his free time.

Connect with Bryan at www.firststepstobusiness.com.

CHAPTER FIFTY-EIGHT

Reinventing Virtual Summits

By Mark Stern

What if I told you that there is a way to launch a new product, ignite your authority, build relationships with influencers, and generate revenue by implementing one simple strategy?

Whether you are brand new to entrepreneurship or a seasoned veteran, there is, in fact, a way to ethically grow and scale your business quickly.

It's through Virtual Summits and in this chapter I'm going to show you how to easily leverage this model to grow and scale your business.

I'm not talking about the traditional high-stress, high-workload model for summits. I'm going to introduce you to a new model that will have you winning with your speakers, affiliates, and participants.

If you're thinking, "I'm not ready for a Virtual Summit. Maybe in a few months I'll be there," all I can say is, "Buckle up!"

You are ready, and you are a prime candidate for this model. So, let's get into it!

In The Beginning

For over 15 years, I was a product of Corporate America. That journey allowed me to collaborate with Fortune 500 companies in retail, healthcare, financial services, fitness, and hospitality. Despite a prospering corporate career, I found myself catching the lifestyle design bug following the discovery of Tim Ferris' *The 4-Hour Work Week.*[47]

I know, I know. Many of us were struck by the idea of being the digital nomad introduced in Ferris' book. But there were two major hurdles I faced:

First, I couldn't comprehend the idea of only working *four hours* in one week; I was surrounded by corporate consultants and venture capitalists who typically clocked over 60 hours per week.

Second, the idea of digital nomads sounded like mythical creatures to me. I had never met one before, and therefore they simply did not exist in my world.

However, in 2013, that all changed. On a whim, I bought a solo ticket to Mindvalley's A-Fest conference, and it was a decision that drastically changed my life forever. This conference was completely made up of digital marketers, nomads, and gamechangers who were living life on their own terms. To say I felt disrupted, shaken up, and completely alone was an understatement. The

---

[47] Ferris, T. (2009), *The Four Hour Work Week*, Harmony Press.

world as I knew it was transformed. My bubble had burst, and I knew nothing would ever be the same. I was hooked – I wanted in.

Despite this desire, there were two other major realities I faced:

- I was $165,000 in debt following getting my MBA at Duke University
- I was committed for a few years to a top-five consulting firm, who owned (by contract) everything I produced within and outside the firm

That's right! Everything I produced outside the firm *was owned by the firm*. In other words, the dream of having a side hustle or small business was merely that: A dream.

When I finally made the leap from Corporate to Entrepreneurship in early 2018, I literally had no funnel, no email list, no influence – nothing. I was virtually invisible to the world of Digital Marketing, and I knew I needed to make a splash fast in order to survive.

Having been a fly on the wall in the digital marketing realm for years, I was familiar with the concept of Virtual Summits, and as a conference junkie, I knew it was the first thing I wanted to do upon leaving the corporate world.

After ten weeks of planning, I launched the CLICKpreneur Summit in October 2018. The result was amazing:

- **Status Elevated:** I built relations and collaborated with over 40 digital marketing influencers who I did not know prior to the event.
- **Leads Generated:** I went from having no email list to thousands of subscribers.
- **Community Activated:** I built a Facebook Community and Messenger Bot with hundreds of followers.
- **Product Launched:** I created a new revenue stream that I was able to monetize quickly following the event

Furthermore, I created a platform that allowed me to showcase my skillset and the value I could bring to the marketplace. And, that was just the beginning.

Podcast hosts started inviting me on their show. Facebook Group owners asked me to lead workshops within their group. And countless Virtual Summit hosts started featuring me on their own virtual events.

I was able to launch several new revenue streams off of the summit; and within six months, I generated my first six-figures as an entrepreneur.

And, despite all this, what was the best part?

The best part was (and is) that these results are not unique to me. They can be easily replicated by anyone who implements this model. I know because I've watched countless clients benefit from it.

What Is A Virtual Summit?

Virtual Summits are online conferences that typically bring together 25or more people interested in a common topic. They're like live conferences, but they don't require all the travel, hotel accommodation, and time away from family and friends.

Via this model, you can participate in the comfort of your own home – all you need is a computer or smart phone and an internet connection. Best of all, Virtual Summits are generally offered for free for a limited time in exchange for an email address, making them one of the most powerful lead-generation tools in the market.

Similar to live conferences, if you miss any of the speaker sessions during a Virtual Summit, you miss the chance to learn from that presenter.

So how can you, as the host, monetize a Virtual Summit?

Typically, Virtual Summit hosts make money in three ways:

- Offering lifetime access to the digital recordings via a *Lifetime Access Pass*
- Selling additional products or services as one- or limited-time offers.
- Offering sponsorships or partnerships.

Reimagining The Virtual Summit Model

Before we outline where to begin when planning a Virtual Summit, let's talk about some of the common pitfalls with the model.

Content Overwhelm: With over 25 experts typically featured on a summit, participants quickly get overwhelmed with too much content.

Speaker Saturation: In this less is more era, influencers are starting to devalue the summit model due to oversaturation of the number of speakers. The model does not elevate status in the capacity it once did.

Host Overwhelm: The amount of work required to put on a traditional summit requires a significant amount of time and resources. When you multiply the workload by 25 or more speakers, you exponentially increase the activities required to deliver the summit. When combined with speaker, affiliate, sponsor, and participant management, you may feel like giving up before you've even started.

This is exactly why so many Virtual Summits are so poorly delivered in the marketplace. As a result, so much opportunity to build strong relationships and generate revenue is left on the table.

But there is a better way to generate massive results and win with all players involved.

Rather than following the rules of the traditional summit model with over 25 speakers, conduct a smaller, more strategic summit with 8-12 influencers. In doing so, you will:

- Reduce content overwhelm and get more participants through your content.
- Be more selective with your speakers, and you'll have more time to invest in activities that increase their status.
- Be able to reduce your own overwhelm and planning while still delivering a high-quality event.

Best of all, you will have created a powerful model that you can repeat a lot more frequently for your audience.

Five Steps Toward Planning Your Virtual Summit

Ready to launch your Virtual Summit? Here are five tips on where to begin planning your Virtual Summit:

1. **Get Massively Clear.**

Outline the three to five objectives you hope to achieve by hosting a summit. What are your goals for your participants? What are the goals for your business?

2. Identify Your Call to Action.

Start with the end in mind. What do you want the participants to do following the event? Do you want them to join your masterclass or attend your live event? Do you want them to buy your course or join your program?

3. Design the Virtual Summit Experience.

Think strategically about how you can lay out the Virtual Summit so people naturally want to take your Call to Action. How many days should it be? What types of topics should be featured to create a quality participant experience?

4. Identify Speakers for Your Summit.

Select speakers who will deliver upon the business objectives and complement the Virtual Summit experience so participants want to take the Call to Action.

5. Cap the Speaker Lineup to 8 to12 Experts/Influencers.

Less is truly more. Spend more time building relationships and repurposing the speaker content. Notice that selecting speakers should be one of the final activities you do when planning a Virtual Summit. As a host, you have a responsibility to your participants: Don't chase influencers simply because of their email list size. Instead, find presenters who will increase the likelihood that people will take your Call to Action.

Moving Forward

Virtual Summits are one of the few platforms that check so many boxes to ignite your business. Master this model, and you'll have a rinse and repeat process to put your content, lead, and revenue generation on autopilot.

A Gift For You

Secrets Revealed! The Ultimate Authority Formula:

Discover the Three Drivers to Help You Stand Out in a Noisy Market, Attract Your Tribe, and Become the Ultimate Authority in Your Niche. www.customboxagency.com

About Mark Stern

Mark Stern is a serial entrepreneur and founder of Rough Streak Digital and LYVE Online. He is also the host of CLICKpreneur.

Prior to becoming an entrepreneur, Mark was a top-tier strategy consultant at Deloitte Consulting, the world's largest consulting firm. While at Deloitte, he was selected from among the firm's 40,000+ US-based employees for a prestigious fellowship with the XPRIZE Foundation. He has spent the last decade working with Fortune 500 leaders across the retail, healthcare, fitness, beverage, and financial services industries.

Mark holds an MBA from Duke University's Fuqua School of Business. He is a four-time Spartan Trifecta holder, SXSW Start-up Mentor, and life-time lover of BBQ. Mark currently lives in Austin, Texas.

CHAPTER FIFTY-NINE

Drop-Shipping and Retail Arbitrage

By Tommy Wang

Everyone seems to want to get into making money online. One reason is because you can start with limited capital, work with little overhead, and start selling quickly. Few are comfortable taking big financial risks, so selling smart is important. Most people don't jump into buying a lot of inventory because there is always the chance that the products won't sell.

Several sales models allow inventory control to be simple and cost-effective. We will examine each in detail and reference other chapters in the book that discuss the specific use of different models.

In The Beginning

I have been designing, creating, sourcing, and selling products for over 20 years. My company has sold over $500m worth of products in the retail marketplace so you could say I understand products pretty well.

Drop-Shipping

To reduce risk and be able to get a business up and running quickly on a small budget, a lot of people start with drop-shipping. Drop-shipping is an arrangement in which a vendor or manufacturer allows you to list their product on your website with a markup and when it sells you forward the order information to them and they ship it directly to the buyer for you. You keep the markup. Technically, you can drop-ship without a website. Some entrepreneurs use drop-shipping and sell on eBay or Amazon. But most people that get into drop-shipping start their own website, often on shopping platforms like WooCommerce and Shopify. Shopping platforms allow you to set up a site in hours and install a plugin (like Oberlo for Shopify and Alidrop-ship for WooCommerce) that allows you to start drop-shipping.

There are a few things that you need to consider before getting into drop-shipping:

Competition

A lot of people have started to drop-ship, so it has become very competitive, unlike it was five or six years ago.

You Must Stand Out

To be successful, you either have to stand out from the crowd or be able to pick excellent sellers (which is very difficult) because, more than likely, a lot of your competition will be selling the same items as you.

Beware of Shipping Costs and Delivery Periods

A lot of buyers look at shipping costs and delivery times when making buying decisions, so be sure you have accurate shipping cost estimates and delivery dates on your items.

Many drop-shippers use manufacturers and suppliers located in China. Shipping times are usually 15 days from there but can be as long as 45 days. Be upfront with your customers so they know they will not be getting their purchases in a few days like domestic suppliers can promise (for example, Amazon Prime).

Product Quality

As a drop-shipping vendor, you rarely, if ever, see the products you're selling. That means you do not actually know the quality of the product, in general, nor can you check items individually for defects or damage. You only have the word of your supplier. You must plan for returns and chargebacks from your customers. Be sure you have a clear return and refund policy for buyers to see.

Domestic companies will drop-ship for you and that has been a trend in recent years but it has become very competitive and the profit margins are typically even smaller than when ordering from overseas.

Many people will tell you that drop-shipping is dying or dead but that far from the truth. There will always be drop-shipping, but it will get more competitive and harder to make money. If you are good at finding sought-after products and you can build a loyal customer base you can make a lot of money from drop-shipping.

Retail Arbitrage

Another method of avoiding a large inventory is using retail arbitrage. It is a fairly simple concept: You look for a store that is selling a product at a good price, you buy a small (or large) inventory of the product from them, and then sell it online at a higher price. With mass discounters and big-box retailers slashing prices to clear inventory in the last few years, retail arbitrage has become very popular.

To get started, find your sources for products. Most people check sales and closeout sections of big retailers such as Walmart, Target, etc. See what is offered and use a Scanner app to scan the items' barcodes to see what the item sells for on Amazon. If the margin or spread is more than enough to cover your shipping costs and fees, then buy the items.

Retail arbitrage has become competitive because it can be a great side hustle. It doesn't require a lot of time and if you get lucky or you're a good shopper you can make quick cash.

If you know your market and what you want to sell, look at other discount retailers like TJ Maxx, Ross Stores, Dollar Stores, and regional discount chains like Burlington Coat or Gabriel Brothers where you can find discounted clothes, shoes, and toys that are overstock or last season. Be warned, however, that if you buy name brands and trying to resell them on sites like Amazon, they might not let you list it because they are worried that the products may be counterfeit.

Another approach is to buy discounted items during big sales like Black Friday or New Year's sales. Because products but are heavily discounted and could be worth it.

With the success of secondhand selling sites like Mercari, Poshmark, Craigslist, and Facebook Marketplace, there is a growing trend in buying secondhand items so look for buying opportunities at flea markets, garage sales, and non-profit organization stores like the Salvation Army and Goodwill. Take note that you need to know the local costs of secondhand items to successfully determine if an item is a good buy or not.

Selling Under Your Own Brand

Once you have some success in buying and selling products and are confident in your business, you may want to grow into selling your own brand. First, find a product that you love and feel confident about. Next, buy your product in volume (remember to negotiate a volume discount with the manufacturer or supplier) and start putting your brand on it. This is called white labeling or private labeling. You are buying a finished product from another company and they (or you) rebrand it with your logo to make it appear as if you had made it. This is usually done with beauty and food products, but it can be done with any product category.

Finally, if you decide that you want to create a product yourself, you can. Start by looking for a manufacturer. Doing this domestically is very costly and you can easily spend too much money rather than making money. Instead, a great way to find a reasonably priced manufacturer is by going overseas and sourcing from China or another southeastern Asian country. There are a few ways to do this:

- Hire a trading company that will handle everything for you including finding the factory and all the negotiations and logistics. For their services, you pay a higher price, but they tend to work with reliable factories and suppliers that they have worked with in the past, which reduces risk.
- Work directly with brokers (who are individuals and not companies) who have relationships with suppliers and factories. The cost of using a broker is lower because they will not be able to provide as many services as a trading company. Also, if there are any problems, brokers will not take on as much liability as a trading company.
- Source products yourself directly from a factory. This method has the highest risk because you will assume all of the liability if something goes awry, but you are in full control of the negotiations.
- To find and source factories, do online research. Websites like Alibaba and EC21 show the manufacturer ratings and reviews. You can also interview factories through online video conferencing.
- Go overseas and meet with factories directly to discuss your needs and negotiate a contract (only travel after doing a lot of research and setting up appointments in advance).

- Go to big trade shows overseas. The biggest one is the Canton Fair and is held twice a year in Guangzhou, China. It has run since 1957 and has three phases (each phase has different product categories that are represented).[48] It goes on for over two weeks. It is huge, so it takes days to see everything. The other big show is the Asian Gifts & Premiums Show in Hong Kong. It also runs twice a year and usually runs around the same time as the Canton Gift Fair. It's much smaller but you can find a lot of new trends and hot products there.

Be very cautious:

There are a lot of companies that claim to be factories that are not. Instead, they are a broker or a trading company pretending to be a factory. If you don't physically fly over and meet them and inspect the factory in person, you will never know if you are dealing with the factory or a middleman.

Moving Forward

There are many ways to sell products online. You must decide which one will work best for you and your situation. The key is to get started. Planning and learning about selling won't make you money. Selling will. Start small with something simple or something that you know something about and grow from there. You may end up running more than one type of business, or all of them, that is up to you, but get started with one of them to start earning money.

[48] n.a. (n.d.). *Introduction of China Import and Export Fair.* Retrieved from https://www.canton-fair.org.cn/html/cantonfair/en/about/2012-09/130.shtml on October 28, 2019.

About Tommy Wang

Tommy Wang has over 20 years of experience in business strategy, corporate finance, and structuring complex deals. His expertise in international commerce has made him a trusted and respected business advisor.

Mr. Wang has the unique ability to envision business opportunities that are not readily apparent and capitalize on them to effectively develop profitable entrepreneurial business ventures.

He started his career by founding iventureLab, one of the first incubator technology firms while working closely with the Center for Technology Transfer at Carnegie Mellon University. The company grew to over 150 employees in under two years. Tommy soon became a board member and consultant to over 50 startup businesses looking to emulate and capitalize on his proven success.

Mr. Wang's keen business insight has proven him to be an effective and accomplished professional. He is versatile and adept in all aspects of business. His expertise transcends many disciplines including operations, finance, logistics, product development, and sales strategies. He has proven knowledge and history in several industries encompassing Technology (IT), Manufacturing, Education, Wholesale/Retail, and Real Estate.

Tommy is a dynamic individual who can translate his unique skills to help businesses develop and thrive. He calls it the *Facts of the Deal* and knows how to structure deals and he consults for many different businesses and industries.

Tommy earned his bachelor's degree in Electrical Computer Engineering graduating with the distinction of summa cum laude. He earned his master's degree in MISM (Masters in Information Systems Management) also from Carnegie Mellon University. Tommy was the first student in Carnegie Mellon University history to complete both an undergraduate and graduate degree program in only three years.

CHAPTER SIXTY

Arbitrage And Amazon

By Nate McCallister

Retail arbitrage involves buying products from brick-and-mortar stores and re-listing the products on Amazon at a higher price. After product costs and shipping fees, you keep the rest as profit. Online arbitrage is the same concept but instead of buying from a physical store, you purchase the products online.

Amazon arbitrage is a great entrepreneurial endeavor and you can get started with very little capital if you want. Savvy buying and keeping on top of shipping details and costs are critical parts of arbitrage.

In The Beginning

I had two copies of *The 4 Hour Body* by Tim Ferriss and I was ready to sell the extra one. I'd heard a story about a couple who were making money buying toys and books and reselling them on Amazon. They claimed to be making over $100,000 a year.

I had to give it a shot. I had just finished my degree in Economics so arbitrage was fresh in my mind, just not at this micro-level.

I created a Seller's Account on Amazon and listed the book. Within minutes, it sold!

I was insanely excited despite making almost no profit. After shipping costs, packaging supplies, and lots of work to determine how to ship it to the buyer, I made about $1. I worked too hard for that tiny dollar but it was the best money I've ever made because it was much more than just a dollar; I realized that I could learn how to sell on Amazon and make much higher profits.

I started going to retail stores every day after work and practiced retail arbitrage. In the store, I'd scan products with my smartphone and use an Amazon sourcing app to check what the products were selling for on Amazon to determine how much profit I could make after costs, how fast the products would sell, and the number of sellers.

After two months, I had surpassed $40,000 in sales with margins of around 25%.

Online Arbitrage

I realized that I needed help finding products to sell. I heard about **online arbitrage**, which was great because I could source products before and after work. Eventually, I hired a virtual assistant who found leads while I slept.

I was excited about the possibility of working for myself full-time. After two consistent months of sales, I quit my day job and started selling on Amazon full-time.

Getting Started

If buying and selling products and being an entrepreneur sounds appealing, here's how to get started:

1. **Open a Professional Amazon Sellers Account**

Although you have the option of creating either a free Individual Seller Plan or a paid Professional Seller Plan, the Professional Seller Plan is superior because of the following benefits:

- Buy Box Eligibility: The buy box appears on the righthand side of a listing. When a customer selects Buy Now and doesn't review other seller options, the buy box seller gets the sale. Buy boxes are awarded based on price, location, and seller feedback.
- Unlimited Listings: The Individual Plan only allows you to sell a maximum of 40 items per month and you must enter each item you offer for sale manually. The Professional Plan allows you to list and sell as many items as you wish.
- New Product Listings: Those on the Individual Plan can only sell products that are already listed on Amazon; they cannot be the first to list a new product. As a Professional Seller, you can broaden your listings to include any product you like at any time. This allows the creation of unique bundles and expansion of your product offerings.

2. **Management Tools For Professional Sellers**

Professional Sellers get Amazon tools that Individual Sellers do not. The tools track orders, listings, sales, inventory, fulfillment, marketing, revenue, returns, and more.

3. **Amazon Advertising and Promotions**

As a Professional Seller, you can participate in Amazon's marketing and promotion services, which include Pay Per Click (PPC) Ads, coupons, discounts, etc.

4. **Value**

Amazon charges Individual Sellers $0.99 per sale. If you sell the maximum number of units allowed, 40, you give Amazon $39.60 per month. The Professional Plan is 39.99 and you can sell as many items as you like.

Thus, as long as you are selling more than 40 items a month, the fee per unit is cheaper (for example, if you sell 1000 items in a month, the cost for fees is only approximately $0.04 per unit).

Fulfillment By Amazon (FBA)

Fulfillment By Amazon (FBA) is a service offered by Amazon in which your inventory is kept at an Amazon warehouse and shipped from there as soon as an order is made.

It's recommended that you use the FBA program rather than the Merchant Fulfillment (MF) option. The FBA program will give you increased control over your time and space requirements.

When using the FBA program, you can take time off and not worry about orders being shipped properly. If you do MF, you have to prepare orders yourself, which is inefficient because you will spend more time filling orders than focusing on your business growth and development.

Read The Rules And Watch Introduction Videos

Although boring, you must start on the right foot. Be sure to review and understand all of the following:

- Prohibited Seller Activities
- Selling Policies and Seller Code of Conduct
- Drop-Shipping Policy
- Condition Guidelines
- Category, Product and Listing Restrictions
- Download an Amazon Sourcing App

As of January 10, 2018, Amazon has 562,382,292 products.[49] A scanning app allows you to scan the barcode of any product and see:

- The product's sales rank on Amazon.
- Estimated fees.
- Estimated Return on Investment (ROI).
- Estimated net profit.
- Whether Amazon sells the product.
- Current buy box price.
- Total sellers.
- Conditions listed for the product.
- Category and if your eligible to sell the product.
- Images of the product (necessary for proper listing).

There are several Amazon sourcing apps but the free Amazon Seller app is more than enough to start. Type *Amazon Seller* into your app store to find it.

What Makes a Good Buy?

This is complex to answer. What makes a good buy varies based on things like your capital, risk tolerance, time, etc. A good buy for you may not be a good buy for someone else.

For now, try looking for the following:

- Products with a profit margin of more than 30%.
- Products that have a minimum net profit of $5 per unit.
- Products with high turn-over; your inventory should sell within two weeks of listing.
- Products that cost less than $50.

---

[49] n.a. (January 10, 2019). *How Many Products Does Amazon Sell?* Retrieved from https://www.scrapehero.com/many-products-amazon-sell-january-2018/ on October 15, 2019.

You'll learn from experience. Don't beat yourself up over bad purchases and don't be afraid to sell mistake products back at cost so you can get your money back to reinvest in better products.

Scan Products Around Your House

Everyone has some extra stuff around their house that they can flip on Amazon. Since you've already paid for them you will make straight profit after fees. I recommend you start with books because they rarely have restrictions and they're easy to ship.

Create Your First Shipment

For retail arbitrage, you'll use MF in the beginning. Once you've listed items to sell, prepare for your first shipment. You will need packing materials (boxes, tape, padding, padded envelopes, etc.). Remove any pricing stickers that may be on the item. Package the item well to avoid damage during shipping that may result in returns. Weigh your shipment (include the packing material) and enter this information on Amazon.

Once an order comes in, create and print shipping labels in Seller Central. Affix the labels to the package. Call UPS or drop the package off at a UPS location to get it on its way.

If you get confused or are unsure of what to do, there are a lot of great tutorials on YouTube. Just make sure that the videos you watch are up-to-date.

Continue Sourcing and Monitoring Sales

Don't be surprised if you make a lot of mistakes. It's a learning process. Don't beat yourself up. Consider this the tuition to learn this money-making skill. Monitor which items are selling and which aren't. Identify why and repeat what works and avoid what doesn't. Be patient. Both your successes and mistakes will make you better each day.

Reinvest Earnings In Inventory And Expand Sourcing Methods

Success on Amazon requires reinvestment of your revenue. You can turn a $1,000 per month business into a $100,000 per month business if you consistently reinvest more than you take out.

Moving Forward

If you're looking for a get rich quick business like those advertised everywhere online, Amazon Arbitrage will not be for you. It takes time, but it is worth it.

Be prepared to expand from retail arbitrage to online arbitrage. There are plenty of tools for online arbitrage available (free and paid), but you don't need them to get started.

A Gift For You

Get my Ultimate Product Sourcing Checklist for free! It will teach you more about the best product-sourcing methods.

AND, If you're interested in getting started with online arbitrage and want to automate the process, visit TacticalArbitrage.com and use code ER10 to get an extended 10-day trial.

Join My Facebook Group: facebook.com/groups/nathan.mccallister/

BONUS:

List of Tools for Online Arbitrage: entreresource.com/complete-guide-online-arbitrage-sourcing-tools-programs/

About Nate McCallister

Nate McCallister is a full-time blogger who focuses on helping others learn the ins and outs of e-Commerce. Selling on Amazon was his gateway into entrepreneurship, and he serves a large community of sellers in his Facebook FBA Today and on his website EntreResource.com.

CHAPTER SIXTY-ONE

Fulfillment By Amazon (FBA)

By Siru Pihlajavesi

mazon is the largest online marketplace on the Internet. In 2017, 50% of the products sold on Amazon were from third-party vendors and, of those, 140,000 made six-figure incomes.[50]

Fulfillment by Amazon (FBA) is an order fulfillment model in which a third-party vendor on Amazon stores their products at an Amazon fulfillment center and Amazon does all the work associated with filling an order for the vendor: inventory management, product storage, picking, packing, shipping, and customer service are all done by Amazon.[51] It assists vendors by taking over a large amount of time-consuming work that vendors normally have to do themselves. This allows the vendor to focus on more important issues, such as:

- Marketing and driving traffic to their store.
- Product research, testing, and procurement.
- Branding.

Using Amazon FBA is not a passive income model, however. I don't believe those exist. Even unicorns need some love and attention. You must keep sourcing products for your store and carrying out marketing to get traffic but FBA allows you to focus on the growth of your company rather than the time-consuming day-to-day operations of it, so your income increases quicker than if you did it all yourself.

Fulfillment By Amazon

Unlike Fulfillment by Merchant (FBM), partnering up with Amazon through FBA eliminates an enormous amount of work for the business owner. Once you have seen samples and approved your final product(s), you may never hold your product(s) again!

Your order will be shipped directly from the manufacturer to Amazon's fulfillment center(s). From there, Amazon is responsible for order fulfillment, returns, and all other customer services, even negative buyer feedback can be removed if there ever is a problem with shipping. Furthermore, Amazon's algorithm favors FBA sellers by improving their listings' ranks for specific keywords, and

---

[50] Dunne, C. (n.d.). Amazon Has 1,029,528 New Sellers This (Plus Other Stats). Retrieved on June 5, 2020 from https://www.feedbackexpress.com/amazon-1029528-new-sellers-year-plus-stats/.

[51] n.a. (August 6, 2019). *What is Fulfillment by Amazon (FBA) and How Does It Work?* Retrieved from https://www.shiprocket.in/blog/fulfillment-by-amazon-fba/ on September 1, 2019.

always providing a Call to Action (buy box). Because FBA sellers automatically qualify for Prime's two-day shipping, customers tend to favor FBA sellers over others.

Tips For Sourcing Products

It is critical, when opening a store on Amazon, to ensure the products you sell will be profitable. Storing items with Amazon that don't sell doesn't make you money, even with FBA.

Whether testing the waters with a single product or planning to build a collection of items for a specific niche, there's a method to the madness of finding a profitable product. It is a formula taught by Mike Gazzola and other Amazon experts. When deciding whether or not to carry a product, you must determine the answers to three questions about the product:

- Does it sell well (is there evidence that the product is in demand)?
- Can I compete (with other vendors)?
- Are the margins there (will I make money in the end)?

Using a Product Information Management (PIM) tool, you can pull up every bit of information on a specific product that is sold on Amazon. The Amazon Seller app can provide lots of sales information. It and other tools show sales volume, number of reviews, number of sellers, estimated profit and fees, best keywords, the average daily giveaways for first-page ranking, and much more. There are many PIMs – many of them free – select those that provide all the information you need to make decisions about what to carry in your store.

You will want to find a product that already does at least five figures in sales each month. To determine if you can compete, make sure there are at least five sellers with less than 200 reviews as this signifies a good entry point. Reviews play a big role in purchases, and 200 reviews are not difficult to gain. Taking into consideration Amazon's warehouse fees, I recommend selling lightweight products that do not take up much space and have at least a 50% Return on Investment (ROI). To start, I recommend you stick with non-seasonal products in unrestricted categories.

You may find a manufacturer directly through sites like Alibaba.com, or choose to go through a sourcing company. I highly recommend finding a sourcing agent in the US and communicating with manufacturers through them.

If you choose to find suppliers on Alibaba yourself, be sure to check that they are Gold-rated suppliers and part of Trade Assurance. To gather data and find the most reasonable deal, send at least 15 quote requests to different manufacturers. You will want to ask for the Minimum Order Quantity (MOQ), turnaround time, and cost of shipping by air and sea. For shipping quotes, it is good to use the Port of Los Angeles or the Amazon fulfillment center where your products are stored as a location so you get accurate, comparable quotes. Always, always request samples of the product(s) you are considering to sell. You should never invest money in a product you have not touched or sell it to a trusting customer who can give poor (or excellent) reviews.

Private Label *Everything*

Private labeling is, in short, branding a product as your own. To create a brand and to stand out, you may engrave logos on your product(s), find beautiful packaging, change colors, textures or materials, or bundle your main product with another item. I recommend looking up the negative reviews given to other sellers of the product to understand what customers have complained about and then asking your manufacturer to make tweaks to address those complaints.

Private labeling also combats hijackers who steal your product listing to sell as their own. Amazon has a hard time catching hijackers but if you can document that the hijacker's product is nothing like your offering, Amazon can take action to protect you and the customer.

Private labeling is important to stay unique and profitable. With my first product, margins without ad spend were roughly 70% after deducting Amazon's fees. It was a simple $20 product in the baby category. By the time I launched, ranked my listing on the first page for major keywords, and received multiple *Amazon's Choice* and *Best Seller* badges, many other sellers had started selling the same product at half the price. Because I hadn't spent enough time private labeling my product, I had to follow suit to avoid falling off the first page. I kissed my healthy margin a sweet goodbye.

I had put my logos on the item but did not create a distinct package so mine just looked like everyone else's. Had I created a beautiful or distinctive package and bundled the product with another item, I would have been able to maintain my $20 price and or raised it since Prime members are prepared to pay more for better quality products. For the matter of a couple of dollars, I could have avoided my lost margins.

Not All Flowers And Roses

You must make the system work for you. Amazon isn't perfect. Many sellers give up and others say, "Only the rich get richer."

I believe two things can be true at once and when you understand how and *why* Amazon works, you can take advantage of it to make money. I believe FBA is the best way to start when a business can only make a small investment in inventory. I also believe it is the easiest way to scale a brand.

There are debates about the benefits of using other Internet marketplaces (e.g., eBay, Etsy, Walmart, Rakuten) but I believe using Amazon's FBA is still advantageous, despite its unpredictability, because no other platform provides a fulfillment service that allows vendors to focus on scaling their business rather than filling orders. Using FBA takes you one step closer to top 10,000 status.

Moving Forward

Amazon FBA is work, but it is fun work. It can allow you the free time you may be looking for and also support a thriving business with limitless scalability. Launching your store and marketing your product(s) are your key focus. Launching is the most fun part, and I have included resources to guide you along. Every topic in this book can be used to help your Amazon business succeed.

I truly hope you'll have success in all that you do, and more importantly, that you have fun with it. If anything, this book will always be a reminder of how likeminded people coming together can have a blast with an otherwise overwhelming project. Whether your next exciting venture is with Amazon FBA or something completely different, I highly suggest joining a mastermind. Having an extra 500-5000 eyes looking out for TOS updates and other changes can save you tons of money in mistakes. Surround yourself with accountability partners and motivated people going over the same hurdles. Take advantage of the connections and support available; it may just be the difference between failure and success.

A Gift For You

Siru has created a FREE starter-kit to Amazon FBA that gets you on the right path and provides amazing resources to guide you through building a profitable Amazon business.

For her FREE Amazon Business Starter-Kit and resources, go to: https://siru.io/playbook

About Siru Pihlajavesi

Siru Pihlajavesi is an online marketer and owner of CoreWorth Consulting, which started as an e-Commerce company and later expanded to digital marketing services including website and sales funnel building and design, SEO strategies, and competitor analysis.

Siru's expertise is in rebranding and bringing companies, products, and visions into the online world, whether it is a complete relaunch of software, rebuilding converting websites, or bringing product to Amazon's marketplace.

Siru has helped hundreds of companies and everyday people to start, build, and scale their Amazon businesses, and she continues to do so today. She works closely with experts in their fields to connect hardworking entrepreneurs with trusted mentors.

Siru moved from Finland to the United States in 2010, and currently lives in New Hampshire with her daughter Cheyenne. The two enjoy traveling around the world, boating on New Hampshire's beautiful lakes, great food and their amazing family and friends.

Learn more about Siru here: www.Siru.io or follow her on Social Media @Sirubaru

CHAPTER SIXTY-TWO

Shopify

By Kim Calera

Kendall Jenner, Kylie Jenner, Kanye West, Adele, Justin Bieber, Logan Paul, Radiohead, Lady Gaga and Jeffree Star Cosmetics... What do all these people have in common?

They all sell products using Shopify.

Shopify is the best platform for e-Commerce because you can easily optimize it for conversions and list products right away, you don't need to build a website first. Before I built stores on Shopify, I used other website builders and there would be so much work required to build the website that I would burn-out before the launch.

One of the most amazing things is that it enables you to work from anywhere. You could literally install some apps to your Shopify store and dropship unbranded products so you're able to fully focus on working on your business, rather than in it, or you can install apps that can send your orders from various warehouses for you, or you can use Shopify's existing tools to create automatic shipping labels for you if you're packing and preparing orders yourself.

In The Beginning

I set up my first store when I became physically disabled. I was able to provide for my family whilst bedridden and working only a few hours a day. I made £134,200 (US$172,780) in a year.

I've tried a lot of e-Commerce platforms, website builders, and marketplaces, but I love that Shopify allows you to remain in full control of your customers' experience and information. Another company doesn't have access to your customers' details. It's also easy to jump on trends or throw in a last-minute sale.

When an injury meant that I couldn't continue my previous career, I replaced my income using Shopify. I started drop-shipping and then branded my best-selling products. I recommend that strategy for anyone wanting to start e-Commerce with Shopify, whether you're an established business or starting from scratch, because:

It allows you to focus on getting customers rather than order fulfillment, which is time-consuming and dilutes your concentration. There's also a low barrier of entry.

Benefits Of Shopify For Entrepreneurs

I believe that Shopify offers some benefits, not offered by other e-Commerce platforms, that are specifically great for entrepreneurs:

- Most importantly, you can work anywhere, anytime, as long as you have a computer/laptop/mobile device and Internet service.
- Build amazing passive online income.
- All customer information and email lists are in your control.
- Install some apps to your Shopify store and dropship unbranded products or send your orders from various warehouses, so you're able to fully focus on working on scaling your business rather than fulfilling orders.
- Use Shopify's existing tools to create automatic shipping labels if you're packing and preparing orders yourself.

Nine Tips About Being A Shopify Entrepreneur

Here are nine useful things I have learned about using Shopify that will help you have success:

1. Choose A Theme Design You Can Handle and Like

Choose one that you'll stick to for at least the first year of business, that isn't too taxing for now, and that will still be good as you scale.

2. Take Imperfect Action; Stick To It Unless There's A Major Problem

Most of my students who come to me with a failing Shopify store have one thing in common: They're constantly tweaking their store website, branding, or thinking about what new products they can list next month or next year. Don't do that. Launch your store, test your products, find your bestseller(s), then scale. You don't need perfect images or the most attractive store in the beginning. You can always perfect it later, if needed.

3. Remove "Powered by Shopify" From The Footer

This statement can put some customers on edge because they wonder if their personal and financial information is being supplied to a third party they can't trust. There is no requirement for that statement to remain on your store to use Shopify, so just remove it.

4. Develop An Amazing Offer

This is the most important! Especially in a niche with lots of competition, you can position yourself the best just by having an amazing offer that's unavailable elsewhere. A bundled offer avoids a price war with the competition, it's unique and no one else offers it so comparing prices isn't possible. Price wars can kill small businesses. Don't be afraid to use scarcity and urgency in your offers too.

5. Get Reviews And Social Proof

Give incentives (freebies, coupons, or discounts), price the product very low in the beginning, or – if you're selling an item made by a manufacturer who collects review – use their reviews (with their permission). Ask followers on social media platforms to share your posts, ads, and sales announcements.

6. Supply The Small Print

Be sure to list all your policies and delivery information. Remember to make delivery costs clear. Carefully consider your purchase terms, returns policy, privacy policy, and legal pages. Be sure they are easy to access and simple to read (use Plain English). Besides building trust between you and your customers, many advertising platforms will not allow you to run ads if you don't have these policies in place.

Place them in the footer, not on your product description. Your product description should focus on selling your products. Most customers know they can find store policies in the footer of a store's site.

7. Market, Market, Market

Trying to do business without advertising is like winking in the dark; you know that you are keeping up a powerful winking, but nobody else has any idea of it.[52]

So many people think if they build it people will come. Even if you have the most revolutionary life-changing product, no one is going to know about it if you or someone else doesn't tell them.

Some marketing methods:

- Social Media Ads
- Social Media Posts (on a business account)
- Search Engine Optimization (SEO)
- Blogging
- Affiliates (pay them a percentage of sales; if no sales, no cost to you)

8. Optimize Your Store for Sales

To convert your shoppers into buyers, focus on good copywriting and organizing your collections. Enter your store as a customer and see if it flows. Install up-selling, down-selling, or cross-selling apps, include it in your product description, or do both.

9. Only Install Shopify Apps You Are Using

The more you add, the slower your website will be. If it takes too long to load, customers will go elsewhere. One app that I highly recommend is the InCart Upsell app. It's perfect for frictionless up-selling in your customer cart. I tested other apps, but customers bounced a lot with up-selling pop-ups, this app doesn't interrupt your customer's journey; it does a great job of raising my average order value.

Moving Forward

Shopify makes e-Commerce simple and you can work from anywhere. You don't need to be a web developer or technology wizard to succeed in e-Commerce, it's now open to everyone. Get started today with my special offer outlined below.

---

[52] Unnamed Editor. (November 8, 1870). *Current Notes.* [Boston] Journal, p. 4. Retrieved from https://www.barrypopik.com/index.php/new_york_city/entry/doing_business_without_advertising_is_like_winking_at_a_girl_in_the_dark/ on October 24, 2019.

A Gift For You

I've created a crazy eCommerce offer bundle just for the readers of this book and I'm giving it away for next to nothing!

This amazing bundle includes:

- Dropship Freedom Course.
- Magical Facebook Marketing Course.
- Facebook Famous Fans + Engagement On Steroids Course.
- BONUS: How to Write Amazing Ads + Ethically Push Your Customers' Hot Buttons.
- BONUS: Facebook Ad copy - Swipe files.
- BONUS: Shared eCommerce Funnels

You can grab it here: https://www.freedominabundancewithkim.com/crazy-offer

About Kim Calera

Kim Calera was a fashion model, but life wasn't always glamorous. She grew up in poverty.

In 2009, after Kim had been a successful model for over six years, she experienced a traumatic assault and subsequently went to model and act in Bollywood.

When her employers mistreated her there, she fled back to London. Because she had no money and nowhere to live, she created a business on the flight home. She used her contacts to manufacture jewelry and sold her pieces at markets. But she remained homeless and had to model again improve her situation.

By 2013, Kim's life was looking up again. She had a house, was modeling regularly in top magazines, and was expecting her first child. But, disaster struck, again, when she became physically disabled and was told she may never work again.

Kim didn't accept that. Instead, she launched her first e-Commerce store.

Connect with Kim on social media at:

- instagram.com/kimcalera
- twitter.com/kimcalera
- facebook.com/kimcaleraofficial

CHAPTER SIXTY-THREE

Etsy

By Kathy Walls

tsy is an e-Commerce platform whose primary focus is on handmade items, crafts, and vintage items. Since its conception in 2005, Etsy has become one of the easiest platforms to use to provide a large market for your business or hobbies.

Most people start by showcasing their hobbies in hopes of making a sale here or there, but there are some that turn Etsy into a money machine and I was one of those people.

In The Beginning

I started using the Etsy platform to tinker and figure out if it was the place for my print-on-demand business. I was not familiar with Etsy or similar platforms because I had stuck to WordPress sites and social media to showcase my products.

Back in 2012, I was looking for a new career. I was completing my business degree in Accounting and Human Resource Management and I had a printing business on the side but I was uncertain how I could scale the side-business so that I could avoid a traditional job after graduation. I searched online and found multiple platforms that already had traffic running to them so I decided to put my products on several of these sites and see how it went.

While working full-time in a tax office, I learned about Etsy and how it worked. I realized that this would be the place for me to develop my business. I studied and implemented for months on end and finally my work paid-off. After a year, attending my full-time job was costing me money. I was pulling-in $8,000 to $10,000 per month in sales. I hired help and formalized the company, which sold products that I designed, printed, and shipped. We shipped products all over the world and the Etsy platform made it all easy.

The Advantages of Etsy

The advantages of Etsy over other platforms are many:

- It is easy to navigate and use.

When new to e-Commerce, using new technologies can become overwhelming and some software requires the owner to build and code to create a store, which is often too complex for the average person. It was and still is too complex for me. I am a designer of products, not a computer programmer/coder. Etsy's dashboard and store builder are so simple that anyone can handle it.

- Customers already know the Etsy name.

As of 2018, close to 39.5 million buyers have purchased goods on Etsy. Using a platform that is already trusted by buyers helps people feel secure about purchasing from your business. It also increases the probability of converting a prospect into a buyer over that of a stand-alone website without brand recognition. People are more at ease and more apt to buy knowing that the site they are buying from has a trustworthy reputation.

- Etsy Pattern gives sellers a separate website for their shop.

This feature allows sellers to use a unique domain name (I.e., www. Yourshop.com) and syncs all the vendor's Etsy product listings to the unique website, which helps with branding. Instead of Etsy.com/yourshop, you are found at yourshop.com.

- Etsy messaging and customer order requests between buyers and sellers.

Customers can email us directly through the conversation feature and request custom orders and ask questions. This allows personalization for your customers, which reduces product return rates, wasted time, and business costs.

- Etsy accepts almost any product.

There are rules and guidelines that must be followed to continue to sell but you can sell digital downloads, handmade, print on demand, vintage items, and so much more. The possibilities are endless.

- Etsy allows promoted listings.

Promoted listings are paid ads for your listings inside the Etsy platform. This will improve your exposure and conversion rates. Etsy also has a way to advertise on Google Shopping. If you don't know how to do this outside of Etsy, this is a great way to appear in Google searches.

- Etsy's integration helps with Search Engine Optimization.

You can link social media platforms to your Etsy shop and find apps that will help measure the quality of your listings and keep track of your income and expenses.

- Etsy has a Sales and Coupon Feature

For those who have favored your items without buying or abandoned their cart without paying, this feature allows you to send coupons after 24 hours that provides a discount if they buy now.

Getting started with Etsy

Getting started on Etsy is a breeze:

1. Go to www.etsy.com and create an account.
2. Click on Sell on Etsy and open your shop.

You will get step-by-step instructions on setting up your store and creating your first product listing.

3. Fill out all the sections in your shop, your terms, policies, info, and procedures
4. Add a banner, logo, etc.
5. When filling out a listing be sure to fill in as much information as possible.
6. Use high-resolution images.
7. Fill out all the product descriptors.

8. Use all 13 tags that are allowed for each listing. Tags help people search for and find your products.
9. Make sure the title is clear and describes your product.
10. Use keywords that you think buyers will use to search for your item in the title.
11. Set up any of the other features you wish to use either now or at a later date (SEO, coupons, promotions, etc.).

Moving Forward

There is much more, but these are the basics of using Etsy; you can learn more once you've started selling. Remember to always treat your Etsy shop like a business rather than a hobby. It's possible to convert a hobby into a full-time business with hired help. I did it and so can you. I make well into six-figures with Etsy

I advise clients who are looking for an online platform on which to start their business not to underestimate the power of Etsy and similar platforms. I am all over online and I do not limit myself to just one platform or another. The more visible one can be the greater the chances of being found. Learning every aspect of the Etsy platform has allowed me the freedom to work from home and be with my children as they grew up. The value of that is priceless.

A Gift For You

Kathy has created a FREE course on how to get your first sale or sign up with the Get Your Groove On Challenge. You can find this at www.getyourgrooveonchallenge.com.For more training and courses please visit https://enhancedtrainingacademy.com.

About Kathy Walls

Kathy L Walls is an e-Commerce and affiliate marketer who got her start on the Etsy platform with a print-on-demand business where she was able to scale her hobby into a six-figure business.

Kathy has taken her knowledge to new heights by teaching those learning to make money online. Her Facebook Group, GrooveNation, is full of likeminded individuals looking to create an online income using social media marketing and platforms such as Groove for e-commerce, affiliate marketing, and network marketing.

Kathy has been married to her husband and business partner, Scott, for 25 years. They have two children, Trevor and Josie, and live in Missouri. Together they love boating and spend as much time as possible on the water, traveling around the U.S., and spending time with friends and family. For more information about Kathy L Walls visit her site here: https://www.kathylwalls.com. Find her group here: https://www.facebook.com/groups/TheGrooveNation.

CHAPTER SIXTY-FOUR

Blogging

By Ilir Salihi

Blogging began in the mid-nineties as people began to publish personal journals or diaries on the Internet. Early bloggers would write about their daily life or topics in which they were interested.

Today, almost any website that focuses on written content is considered a blog. From The Huffington Post to TechCrunch, blogs are some of the most popular destinations on the Internet.

When it comes to blogging, it costs almost nothing to launch, you can write on just about any topic, and there are multiple ways to make money. Plus, you can run a blog from anywhere. With only a wi-fi connection, the world becomes your office.

In The Beginning

I started my first affiliate blog, as a side hustle, in late 2013.While it took several months of hard work, I vividly remember the first month I made more money than working my 50-hour-a-week day job. I was hooked.

I'm convinced that blogging is the best platform for building your brand, boosting your online visibility, and obtaining multiple income streams.

The Benefits Of Blogging

The benefits of blogging are many. I'm listing the best ones here.

Establish Trust And Authority

To position yourself as an expert in your field, post informative, valuable content for your audience. Interact with your readers by responding to questions and comments. The more you demonstrate that you're a useful and reliable resource, the more likely readers are to trust and turn to you when they need your products or services.

Organic Traffic

People search for content related to your topic every day. Blogging regularly can boost your organic traffic in many ways:

- Fresh Content: Google gives more exposure to fresh content. An active blog signals that your content is relevant and up-to-date and they will reward you for that by showing your blog early in the search results.
- Keywords: A regularly updated blog is going to naturally start ranking for searches related to your topic.
- Backlinks: The more content that you publish, the higher your chances that other websites will link to your blog. Backlinks from reputable websites improve ranking in the Search Engine Result Pages (SERPs).

Content For Social Media

Social networks crave blog content. Each new article that you publish has the potential to get shared, go viral, and expose your brand to new audiences.

Multiple Streams Of Blogging Income

Blogging opens the door to lucrative income opportunities. There are several ways to monetize a blog. As you build authority, learn what your readers want, and can determine the options that make sense for you. Here are a few examples of how to monetize a blog.

Affiliate marketing: You do not need your own products or services to sell. Businesses from Amazon to Target and Home Depot have an affiliate program. You just need to find products that complement your niche.

Sell Digital Products: Digital products can be guides, e-books, online courses, and apps. Digital products have no storage, shipping, or fulfillment costs. If you can solve a problem or fill a void in your niche, you should consider selling digital products.

Email Marketing: Your blog is one of the best platforms for building your email list. This list can be used to promote new blog updates, affiliate offers, or your own products.

Speaking/Coaching Services: This doesn't always mean coaching in the traditional sense of the word. You can offer a service that allows you to connect with (and help) your audience in a one-to-one or small group setting. For example, if you're blogging about:

- SEO – offer website audits, feedback, or consultation
- Keto lifestyle – sell diet plans and one-to-one support
- Budget travel – create personalized travel itineraries

I started an Internet marketing blog less than a year ago. I do not list services anywhere on my site but have been contacted for mentoring, funnel building, and Search Engine Optimization (SEO). I've been asked to appear on podcasts and virtual summits. As your website grows, so will new opportunities.

Passive Income: A monetized blog post can bring an incredible return on investment. Each article can bring in leads or sales for years to come. For example, in 2015, I wrote an article for a financial blog. The article links to an affiliate offer that pays (on average) $1,980 a sale.

Four years later, that article is still online. Last month, it made $1,379 in commissions. The few hours invested in writing that article may continue to bring in sales for years.

Can you make a full-time income blogging? Each person you talk to will define a full-time income differently. According to the U.S. Census Bureau, the median household income in the United States in 2017 was $61,372.

Let's look at the finance blog just mentioned. One affiliate offer averages $1,980 in commission. If you were to promote just this one product, you'd need roughly thirty-one sales in an entire year to reach an average full-time income. Of course, your blog would not be limited to promoting just one product and you may have many blogs with other affiliate offers. If you think that thirty-one sales in a year are feasible, you'll be making a full-time income (or more).

Advertisements/Sponsored Content: You may consider adding display ads such as Google Adsense to your blog. You can also work with companies directly and negotiate fees for banner ads, advertorials, or other sponsored posts. Just make sure that any sponsored content is clearly labeled as such.

How To Start A Blog

You don't need to be a tech genius to start a blog. I'll walk through the process. With minimal computer skills, you can have your site up and running in under thirty minutes.

1. Choose Software

There are several free website building solutions such as Wordpress.com or Tumblr. Free may sound great but it isn't. Wordpress.com, for example, highly limits the look and functionality of your website. You're limited in themes, they don't allow plug-ins or any third-party web analytics, and they even limit your monetization options.

If you want full control over your website (which I recommend), build your site with Wordpress.org. It's important to note that WordPress.org and WordPress.com are two very different platforms.

Wordpress.org is an open-source free blogging platform. It's the most widely used blogging software in the world; 30% of all websites on the internet are powered by Wordpress.org.

The only downside is that you will have to pay for your domain name (YourWebsiteName.Com) and web hosting. While hosting your domain is not a free solution, it's worth the small fee to own your website.

2. Choose a Domain Name

Choose a domain name (also known as a URL) for your blog. Your URL should make sense for your specific business, brand, or industry. If blogging for an established business, you may want the domain to match your company name. If you plan on creating a personal blog for a variety of topics, then you might want to blog using your name (or a variation of it).

Once you have ideas, you'll have to consider the domain extension. The .com extension is usually the first choice, but a .net or .org are also good options. There are several great domain registrars you can use to search for and purchase a domain.

3. Get Hosting For Your Site

Once you've purchased your domain, you will need a hosting provider. This is where your blog lives on the Internet. The good news is that you can find high-quality blog hosting for around the cost of a large latte every month. Some hosting providers even include a free domain name with your hosting plan.

4. Install WordPress

You don't need to be tech-savvy to do this. Wordpress.org is pretty much a one-click install. You should also install an SSL certificate (indicate by HTTPS at the beginning of your URL) to add security to and build trust in your site. This also can be done in just a few minutes. Most hosting companies have support agents available via chat. Sometimes if you get stuck on something, support will even log in and just do it all for you.

5. **Navigate WordPress and Customize Your Blog**

Once you're up and running, log into your new website. Get familiar with the WordPress dashboard. Start browsing different themes to customize the appearance of your website. You will also want to install a few plug-ins and add Google Analytics. If this sounds too technical, check out the A Gift For You box, below.

Moving Forward

While there are many pieces to the digital marketing puzzle, a blog is a great content hub for your online brand.

Have patience and realize that blogging results do not appear overnight. It will take time for a website to start ranking, getting traffic, and for people to take notice. It took roughly five months for me to start seeing affiliate sales back in 2014. If you're willing to stay the course, you'll reap the benefits.

A Gift For You

To Get Secrets To Blogging Your Way To A Six-Figure Income including:

- Step-By-Step Guide To Launch Your New Blog
- Tips And Tricks To Install Google Analytics
- List Of Free Plug-Ins To Install On Your Blog
- Master List Of High-Paying Affiliate Programs
- Six-Figure Case Studies: Insider Look At Highly-Profitable Blogs
- Access To My Facebook Mastermind Community Of Bloggers and Digital Marketers

Go to freedomrep.com/playbook

About Ilir Salihi

Ilir Salihi is a digital marketer, consultant, and blogger. He helps entrepreneurs and small businesses design and launch wildly lucrative content marketing campaigns. He is also a buy-and-hold real estate investor, entrepreneur, father, and husband.

CHAPTER SIXTY-FIVE

Starting A Digital Agency

By Serena Schwartz

You're thinking about starting your own digital agency? Not a bad idea, considering 2.34 billion people are using social media accounts worldwide to make decisions on what to buy and what businesses to frequent so let's dive right in.

Here is a checklist you should have completed before going out and landing clients.

- Create company name & logo
- Obtain business license
- Create LLC
- Create business bank account
- Build company website

#1 - Simplify

Let's start off by clearing one thing up, our ONLY goal is to get clients who pay every single month for a premium service, not a "one time service." So, don't offer every service! When I started, I offered every service you can dream of: social media management, Facebook ads, website design, graphic design, photography, videography. I WAS THE JACK OF ALL TRADES MASTER OF NONE!

You may think offering every possible service makes you indispensable, but you'd be wrong. Don't reinvent the wheel, or learn everything there is to know, but simply master ONE very in demand service, and concentrate almost solely on it. You're probably wondering... What is this magical in demand service that gets our clients great results?

LEAD GENERATION - What business can you think of that doesn't want more customers?

Your lead generation agency will work with clients to create an offer people are willing to exchange their information for. This will include full name, email, and phone number for EVERY opt-in.

When someone provides their information through your funnel, your client gains a lead. An important element of any agency is to have a guarantee. Example guarantee, if you don't get your client at least 30+ customer opportunities, the next month is 1/2 off. Having a guarantee is a good way to gain instant trust, and to create the best client experience.

Lead generation includes ad spend, a sales funnel promoting the client's offer, Facebook ads to drive traffic to the funnel, and email & SMS automation to follow-up with people who have opted-in to the offer so they become paying customers. Not a bad strategy, eh?

#2 - Prospecting

- Attend Networking Events.
- Facebook Value Videos.
- Send Cold Calls/Emails.

Don't waste your money on ads for yourself! Instead, go to networking events in person and talk to real people - it works. You are 7x more likely to get a "yes" in person!

Attend Networking Events

#1: Do Not Sell - Be authentic in attending simply to make connections. Ask people about themselves and get to know others. If they ask you what you do, tell them.

#2: Give Value, Always - When you do make a connection, offer to go over their current ads and give feedback.

#3: Teach - Networking events are always looking for presenters, so teach a presentation in your local area about successful social media ad campaigns. This pivots you as the expert and gets clients to come to you. Word of mouth is powerful, and this is a great way to stand out.

Facebook Value Videos

Use this prospecting method to not only stand out, but to give a lot of value without any expectation. This creates trust as well, which is something hard earned when approaching a stranger online.

- Go to Facebook and search your target location and desired niche.
- Scroll to the bottom of their business page and hit "Info and Ads."
- Download a free extension called Loom from the Google store.
- Go back to the "Info and Ads" section of your prospect's Facebook page; pick one of their ads, and record a video using loom of yourself giving value. Make sure to use our "compliment sandwich" method below:
    1. Compliment them.
    2. Very respectfully tell them what adjustments you would make to their ad.
    3. End the video with "I hope this has been helpful! If you have any questions, please don't hesitate to reach out."

Starting out, you should concentrate on prospects who already have ads running. If they don't currently have an ad running, you could suggest tips for their page and benefits of ads.

Send Cold Calls/Emails

The other prospecting methods seem to have the best conversion rates, however, do not discount cold calls and emails. You can easily find that information on their Google listing.

#3 - Introductory Meeting

Your introductory meeting is to learn about the prospect. You'll ask about their business and goals. Once you have a clear picture of their business and how you can help them, you can pitch your service to them, potentially signing them as a client.

Here are a few questions you can ask in your discovery meetings:

- What marketing tactics have worked the best/worst for you?

- How much do you currently spend monthly on advertising?
- How much of a priority is growth for your business and where do you want to be in 6 months?

Once you have a clear idea of their mindset and goals, offer your proposal/pitch and go for the close. This is the most crucial time do this. You have their trust, and emotions are running high from asking them all the right questions.

#4 - Value Ladder & Research

A value ladder is a visual map of a company's products or services ascending in both price and value. Typically, the first step in a value ladder is something accessible (something of high perceived value to the customer, but of low cost to your client) to draw new customers into our client's value ladder.

Once you've on-boarded a client; set up a short meeting to create or learn about their value ladder. It is VERY important when someone enters into a value ladder they have a great first impression. By doing this, they will ascend the value ladder, and maximize our client's ROI.

Why do research? Research helps us figure out the emotions connected to your client's niche, and your client's potential customers. Take what they say, and use it in your ad copy.

What's the point? People take action when their emotions are high. If we can present the prospect with your client's solution at the right time, they are the most likely to take action.

#5 - Access & Content

In order to run ads for your client, you will need to be granted access to their Facebook business page.

Use Loom to make a simple walkthrough for your clients on how to grant you the proper access to their accounts, and make the client experience as seamless as possible.

Once you have access to your client's FB page, you will want to create an ad account for their business within YOUR business manager. Why? If you use their ad account, instead of creating your own for them within your business manager, they can see everything. Nothing is stopping them from just copying your ads, then canceling your service.

What content do you request from your client? Request photos that show these are REAL people, and not just another business. Don't bother with stock photos unless you are going for a pattern interrupt effect.

#6 - Campaign Setup

What is needed? Key elements:

- Craft a front end and thank you offer that your campaign will revolve around.
- Build a funnel to collect opt-ins. Collect names, emails, and phone numbers for your offers.
- Connect an email autoresponder to your funnel that will deliver the offer voucher and follow-up email sequence to your new lead's.
- Nurture those leads! Connect automatic text and email notifications to your funnel. Your client gets alerted the moment they receive new leads so they can follow-up immediately. Also, the lead gets sent both texts and email reminders about their voucher.

#7 - Campaign Launch

If you don't already have a good idea how to run effective Facebook ads, you WILL need to find some courses to take. So, I'm just going to share my top campaign objective choices:

- Traffic
- Lead Generation
- Conversions

#8 - Client Strategy Sessions

Your clients should have your contact information and a clear timeline of what hours you are available. They should feel confident they can reach you via email, phone, or text to answer any questions or concerns they have.

These sessions help the team run smoothly, and should take place bi-weekly. Use these sessions to discuss what is and isn't working, and any other agenda items from either party.

It's important to keep your client involved not only with the entire campaign, but to make sure you are always nurturing your client relationships. Retention and referrals are a big deal in this business, so make a habit of truly helping people and being genuine.

Moving Forward

I'll leave you with a few last things:

Pro Tips:

- Split test, Split Test, Spit Test!
- Prospect, Always!
- Keep Learning!

A Gift For You

If you want a copy of my free 8-Step Guide to Starting A Digital Agency, the full version – complete with lots of plug & play templates and bonus information – is available at TalkNerdyMarketingCourses.com

You can also join my Facebook group: www.facebook.com/groups/TalkNerdyToMeDigitalMarketingHacks/

About Serena Schwartz

Serena Schwartz is an entrepreneur who has started two successful companies while being a stay-at-home mom of two children under three. From starting out managing many successful corporate salons to starting a family to creating a successful Digital Marketing Agency and thriving CBD company, she is a reminder that you can always change and adapt your career to your life.

Her biggest passion is helping others operate at their best. Whether it's helping clients to get more customers for their business or helping others learn the amazing physical wellness benefits of CBD: Her entire goal is to help others to find their freedom to spend time with their family and have a work/life balance that leaves them happy and content. She is also currently a part of her local Chamber of Commerce and has been an active speaker and trainer in her field.

CHAPTER SIXTY-SIX

Print On Demand

By Cody Neer

If you have or have spent time around young kids, you know that one of the best things about them is their natural optimism and excitement for the little things in life. They're not yet affected by debt, daily news, or world catastrophes. Kids wake up every day and believe they can do, see, and have anything they want out of life. It's refreshing.

In The Beginning

When I was three years old, I became obsessed with baseball. I'd wake up starry-eyed with happy optimism because I found the one thing I loved, baseball. Playing in the major leagues one day became my dream. It wasn't an *if* but a *when*. I quickly developed tunnel-vision and started obsessing on building my talents in the sport.

Things were on track because I ranked as one of the top high school players in the world and the best high school catcher in 2005. After my senior season, I was offered to play for The University of Florida on a scholarship or go into the Minor Leagues and pursue my dream. I chose college.

To be honest, I felt more invincible then than I did when I was three. The University of Florida was coming off a College World Series appearance and I was in line to join a list of players who'd make a quick three-year stop in college before making their MLB debut.

Playing at the highest level and finally seeing nearly two decades of hard work start paying off tends to give you a boost in confidence that tells you, "It's ok, you can breathe, you've made it now."

The only problem was, I hadn't. Success is never promised, it's earned.

After college, I turned professional only to get cut from the team after a few seasons, and I had to answer the question, "What do I do now?"

A simple question to answer in most daily scenarios, it can also be the most difficult question to answer. It's one that your subconscious mind often answers for you, as you try the avoid the stress of formulating a strategic answer.

But when my coach told me I was being let go from the team, I knew I had to figure out an answer that would help me reach financial freedom. I realized I never wanted to rely on someone else for a paycheck again. I did not know how that would happen, but the most important thing to occur in my life was being forced to end my life's dream.

Despite the confusion, fear, and endless *what-ifs* that racked my brain, I maintained my competitive spirit and devised a plan to make money ASAP (and promptly exit the pity party I was in). I became an entrepreneur.

Within a few short months, I was a co-founder of what became a $13,000,000 online company. I was one of nine founding partners and, as the youngest on the team, I was only a 3% equity partner. I thought that was amazing until they sold the company and I only received 3% of the proceeds.

Boy, did I learn a tough lesson in business at that moment! Having been one of the most important factors in driving its sales, I did not reap the financial benefits of the other partners. After the company sold, I was left hungry for more and the desire to do something big.

I interviewed with fortune 100 companies and Target Corporation took notice of my newly acquired online advertising and marketing skills. They hired me to lead their new paid social media advertising team and launch their first Facebook Ads to drive sales on Target.com and to help launch their new app called Cartwheel.

After nearly spending $56 million on advertising, I generated over $350 million in gross revenue for Target and converted over 100,000 customers to the Cartwheel app in the first few years. I remember staring at the results and wondering what would happen if I tried to recreate them for myself; I decided to give it a shot and launch an e-Commerce store and my world changed forever.

Two years later, the store crossed seven-figures and I surpassed $1 million in sales. The success of that business caught the attention of Shark Tank TV personality and investor Kevin Harrington, who I partnered with to build another e-Commerce brand that did nearly $4 million in five months.

As mind-boggling as that was, it was only the beginning. In that year alone I sourced products from around the world and built over a dozen of my own e-Commerce brands that generated over eight-figures in gross sales. I sold those stores for six- and seven-figure paydays and I created a partnership with incomestore.com to build and scale hundreds of e-Commerce brands from scratch to six- and seven-figures.

I'm not boasting. I want to demonstrate that what you're about to discover has been tried and tested over a decade of learning and perfecting. And, it's not rocket science.

Print On Demand Simplified

Print On Demand (POD). is a low-risk way to sell custom products online. The biggest benefit of starting a POD store is the ability to bypass the time, investment, and risk of holding your inventory because the manufacturer prints one item at a time. Traditional retailers and product sellers used to buy and hold their inventory, often leaving them with a pile of products that didn't sell. Thanks to POD, you can now sell your products at a fraction of the cost. Whether you're an entrepreneur, designer, parent, writer, or artist, POD offers the lowest-risk, most time-efficient, and profitable way to sell custom products.

How POD Works

In a nutshell, POD involves working with a supplier to customize white label products (t-shirts, hats, or mugs) with your designs. You sell them from your brand, on a per-order basis, meaning you don't pay for the product until after someone buys it.

After someone buys your product, everything from printing to shipping is handled by your supplier. Once you've chosen your products and gotten your store set up, it only takes a few clicks for your supplier to fulfill an order every time you make a sale. This means you get to sit back and relax, knowing your customers are being taken care of and money is hitting your bank account. A POD store is an easily accessible business model that doesn't require hundreds to thousands of dollars in upfront costs.

Choosing Products

When it comes to POD, choosing the right products is only one part of ensuring your store will be profitable and grow to five-, six-, and seven-figures. It's the first part and one that I've spent over a decade demystifying. I've had stores that took months to make the first sale, and I've had stores that took minutes. The difference is choosing the right products for the right niche.

One proven method I've used to find the most profitable products for my stores and my clients is called The Jungle Scout app, which is an app available on Amazon that tells you what products are selling and when. I strongly recommend starting there to get a data-backed understanding of what kind of products are already selling well in your industry. The biggest mistake most e-Commerce beginners make is assuming a product will sell. Never assume - always verify. The Jungle Scout app will help you do this.

Once you verify what sells, you can place your product right next to the other ones on Amazon that are proven to sell. Allowing Amazon to become your advertiser and provide the traffic to your products helps ease you into learning the paid advertising part of the business (which is how you scale to seven-figures).

Entering The Market

You don't have to be an experienced marketer, Facebook Ads expert, or tech-guru to make a comfortable living with an e-Commerce store. A lot of experts make e-Commerce sound more complex than it is. If you have access to a computer, an Internet connection, and a basic understanding of what I described in the last few paragraphs, you can get started today.

Thanks to platforms like Shopify and Etsy that take the stress out of designing your store, you can get your store up and running in less than a day. POD allows you to create a product and put it up for sale in minutes. To reiterate the benefits: shipping is taken care of by your supplier, you face low investment and low risk since you're not physically holding any inventory, and it's easy to add or remove products or test new ideas.

Moving Forward

I have presented the first step in my three-step program to eCommerce financial success, which is the best way to get started making money. Once you have set up your supplier(s) and store and everything is running smoothly, you will have time to start looking at scaling your business by getting more customers to your products using social media and then creating a sales funnel to send new customers to your store(s) round the clock, even when you are sleeping.

A Gift For You

I've just presented the first part of my three-part formula to grow any store from zero to a million dollars, how to find the right products.

The second and third parts include how to drive traffic to your store and how to create an automated sales funnel that runs and scales your store passively.

Inside the eCommerce Brand Academy is where I currently teach over 300 people how to do this step by step. For more details and to see if the academy is right for you, head over to www.ecommercebrandacademy.com and watch my video where I share those three steps for free.

About Cody Neer

Accomplished and innovative Digital Marketing Expert with a career history of architecting automated digital sales environments, building creative business teams, and launching products globally. Cody Neer founded his first business in the digital payment processing industry helping pioneer the electronic check industry at the age of 22.

As a serial entrepreneur, Cody enjoys building online assets that produce recurring income opportunities for investors. Cody currently owns an 8-figure e-Commerce business selling print on demand fishing poles, and hunting gear.

CHAPTER SIXTY-SEVEN

Affiliate Marketing

By Paul Mottley

ffiliate marketing might be new to you or you may have heard various things about it, but I'm going to describe how I've achieved sales of over $100,000 in the last six months and won a new car bonus without owning a product or service.

Affiliate Marketing Explained

Affiliate marketing involves earning a commission from companies to which you provide visitors (leads) or customers (buyers) through your efforts such as lead-sourcing, marketing, sales, etc.[53]

Regardless of your skill level, affiliate marketing is one of the most attractive ways to make money online. You don't have to be a great speaker, design outstanding courses, be a coach, or run an agency. With affiliate marketing, you are simply getting a commission for selling other people's products and services. In a sense, you are a salesperson, but for many different companies rather than one.

The most professional affiliate marketers constantly build email lists of those who would be interested in buying their affiliates' products and services. If you can narrow the lists down to particular niches, even better. For example, having a list of people who like pets in general is one market, but if you are promoting dog products then having a list of dog owners will get far better sales than the more general list.

Creating Lists

There are many different kinds of lists you can build, four of my favorite list-building sources are email, Messenger, Facebook Groups, and YouTube

Email Lists

As an affiliate marketer, this is the oldest and still the surest way to make money long-term on the Internet. The rule-of-thumb is that you can make, on average, $1 per email subscriber per month. So obviously having large email lists can be amazing.

---

[53] n.a.(n.d.). *Affiliate Marketing.* Retrieved from https://en.wikipedia.org/wiki/Affiliate_marketing on October 16, 2019.

It is critical to capture an email address. By supplying an email address, the user is permitting you to keep sending them offers. Although you should always provide an option for unsubscribing from the list, many remain on the list in hopes of receiving a great offer from you.

To collect email, you will need two things, some kind of website where you can create your opt-in form and email list software.

I use ClickFunnels (CF) as my opt-in forms: it is the easiest to set up and the pages convert extremely well (over the last five years, I've tried almost every type of software and still haven't found anything better than CF). ActiveCampaign is my favorite software for collecting and storing my email lists.

People are no longer as willing to provide email addresses as they once were, so an incentive is needed. Try giving them a free report, a free trial, a discount voucher, an e-Book, or a free training/coaching session to win their personal information.

Note that the more the look and feel of these lead magnets match the look and feel of the affiliate product or service you're promoting, the more trust the leads will feel tabout sharing their personal information and conversion rates will be higher as well.

Messenger

This list is will only capture people who are on Facebook but with 2.41 billion users, that is a lot of people.[54] Messenger efforts are beneficial because the open rate on Messenger is higher than that of regular email.

Use a third-party app such as ManyChat or Opesta to gather people onto your list. Using the growth tool allows you to offer something of value to readers in exchange for their name and email address, just like landing pages gather email addresses. You can narrow your targeting on Messenger by using the comment tool in the apps to narrow the message recipients down to those who are more likely to buy because they use certain keywords.

Send a broadcast to those on your bot list – either simple messages with a Call to Action (CTA)or a complex series of messages that are triggered by their actions – to learn their preferences. Use this information to segment people and tag them so that when you have something that will be a close match to a particular segment you can expect high conversion.

Facebook Groups

Having a Facebook Group (FBG) helps build your authority within your niche. Encourage membership by inviting friends and followers to join and posting a link to your FBG on social media posts. It's been common practice for a few years to include an incentive for people to join FBGs and having a link directly from your Facebook profile to show off that opportunity.

Inside of your group you build relationships, and post reviews or recommendations for related affiliate products. It's a great way to show you are an expert and offer help to as many as possible. This often results in some people actively asking for your affiliate link for a tool or service they want to buy as a thank you.

When people organically ask to join your group, offer your incentive and collect their email address plus get them on your Messenger bot list at the same time.

---

[54] n.a.(n.d.). The number of Monthly Facebook Users Worldwide As Of 2nd Quarter 2019. Retrieved from https://www.statista.com/statistics/264810/number-of-monthly-active-facebook-users-worldwide/ on October 16, 2019.

YouTube Subscribers

When people subscribe to your YouTube channel they are more likely to see your new videos. If they also hit the notification bell for your channel, YouTube will let them know soon as you upload. The most common way to gain subscribers is to ask viewers to subscribe to your channel within the opening few minutes of your videos. Remember to add your affiliate links to your video descriptions (I recommend you use a URL-shortener to track which video links get sales). The best types of videos are reviews of the product or service, a user guide (how-to video), or those that offer extra incentives if viewers use the link at the end of the video.

Moving Forward

Once you've started building lists, increasing affiliate sales can be as simple as sending out an email or a bot broadcast, posting in your FBG or profile, and adding a new YouTube video. Using Bridge Pages is even more profitable, even though they are prohibited in Google AdWords.

The bridge page is a site that simply forwards visitors to another site. It functions in many ways: you can introduce yourself; you can use it to build your email or bot list by asking people to opt-in and then sends them to the affiliate product or service.

Try to get people to follow you on as many different platforms as possible. Then use them all. Here's an example, you upload a new YouTube video and email it to your email list, send out a bot broadcast, and post it in your FBG and profile. If followers are on more than one list, chances are they will end up watching your video once they see it offered more than once. Those who follow you on multiple platforms are more likely to buy from you.

A Gift For You

I help affiliates start and grow an affiliate business of their dreams. Get my 7-Day Mentoring Bootcamp Training Series by heading to: https://www.highticketleadmachine.com/blueprint

About Paul Mottley

Paul Mottley is from the UK and a proud Dad of three boys. He has been a local business owner for the last 24 years.

Now turned affiliate marketer. After struggling for years he decided to get more serious in 2018. The successes started to follow and in June 2019, Paul won the Clickfunnels Dream Car Award for achieving over 100 account sales.

A keen member of many facebook groups, Paul has taught – directly or indirectly -- hundreds of budding entrepreneurs. He has a general ethos of helping as many people achieve their goals and dreams in life as possible.

Paul's passion is soccer and he has played at an (almost) semi-professional level. He later went on to couch kids and has a FA coaching badge. Spare time is spent with his family and playing the odd game of golf!

CHAPTER SIXTY-EIGHT

How To Create A Successful Online Course

By Melissa Duran

Online education is a growing industry and is the perfect way for entrepreneurs to streamline, automate, and expand their reach. e-Learning is expected to reach $325 billion by 2025 and it is important to note that online courses are a large portion of the industry. As a lifelong learner, I enjoy learning and online courses have widened my learning opportunities.

In The Beginning

I have taken several online courses. The best was *CF Design School*. Using what I learned there and my existing knowledge, I helped a client create her first online course. I loved the entire process and I dove into the foundation, strategy, and design processes that are the key elements of my *A»B Method* for e-course creation.

The *A»B Method* guides people, one-on-one, through the foundations, strategy, and design phases of online course creation. Most people jump right into creating their course without laying the proper foundation, determining a strategy, or considering the design of their offering.

Why Create An Online Course?

You may be asking why you should consider an online course for your business. There are five big reasons people create online courses:

- To automate their current teaching/coaching methods.
- To start a movement or revolution.
- To reach more people than they could one-on-one.
- To fill a hole in their current value ladder.
- To create passive income (note that putting together a course is anything but passive, but once created, it can become a source of passive income).

There may be other reasons you're creating an online course and that's OK, too.

Five Steps For Creating Successful Online Course

Here are five steps to help you get started on your online course creation:

1. **Determine your ideal student.**

Your ideal student may match your target audience (your Avatar) or may be a slight variation of your target audience. The key is to identify the problem or problems you are going to solve for them.

By determining the ideal student, you can start to envision the course development. You'll be able to set the right foundation to serve those students and determine the content they want and need and what they may not need. Clarity of your ideal student will help you market your target audience, as well.

2. **Determine the results the students should experience.**

The results they experience should include solving the problem that brought them to your course. Because each course addresses different problems, the result for each course you create will be different, even if the ideal student is the same.

Take your time determining the intended outcome; there may be both a primary and a secondary result your students could experience.

A primary result is directly related to the problem your course is addressing. It will be the "big result" that you want them to achieve. You may even measure the success of the course by this result. It might be learning a skill or process, changing a behavior, or understanding an app. These skills can often be measured qualitatively to measure the success of the class.

A secondary result is something the students will learn without directly addressing the topic. It might be increased earnings, improved confidence, new understandings, or changed paradigms. These results are often difficult to measure quantitatively and a qualitative evaluation may be necessary if you want to measure secondary results.

3. **Take 20 minutes to write down all of the ideas that you have for your course.**

Write down *every* idea; there are no wrong answers. Once you've got the list, you may need to do one or both of two things.

The first is to narrow down your ideas. Look for patterns in your ideas. Look for the natural flow of information as you write. Narrowing things down will help you focus on the structure of the course.

The second thing is to complete another session of 20 minutes. This second session might help you to refine your ideas and help you to determine how to group your information into modules. Once you get your thoughts organized, you can outline your course including the modules and lesson titles.

4. **Create the course materials and lessons (videos, worksheets, or digital assets).**

This is the content of your course and it will set you apart from the other courses your students may have taken or are taking. Think about how you are going to deliver the content and choose what is best for the student, not you! If your audience prefers watching videos, create video lessons. If they prefer slides, use PowerPoint or other slide software to create a slide show.

Like a website, the success of a course lies in its content and the delivery of that content: everything from the flow of the lessons to the quality of the content to the design and how successfully the course solved the problem it promised to.

Having a great sales funnel is wonderful but if it leads to a course that isn't put together well, word will start to get out and your sales will decline.

5. **Launch!**

If only it were as easy as saying, "Launch!" and people started clamoring for your course. There are several ways to launch and market a course. While the list is long, I will cover three of them in this section.

Three ways to launch your course:

- The Beta launch.

A beta version of your course is a test version for which students get a discounted rate and you build the course out as they access it. There are several reasons people decide to go through a beta launch including immediate student feedback, the ability to build as you go, and having testimonials for when the big launch happens.

- Organic and Paid Traffic.

This involves using your email list or paid advertising to launch your course. Each launch is unique, so reaching the right audience is important. This organic source of traffic is great because it is your warm network who already know, like, and trust you. Paid traffic allows you to focus your advertising dollars on your ideal student.

- Affiliate or Joint Ventures.

Leveraging those who have an audience that matches your ideal student is a great way to get the word out about your course. The most successful joint partnerships will be one that has the students' needs at the forefront of the partnership.

Moving Forward

One thing I've noticed about entrepreneurs looking at creating an online course is that they sometimes think that they aren't ready, don't know enough, or aren't as good as the competition. There will always be someone out there who has done things differently or who believe a lot of experience is required before teaching a course.

If you are facing these fears, remember Vince Lombardi.

Vince Lombardi was a football player in the 1930s who never won any championships as a player. He began coaching and went on to win several championships and he coached his students (his players) to win Super Bowl I and II. The impact a coach or a teacher can have on their students can be invaluable.

Who you are, your background, and your experiences make you uniquely qualified to create and launch a course to change lives or the world. You are qualified to create a course based on your experiences, your passions, and your perspective. The world needs you; start teaching today!

A Gift For You

If you are looking to get started on the right path, head on over to https://melissacduran.com/outline and get a free downloadable PDF, From Overwhlemed to Outlined.

About Melissa Duran

Melissa Duran, creator of the A»B Method, has a passion for helping others create their online courses.

Originally from Los Angeles, CA, she currently resides in Mesa, Arizona, with her husband and their four kids.

When asked what she wanted to be when she grew up, Melissa would always say, "Mom." Little did she know that it would be her greatest enjoyment, as well as the source of her second passion in entrepreneurship.

If you're ready to work with Melissa directly and want to use her as your pathfinder, head on over to melissacduran.com where you can apply to work with Melissa one-on-one.

CHAPTER SIXTY-NINE

LinkedIn

By Lindsay Mustain

Imagine being invited to the most epic networking party in existence. I want you to picture Fortune 1000 CEOs, corporate decision-makers, and both large and small business owners from all industries together in the same room. Would you want an invite to that party? Consider this your personal invitation to that party which is being held every single day on LinkedIn.

LinkedIn was founded to leverage and grow your professional connections through social networking. Most business owners know the power of utilizing your network and their referrals to grow a business. Envision finding a place where you could build relationships instantly online and with people who are on this platform because they want to hear from you. It's not a dream; this is the reality of how LinkedIn can absolutely transform your business.

LinkedIn was formed in 2002, long before the concept of Facebook existed. The premise was applying the 6 degrees principle to your professional network; you would be connected to anyone in the world within six connection points. Today, LinkedIn boasts over 625 million users, half of which are logging on every month.

I've been on LinkedIn since 2005 as an early adopter and someone who professionally sought out the best and brightest people to recruit to 25 companies within the Fortune 500. Long before I had Myspace or Facebook - LinkedIn was my social network of choice. I learned quickly in my career that LinkedIn is a huge asset to your career and to building relationships. During my time I worked at Amazon, I became their most visible employee on that platform. Ultimately, as an individual, I received more engagement and profile views than any other person inside the company and even more profile visits than the Amazon company page. I've been called a LinkedIn Celebrity, Top Voice, and Queen of LinkedIn. LinkedIn is the main driver of revenue in my business. To date, I've generated over $500,000 from organic marketing traffic.

5 Reasons You're Leaving Money on the Table by Not Using LinkedIn

1. **Easily Connect with Real Decision Makers**. LinkedIn wasn't built to share photos of sunsets, beaches, or complain about grandma's tuna casserole. LinkedIn is the largest professional networking site in existence with 625 million professional users. The beauty of this platform is that people join to build their network. If you want to be networked with someone, you need only send them a connection request. It's truly that easy.

2. **Quality of the User**. Decision makers and influencers congregate on LinkedIn. On most social media, you must sift through thousands of profiles to find the ideal client for your business. There is a reason that LinkedIn is the best social media site to drive B2B leads and sales: 90 Million users are senior level influencers and 63 Million users are in decision making positions. That means 25%

of the users who are using this platform are the people are the highest caliber of clientele with financial resources and decision-making capacity. For those that offer B2C services, nearly half (49%) make over $75K annually. In short, if you want influential or consumers who can afford a higher price tag, you should be on LinkedIn.

3. **Drive Revenue**. I'm going to hit you with a staggering statistic. LinkedIn originates more than 50% of all social media originated traffic to B2B websites and blogs. That's more than Facebook, Instagram and Twitter combined. There is easy lead and revenue generation happening on LinkedIn and you're just leaving money on the table if you're not using this platform.

4. **Establish Thought Leadership.** One of my personal favorite aspects of LinkedIn is the ability to build credibility and thought leadership easily. Most of the Fortune 500 executives and decision makers are spending their free moments on this platform and 91% rated LinkedIn as their top content source for their business. There are two ways you can contribute to building this authority through content on LinkedIn. One is a post (which is like a Facebook status update). The second is an article.

How is it so effective to use a content strategy on LinkedIn? Of the 625+ million people on LinkedIn, only 3 million users share content weekly and less than 1% of users have written an article. In fact, the revenue I have driven to my business has solely been through content marketing on this platform.

5. **Still the Wild Wild West of Social Media.** LinkedIn has not become an overpriced and oversaturated market like Facebook. People can easily establish their expertise, connect with the right people, and drive sales in a very blue ocean. It's not difficult to build these things yet, because most businesses don't understand what an untapped gold mine LinkedIn is. So, start now, because with enough expertise and thought leadership under your LinkedIn belt - you'll be prepared for the waves of people who are joining the platform every day.

Now that you can see the power of this social media platform, let's dive in and talk about how you can get started on maximizing this platform to build thought leadership, drive sales leads, and generate revenue.

5 Ways to Start Making Money from LinkedIn

1. **Begin with Your Profile**. Optimizing your profile is step one in the process of making money from LinkedIn. There are six places on your profile that you should be optimizing. Don't scrimp on this; if you don't have a compelling profile that solidifies a user's opinion for what you do, you'll never see that turn into a sale.

A) *Your Cover Photo* - choose something that relates to your field. Make sure it makes sense with who you are professionally and what you are offering.

B) *Your Profile Photo* - profiles with photos get 21x more views. Make sure it is both a welcoming and professional headshot.

C) *Your Headline* - This is key to getting people to click to learn more about you. Your goal is to tell them what you offer. Example: Driving Organic Sales Through Digital Marketing Strategy or Digital Marketing | Facebook Ads | Best-Selling Author

D) *Your Summary* - This section is the "make or break" one for your profile. Your first goal is to tell them what you do. Example: "I help entrepreneurs create digital marketing strategies that drive automatic sales effortlessly." After that, describe how you got into this field, why you're passionate about it, and how they can contact you. You can also add a link to a sales funnel or website here.

E) *Your Experience* - Include what you have done professionally. That means tell them what kinds of accomplishments you have under your belt and results for your clients (or the businesses you worked under).

F) *Your Media* - You can add media, meaning pictures, videos, links to your summary and to your experience section. I HIGHLY recommend you do this as it will showcase your business and give them a place to learn more about you and convert them into a lead without any effort!

2. **Create and Optimize Your Business Page**. Unless you have an existing business page on LinkedIn, when you input your experience, you will likely show a default image of a gray building. You do not want this. It reduces your credibility as an expert and as a business. You must set up a page for your business on LinkedIn. It's easy, free, and builds your reputation. Just like your personal profile page, input a summary that discusses what your business offers and with a third-person voice. Last, you should upload your business logo.

3. **Build Connections.** The power of LinkedIn is in your connections. It's actually not just in your first-degree connections, but in your second degree. The maximum number of connections you can have is 30,000, but you can have unlimited followers once you hit your max. Let's do the math: I have 30,000 connections. The average LinkedIn user has 150 connections. Take my 30,000 connections and multiply it by 150 (my connections' connections) and we get 4,500,000 as my potential audience. It becomes even bigger when you have a following! Adding connections will be the first step to getting more visibility on LinkedIn. All you must do is select 'Send Connection Request' on someone's profile. 97% of people do not personalize this request. Of those 3 percent that do, most will pitch something. Do not leave it blank and do not pitch anything. Send a personalized note about what interested you in them and be sure to use their name and do NOT sell anything.

4. **Provide Value vs Selling.** Your goal is not to get a large number of connections. Your goal is to get a large number of people with whom you can build a relationship. Most people jump immediately onto a newly accepted connection and assault them by asking them all sorts of questions about their business. It's the fastest way to lose a contact and kill that lead. When someone accepts your connection request, reply and tell them "thank you and it's a pleasure to be connected". Your next move should be to tell them what you enjoyed learning about them from their profile. Make it personalized and interesting so that they want to reply. After you have begun a dialogue, the next step is to mention that you "saw that they had (insert need or business) and that you have created a (insert resource/video/pdf/etc.) to help (types of business owners your lead is) to help (insert the result)". Ask if they are interested in this free resource. If you have built enough rapport, they will likely say yes. Drop the link to your opt-in/lead magnet and let them have time to review the material. On the next business day, follow up and say, "I hope you found some value in (item you delivered to them). Is there anything you think that I may not have covered in detail that will help (insert type of business owners that this lead is?)". Your goal is to begin an open-ended, no-pressure conversation with them so they feel that you are providing value and help. Never hard sell. Ultimately, you should gently push them to the next step of the selling process which could be a call or even a training you're offering. Always approach any new connection with the mindset of "how can I serve?"

5. **Publish Content.** Content should always be based around that idea of "how can I serve my ideal clientele"? Information, how-tos, lists, stories, testimonials, and asking questions are my favorite content formats. I like to include a link to a sales funnel in the text itself or in the first comment. This is how I add 500 new leads every single week without paying a dime! Once you have achieved some comfort with publishing on LinkedIn, I recommend you write an article for the #1 question or topic that people ask you about. This is the beginning of you becoming a serious influencer on this platform and building your business brand online.

I've used the strategies above to create a total connection and follower reach of over 9,000,000 people and generate $500,000 without any ad spend. I can easily help to inform, inspire, or create a call to action that drives people to my sales funnel where I can begin to form a more personal relationship with them. I continue to add new content and resources that clients can get at no cost. With the free resources, I help my connections or followers get a quick win, which helps me easily earn trust and invite them to work more closely with me if they desire. Follow the strategies above and you'll find the most impactful and free ways you can use LinkedIn to grow your business and generate revenue with very little effort.

About Lindsay Mustain

Lindsay Mustain is a best-selling author, keynote speaker, and has been called the Queen of LinkedIn. After a successful corporate career helping Fortune 100 companies find the best talent in the marketplace, Lindsay founded her own company, Talent Paradigm LLC. Today she teaches students how to find their dream job using LinkedIn and shows businesses how to duplicate her success with organic viral LinkedIn strategies. She's been featured in Entrepreneur, Mental Floss, Glass Door, SHRM, ERE, and SparkHire and has been hired by Fortune 25 organizations to teach their executive teams the power of leveraging LinkedIn to build their personal brand.

CHAPTER SEVENTY

Door-To-Door Sales Funnels

By Jackson Rucker

If you're a digital marketer, I'm going to introduce a new source of customers. If you're in the door-to-door industry, congrats on picking up and reading this book. I'm going to introduce you to the benefits of using the Internet and social media to improve your profits.

Stop trying to sell to everyone. You must focus on specific things to say and do that will engage someone's desire to buy your product or join your team. You're not in the convincing game. You're looking for people who will give you an audience because they want what you're offering.

I had to keep saying that to myself in my early days as a door-to-door salesman. Remembering this has helped me discover the secret I'd like to share with you today.

Those in the door-to-door industry want to sell their product or service more effectively but many door-to-door recruiters and trainers are behind the times and aren't using internet marketing to support their businesses. Slowly, the door-to-door industry is starting to come online with everyone else. That means there's an entire industry that needs help from digital marketers.

In The Beginning

During my college years, I spent a few summers as a door-to-door salesman. I realized neither my college professors nor my summer sales managers suggested leveraging the Internet and social media for door-to-door sales.

After several failed attempts at recruiting on my own, I began looking at how to make my team more attractive to prospective salespeople through marketing. I knew success in selling and recruiting in the door-to-door industry comes down to talking to more of the right people. But finding the right people simply by knocking on doors was not terribly productive and no one was doing anything to fix it!

The Industry Today

Door-to-door sales, the job, has become a kind of necessary evil to getting paid. A necessary evil that often pays extremely well. When doing it, it's painful for a while and then it becomes enjoyable once you get the hang of it. As the career of choice for many, what makes it worthwhile year after year are the results and the lessons learned.

There are plenty of people who have become successful in the door-to-door industry. They have worked themselves up the leadership and financial hierarchy in the traditional manner. Most successful door-to-door salesmen eventually leave the daily grind of door-to-door sales in one way or another: some become sales rep managers for an existing company; others become entrepreneurs. The problem is, there is no special training for progressing to entrepreneurship.

While people continue to live in buildings with doors, there will continue to be people who knock on those doors and try to sell the residents something. Most door-to-door salesmen love their job, but I've found 100% would rather have people calling them to buy, or to be recruited, than finding the sale, or recruit, for themselves.

The door-to-door sales industry market is saturated and competitive. It occurred to me that the top talent in the door-to-door industry needs to have automation set up to enhance their sales message and reach more customers. This is where the Internet can help.

Moving Online

The way to establish credibility and become an expert online is through the production of quality content. When top-quality content is frequent and consistent, the person or company supplying the content becomes an influencer. Publicly sharing knowledge and expertise with ideal customers creates an opportunity to capture new clients. By giving value to their customers online, door-to-door salespeople can prosper more than by knocking on doors alone.

I believed that I'd never have similar success as online entrepreneurs until, with the help of my mentors and friends, I understood the secret to make my team attractive rested in developing a marketing system. A system that uses marketing principles proven in similar industries. I figured, "If marketing systems work for Multi-Level Marketing, why not apply them to the door-to-door industry?"

I quickly understood that the door-to-door industry, as a whole, needed sales funnels and digital marketing to truly allow door-to-door salesmen to differentiate themselves from one another. Salespeople need to leverage automated systems that bring pre-qualified leads. It is more productive with less waste than traditional customer recruiting methods. Individuals using a multi-faceted approach accrue higher revenues. Subsequently, they can then outspend their competitors to acquire a customer or recruit.

Most door-to-door recruiters fear that their sales reps will be distracted with online marketing tactics. They want reps to focus on traditional in-person methods that are known to be tried and true. Digital marketing in the door-to-door industry is not readily understood by many.

Luckily, a handful of door-to-door entrepreneurs are changing the path to success. They come from the grassroots of the old door-to-door methods but have the vision to see what is needed to be successful in the 21st century. They blend the best parts of door-to-door sales and digital marketing to create the perfect recipe for success.

So, if you're looking for new customers (and who isn't) and wondering where to look next, let me ask you, "Do you sell things to door-to-door salesmen?"

A Gift For You

The most valuable thing you could do is share this chapter with a door-to-door salesman or recruiter!

Earn Affiliate CASH by spreading the message!

Get your Affiliate link & pre-built assets at https://jacksonrucker.com/book

About Jackson Rucker

After three years of selling door-to-door pest-control, Jackson realized the popular ways of recruiting, selling, and training in the door-to-door industry were set up for failure in today's online world.

His message for the door-to-door industry is recruiters need to focus on building their business and team by harvesting the benefits of both worlds.

Jackson helps door-to-door recruiters who want to dominate their market become entrepreneurs.

Made in the USA
Middletown, DE
08 July 2021

43679674R00177